MYSTERY AT THE BLUE SEA COTTAGE

A TRUE STORY OF MURDER IN SAN DIEGO'S JAZZ AGE

JAMES STEWART

WILDBLUE PRESS

WildBluePress.com

MYSTERY AT THE BLUE SEA COTTAGE published by:
WILDBLUE PRESS
P.O. Box 102440
Denver, Colorado 80250

WILDBLUE PRESS is registered at the U.S. Patent and Trademark Offices.

ISBN 978-1-952225-78-9 Trade Paperback
ISBN 978-1-952225-77-2 eBook

Cover design © 2021 WildBlue Press. All rights reserved.

Interior Formatting/Cover Design by Elijah Toten
www.totencreative.com

MYSTERY AT THE
BLUE SEA COTTAGE

Dedication

For Mom and Dad, from whom I inherited my love of books.

Table of Contents

Preface

This book is about the unsolved murder of Fritzie Mann in 1923 San Diego. In the era of yellow journalism, sensation mattered more than accuracy and this story had all the elements needed to sell newspapers: the body of a beautiful interpretive dancer found scantily clad, a murder mystery, intriguing suspects, a sex scandal, Hollywood connections. The San Diego and Los Angeles papers hyped the story and it spread, often distorted, to front pages across the country. Later that year, the story ended without resolution and disappeared from history until 2011, when San Diego historian and author Rick Crawford resurrected it with a piece in the *San Diego Union-Tribune*.

This book is also about a place and time, southern California in the Jazz Age. San Diego, then a small but rapidly growing tourist town, border town, military town, and seaport, faced unique law enforcement challenges even before Prohibition inundated the city with illegal vice and corruption. Prohibition was one of a confluence of forces that drove rapid social change in the early 1920s and shaped the events surrounding Fritzie's death. Another of those forces, motion pictures, made an outsized impact on popular culture by featuring what traditionalists considered decadent themes. And another, a more aggressive women's movement, produced feminist archetypes in the form of the New Woman and the flapper that pushed the boundaries of gender norms, outraging the patriarchal society. The younger set's liberated outlook ran headlong into a Victorian moral code and laws against birth control and abortion. Waking to the Problem of the Younger Generation, as Frederick Lewis Allen phrased it in *Only Yesterday, An Informal History of the 1920's*, conservatives came to believe "that if the Constitution were not in danger, the moral code of the country certainly was." And so came the backlash. The culture wars in the early 1920s looked much like those one century later. Other than the addition of LGBTQ+ rights, the flash points—gender, race, abortion, immigration—haven't changed, nor has the rhetoric.

This book is also about an immigrant Jewish family whose dreams for a better life ended in San Diego after a series of tragedies. And about the baby of that family, a high-spirited and talented young woman who practiced a now-forgotten art and loved the wrong man.

***

I first learned about Fritzie's story in 2012 while looking for a thesis topic for an MFA program I was about to start. I wanted to write a narrative nonfiction book about an old crime, preferably obscure and unsolved, set in San Diego. A few people mentioned the Fritzie Mann case; a Google search brought up Rick Crawford's article. I found and considered other stories that met my criteria, but none as interesting or as widely covered as this one. As I began what proved to be a daunting research project, I learned that the story of Fritzie's tragic death was much more than an intriguing Jazz Age murder mystery; in many ways, it defined one of the most fascinating eras in U.S. history.

But telling the story proved to be more challenging than I'd anticipated. In some cases I found annoying, hard-to-fill gaps in the historical record, in others an abundance of information but of questionable veracity. I learned some hard lessons about writing a narrative nonfiction book, at least one about an obscure hundred-year-old murder mystery. The most important: Real-world events don't always cooperate with story-telling essentials and those pesky facts can get in the way of a good true story. Solving these problems required me to get creative with how I told the story without getting creative with the facts. It took me nine years to figure it out.

This is a work of nonfiction based on years of research. I didn't make anything up. Primary sources include trial transcripts and other court documents, contemporary newspaper accounts, and documents from the archives of government agencies, universities, and historical societies. Other sources include books, maps, city directories, consultations with experts, and the recollections of relatives and friends of some of the characters. All quotes, including dialogue, are given verbatim from primary sources except for slight edits to dialogue for readability and clarity. At times I knew the substance of a conversation but not the words used; in those cases, I paraphrase the dialogue or put the information in dialogue format without quotation marks.

***

Prologue – A House Party In Del Mar

On the morning of Monday, January 8, 1923, after performing in Los Angeles for two months, Frieda Mann rode the midnight train home to San Diego dressed like a flapper.

The outfit shocked her mother, Amelia. A party dress of brown silk crepe fringed with rows of copper beads and a brown hat with a tan ostrich feather? Who wears a get-up like that on an overnight train ride? Not her daughter, usually. Frieda said she'd borrowed the outfit from her friend in Long Beach for a house party on Sunday evening. It seemed odd to Amelia. She scolded Frieda for being careless with her friend's fancy outfit, then put it away and told her to wear her own clothes.

Frieda behaved oddly for the rest of the week, but Amelia saw no hint of melancholy. If anything, the girl acted too cheerful, too much like herself, especially that last day.

"She was joking around the whole day and making happy her sick sister," Amelia Mann said later in her thick Hungarian accent, "…and she made jokes, take her bath, and was lively—don't show a thing—nobody can say this girl had something in her heart, because she was happy, and she always was a jolly kid."

That jolly kid, twenty years old, went by a stage name better suited to her personality and profession: Fritzie. She remained jolly to the end, Amelia insisted, despite what some would claim. Still, something new seemed to be weighing on Fritzie.

What had she been up to in Los Angeles for the past two months? Filling dancing engagements and visiting friends, or so she said. Her visit home was supposed to be short—long enough to break a contract with her employers in San Diego and perhaps tie up some loose ends—then return to L.A. for work and from there on to San Francisco. But maybe she'd been doing something else, like consorting with the wrong kind of people, a danger in the interpretive dance world. Or, more dangerous still, trying to break into Hollywood, again.

Don't worry, Mother, Fritzie said when Amelia asked her to share her troubles. Everything will work out.

But Amelia did worry, perhaps more than she would have before now that her older daughter, Helen, lay dying in a sanitarium, the consumption killing her by degrees as it had her husband three years before. Fritzie's cageyness about her plans for Sunday evening bothered Amelia the most. She mentioned the house party more than once but refused to share details.

"Between Del Mar and Los Angeles," Fritzie said when Amelia asked where the party would be held, which meant nothing—it was a hundred miles between Del Mar and L.A. At other times she answered, "in Del Mar."

"Tell me the man with who you go," Amelia said.

"A man from L.A."

Each time Amelia asked, Fritzie refused to give the man's name or pretended she didn't know. She'd never done that before.

There were enough reasons to worry about a young daughter without her keeping secrets. Times had changed in the few years since the Great War and not all in a good way. The shifting gender norms and rambunctious behavior of the younger set—the late-night drinking and dancing, the permissive attitudes towards sex—had come too far and too fast for traditionalists. There were no safeguards anymore.

Suitors no longer called on a young woman at her home, where her parents could keep an eye on her; now the man picked her up in his automobile and took her out on a "date," ostensibly to a restaurant, a moving picture, or a jazz dance. But they might end up at a speakeasy or a hotel.

Amelia had scrutinized Fritzie's dates as much as any mother would, always asking questions and writing down the man's name. Some of the men had seemed respectable enough. The soft-spoken Jewish doctor from the Veteran's hospital, who Fritzie had dated on and off since the previous spring, fit into this category. Fritzie had seemed to care for him, at least before she left for L.A. last November. Was he the house party mystery man? Maybe. The doctor had telephoned her almost every day since she returned home so they must still be seeing one another. But he lived in San Diego, not L.A., and Fritzie would've had no reason to hide his identity.

Other suitors had vexed Amelia, one a man Fritzie had dated the previous fall. She had seemed smitten though it hadn't lasted long—thank God. Supposedly an actor and director, the man never entered the house or stepped onto the porch, just waited on the street in his pretentious Marmon touring car and summoned her with that damn *ahooga* horn. One morning he'd picked up Fritzie for a drive south of the border to Tijuana. Amelia hadn't liked the idea one bit—nothing good happened in TJ, a place that teemed with bars and brothels. To size the man up, Amelia had created a pretext; she asked him to drop her off at the Paradise Hills sanitarium, where Helen was being treated at the time, on their way south. Riding in the back seat of the ritzy machine, Amelia had jotted down the man's physical description, just in case. Was he the mystery man from L.A.? He lived there and worked in the motion picture business, a business Fritzie wanted to join. Hopefully not. Fritzie's troubles had seemed to start around the time she met him.

Not that Amelia had much control over Fritzie anymore, least of all her dating life and aspirations. Modern young women, the ones they called New Women and flappers, tended to do as they pleased, tradition and consequences be damned. Fritzie had been around more than most women her age anyway, especially for a place like San Diego, a rather provincial city of 80,000. She'd spent her early childhood in Europe, spoke several languages, and danced before large audiences in San Diego, Denver, and L.A. But if Fritzie's independence and self-assurance gave her certain New Woman sensibilities, no one could call her a flapper—she didn't smoke cigarettes or hang out in speakeasies or sleep around or do other things flappers did on the big screen. Fritzie danced on stage, not on tables. She was a sensible girl who helped to pay her sister's medical bills and pursued a career as a dancer on her own. And if interpretive dance had naughty undertones in some quarters, Fritzie considered herself a serious artist and any salaciousness rested in the minds of people who had such thoughts. But she had a twenty-year-old's overconfidence and naiveté and moved in risky circles, the night world of the cabaret and on the fringes of Hollywood. A young lady could get herself into trouble if she weren't careful. Her attitude and behavior may have changed; in many ways, things had not.

***

On Sunday afternoon, January 14, 1923, as she watched her daughter get ready for the house party in Del Mar or wherever she was going, Amelia's anxiety grew. Was Fritzie really going to a party? She seemed to be getting ready for one, putting on a real flapper outfit. She dolled herself up with makeup and curled her hair and donned her Long Beach friend's glad rags, as the younger set called their fancy outfits. To the brown hat and dress, she added brown satin shoes and silk stockings. She accentuated the outfit with a necklace of black and white beads, a gold bar pin on her left breast, and a barrette pinning her hair on the left side. She topped it off with an electric blue coat. She packed an overnight bag with a pink satin night shirt and underwear, makeup, and a sheer peacock blue nightgown with longish sleeves and gray fur trim.

If I'm not home by noon tomorrow, Fritzie assured her mother, I'll call.

At 5:15 p.m., ten minutes after sunset, Fritzie grabbed her handbag and vanity case. With her usual flippant goodbye wave to her older brother William, she headed out the front door of their tiny rental house on Spruce Street, near the northeast corner of Balboa Park. Amelia, a small woman, walked with her daughter in the cool January twilight under a cloudy sky, past the California Bungalow-styled homes of the modest neighborhood, two blocks to the streetcar stop at 30th and Redwood. On the way, Amelia's trepidation grew into a premonition. She implored Fritzie to stay home.

"Tell me who is the man who takes you out," Amelia said.

"He is a man from Los Angeles," Fritzie said.

"Tell me the name."

"I don't know his name."

"You told me always who you go out with and now you don't want to tell me."

Amelia continued to nag but at the trolley stop Fritzie gave her a quick hug and stepped up onto the streetcar.

Photographs of Fritzie Mann, most of which show her in an exotic dance costume, reveal a pretty woman with delicate features whose self-assured, vibrant temperament is evident. Her dark brown hair, often tinted auburn by the red hairnets she wore, wasn't cut in a flapper bob, but she kept it short in line with Jazz Age fashion and the preferred style of the New Woman. Having seen these pictures, it's easy to imagine her waving goodbye to her mother, confident that she had everything under control. No photographs of

Amelia survive, but it's not hard to imagine her face as she watched the streetcar disappear into the gathering darkness, the trolley pole sparking on the overhead wire: The worried look of a mother who knew or suspected that her youngest child had gotten herself into a fix and feared it was about to end badly.

Fritzie likely caught a south-bound streetcar, the shortest route to downtown. From there the car would've rattled down 30th Street on the eastern edge of Balboa Park, zigzagged around the corner of the park through Golden Hill, and then due west along Broadway into downtown. Fritzie had kept the rendezvous point to herself, mentioning only that she was meeting the mystery man downtown. It might've been the U.S. Grant Hotel, a gathering place for the younger set in the heart of downtown that Fritzie and her chums frequented. Or the Golden Lion Tavern, another hangout. Or, if the man was coming by train, the Santa Fe depot.

Twenty minutes later Fritzie called Amelia.

"Mother, that party will not be between Del Mar and Los Angeles," Fritzie said. "It will be in La Jolla."

A strange phone call on top of the other strangeness. Did the house party change venues at the last minute? La Jolla was nine miles south of Del Mar, somewhat closer to home. If Fritzie hoped to allay her mother's fears with this information, it didn't work.

"You might think you know the place where you are going," Amelia said. "I don't. You don't told me who you go, and I don't know."

Don't worry, Fritzie said. "It is a very quiet place."

***

Part I – Conundrum

Chapter One – I Am Fritzie Mann

Driving south on the coast highway through Del Mar, a little seaside resort twenty miles north of San Diego, John Chase and his wife decided to stop for a beach picnic lunch with their three children. They had travelled some one hundred and twenty miles from their home in San Fernando, north of Los Angeles. It was a substantial trip given that many automobiles were open to the elements and most roads remained unpaved and turned rutted and muddy after winter rains. Road trips were the latest thing. With the economy thriving and Model T's rolling off Henry Ford's assembly lines at $319 retail, ordinary families like the Chases could now purchase "machines" and take road trips for pleasure.

Few road trips could be more pleasant than this, motoring down the paved highway on a stretch of coast renowned for its beauty on a warm, partly sunny Monday in January. As they descended the southern edge of the Del Mar mesa, a gorgeous vista opened looking across to the Torrey Pines Grade a mile away, and down the coast in the haze, Mount Soledad and the La Jolla peninsula. To the left lay the Soledad Lagoon, a salt marsh estuary. To the right, the blue expanse of the Pacific. Separating the lagoon from the beach, as sharp as a blade, ran a straight half-mile stretch of paved highway hugging Torrey Pines beach. At the bottom of the hill, they drove past the Torrey Pines Garage and a small cluster of houses on the edge of the lagoon, through a railroad track viaduct, and across a wooden bridge spanning the Sorrento Slough. They pulled off the road at the southern end of the bridge and parked near a Chevrolet sign.

As the car rolled to a stop, Chase's nine-year-old son, Russell, hopped out and disappeared over the rocky embankment that led down to the beach. John Chase, a tall man with light brown hair, stepped out of the car into the fresh salt air. A bookkeeper in the fruit packing business, he was no stranger to the area and its ideal climate. The Chases had lived in Lemon Grove, a rural town east of San Diego, until a couple of years before, when John had taken a job in the lemon groves of the San Fernando Valley. John began to eat a sandwich. He had barely taken a bite when Russell came running back up the embankment.

There is a boy on the beach, Russell said. "He is laying very still."

The edge of the embankment blocked Chase's view of the beach below. He stepped onto the car's running board for a higher vantage point and spotted a human form lying a few hundred feet to the northwest near the surf. He told Russell to stay with his mother and began walking toward the figure, still holding his sandwich.

Torrey Pines Beach, though a popular bathing spot, was deserted at 12:30 p.m. on a Monday in January. The onshore breeze was strangely calm, the silence broken only by the light rush of the breakers and periodic seagull squawks. Near the bottom of the embankment, Chase walked past a dark-brown beaded dress lying alongside a mound of pebbles and weeds. The dress lay flat and stretched out on a line toward the body, as though someone had dropped it and dragged it across the dry sand. As he neared the figure, he realized that it wasn't a boy, but a young woman wearing only a pink silk teddy and garters, dark-brown silk stockings, and matching satin pumps.

The obviously dead woman appeared to be in her early twenties. She lay on her back parallel to the beach, ten or fifteen feet from the water's edge, embedded about one and a half inches into the wet sand, her legs to the south towards La Jolla, her feet close together and her arms across her torso. Her dark wet hair lay loose and splayed out, mixed with sand and strings of kelp. Her bloodshot, partially opened eyes stared skyward. Her tongue protruded between her teeth. There was a small bluish bruise over her right eyebrow. The sand in the vicinity of the body had been washed smooth by the waves.

Chase walked back to the road, the partially eaten sandwich still in his hand. He never did finish it. He and Russell flagged down a passing car, asking the driver to stop at the garage up the road toward Del Mar and call the police.

***

Harley Sachs, owner of the Torrey Pines Garage, didn't get excited about the report of a body on the beach— probably a mistake or a hoax, he figured. He decided to check it out before ringing the police and wasting their time. John Chase walked with Sachs and three of his employees out to the body. Sachs noted a mark over one of the woman's eyes and her hands folded neatly across her upper abdomen, one over the other. Sachs drove back to the garage and called the police. He and the other garage men soon returned and covered the body from head to knees with a piece of burlap, weighting down the corners with sand to prevent it from blowing away in the sea breeze.

County motorcycle officers Clarence Matthews and Robert Bowman, the first police on the scene, lifted a corner of the burlap. They noted, or later recalled, more precise details than the other witnesses. The woman's feet were five or six inches apart. The right strap of the pink teddy was down on her shoulder, partially exposing her breast. A "half a thimble full" of blood, Matthews estimated, had pooled in the inside corner of her right eye. A froth of fine bubbles, resembling shaving soap lather flecked with enough blood to give it a slight reddish tinge, had oozed out of her mouth and nostrils. Matthews' observations of the woman's tongue starkly contradicted those of Chase and Sachs. The tongue, in fact, did not protrude slightly out of her mouth, as those men had observed, but way out, farther than Matthews had ever seen a tongue hang from a person's mouth. As he described it, as if "she had throwed up her tongue."

Curiosity seekers began to assemble along the slough bridge rail and at the makeshift parking area south of the bridge. Some people wandered onto the beach. The motorcycle officers tried to keep them away from the body and the dress, assumed to belong to the dead woman. Harley Sachs and a few other men waited with the cops for the coroner to arrive, anxiously watching the waves. The waves broke, spread across the sand, and dissipated with a sizzle, inching ever closer to the body as the tide began to come back in.

"If the coroner doesn't hurry up," one of the garage men said, "the water will be up over the body."

***

The law did not require the San Diego County coroner, the elected official responsible for determining the cause and manner of suspicious deaths, to have a medical background, and Coroner Schuyler Kelly did not. A square-jawed, gray-haired man in his mid-fifties, Kelly had spent most of his life in the newspaper trade. He'd worked at the *Kansas City Star* in his youth and held editorial jobs at two small San Diego newspapers. In five years in the coroner's job, he'd recovered corpses all over the big county. He spent "many a night in the mountains, traveling in mud, rain, and snow, on an errand of death, bringing the body of some poor unfortunate person," according to a *San Diego Union* profile.

Now he stood over the body of another unfortunate person and pronounced her dead.

"Do any of you men recognize this woman?" he asked those assembled, who at this point included the garage men, the motorcycle cops, an ambulance driver, and Deputy Sheriff John Bludworth from Del Mar. No one recognized her.

"Well, boys," Kelly said, "there ought to be some more clothes around here some place…a hat or something…" Something they could use to identify the woman.

The men searched the beach in the vicinity of the body and nearby areas, around a large, abandoned rock crushing machine and under the curving bridge over the slough entrance. They found nothing of interest.

Kelly feared the tide might be coming in to reclaim the body. He made a quick, general examination. He found rigor mortis "very decided." He saw no marks on the woman's arms or chest, but observed small scratches on the face, which he attributed to crab bites. He didn't notice—or later couldn't recall—a discharge emanating from the mouth or nose but noted a white substance across the lips. He thought this might be dried saliva or the residue of a poison, possibly cyanide.

Deputy Sheriff Bludworth noted a bruise over the eye, a drop of blood in the corner of one eye, and a foamy discharge on the face, which seemed to still be oozing from the nose and mouth. The tongue protruded about an inch out of the left side of the mouth, he thought.

The ambulance driver placed a stretcher alongside the body. He grasped the dead woman's shoulders and the coroner held her by the ankles. They eased her onto the stretcher and covered her with a sheet. The woman's body left an impression in the damp sand, a fleeting trace of her the surf would soon wash away.

***

The *San Diego Evening Tribune* once described sixty-year-old Deputy Sheriff John Bludworth as one of the last "remaining picturesque characters of the old, two-gun west." The longest-serving law officer in the county, Bludworth had joined the San Diego Sheriff's Office in the 1880s, almost back to the day Wyatt Earp ran saloons and gambling halls downtown. He looked the part. His standard attire consisted of a white shirt, dark tie, black Stetson, and a dark vest with a watch chain dangling from the pocket. He carried a .38 Colt Police Positive revolver on his hip and wore the weathered visage of a law man with too much mileage on him.

He'd watched times—and bad guys—change since the days of Wyatt Earp.

"In the old days you had the best horse and the best gun or you didn't get your man," Bludworth once said. "You're hunting gentlemen these days."

He'd replaced his best horse with a Model T. These days he often waited in his machine at the Hotel Del Mar, which dominated the town, until the sheriff alerted him with instructions to intercept a bad guy, usually a bootlegger or a dope runner heading north on the coast highway, few of them actual gentlemen.

After the coroner had removed the woman's body from the beach, Bludworth went home. Soon Harley Sachs called him back to the scene. He arrived to find Sachs and two other men combing the beach in the late-evening sunlight. They pointed out a spot some five hundred yards south of the bridge. The embankment, comprised of a thick bed of earth and crushed rock that kept the highway dry from the highest tide, was so steep at this point that the men had to half-walk, half-slide the thirty feet down to the sand. Four or five feet from the bottom of the embankment, above the most recent high tide line, lay a small metal vanity case. Two feet away lay an imitation leather handbag.

Bludworth asked the men if they'd touched anything. They all said no.

He saw no foot tracks near the items. He noticed an indentation, roughly the width of the vanity case, in the dry sand, apparently an impact mark. One corner of the case lid had sprung open, also indicating a possible impact. It appeared that someone had tossed the items out of a moving machine.

Bludworth glimpsed a blue garment inside of the partially open handbag but didn't investigate the contents further. He opened the vanity case. The mirror on the inside of the cover was cracked. Inside, he found several business cards, a photograph of a dark-haired woman who resembled the deceased, and various feminine items. A white card listed several names on one side. On the other side it bore a handwritten note in black ink:

I am
Fritzie Mann
2773 A Street

***

Chapter Two – A Delicate Condition

The coroner lacked his own morgue. This forced his autopsy surgeon to perform post-mortem examinations at funeral parlors under mediocre or worse conditions. A long-standing agreement obliged the coroner to deliver an equal number of the corpses he collected to each of the eight local funeral parlors. This arrangement had caused controversy on occasion. In the most egregious example, Schuyler Kelly had stood trial the year before, charged with accepting bribes to deliver a disproportionate number of bodies to one undertaker and for stealing jewelry off a corpse. The charges didn't mean much in themselves in a city rife with Prohibition graft—people were always accusing each other of taking bribes. Kelly called it a charade, the personal vendetta of a disgruntled undertaker. The jury ultimately acquitted him. More often, the lack of autopsy facilities created practical problems that might undermine the veracity of an autopsy and criminal investigation. Such was the case with the autopsy of the unknown woman found on Torrey Pines beach.

Dr. John Shea arrived at the Smith, Goodbody & Dunn funeral home around 5:00 p.m. on the evening of Monday, January 15, 1923. A distinguished-looking man with small round wire-rimmed glasses, carefully parted hair and a neat moustache, Shea had served as Schuyler Kelly's autopsy surgeon for the past five years. He didn't seem to like working for a non-medical coroner. Years later Shea would run a losing campaign for his old boss' job under the campaign slogan, "A doctor should be coroner." In the meantime, the Harvard Medical School graduate worked for a former newspaper man.

A funeral parlor preparation room of the 1920s might be all white with a black and white checkered ceramic floor. Bottles of yellow, orange, and green embalming fluids would be stacked on shelves or in a cabinet along with other materials of the dismal trade. A familiar scent greeted Dr. Shea as he entered the room, an acrid blend of antiseptic, embalming fluid, mortuary powder, and death. What he saw on the embalming table stunned him: A tube inserted into the axillary vein under the woman's armpit was draining her blood into an enameled pan beneath the embalming table. Even though the coroner had delivered the body, the undertaker somehow didn't get the word that this case required an autopsy. He'd already drained most of the blood in preparation for an infusion of embalming fluid. Asked later if this precluded a definitive determination of cause of death, Dr. Shea replied, "Well, it handicaps a man."

Shea took notes on a card as he performed the autopsy. The body, that of a well-developed, well-nourished Caucasian female with dark brown hair and blue eyes, aged approximately twenty-two, measured five feet, four inches in height and weighed about 130 pounds. The body was pale except for a congested (red) appearance of the face. The teeth were "all sound, well kept; second molars, right and left side, missing."

Shea's external examination revealed no abnormalities or identifying marks. He noted fresh slight abrasions on the elbows, as though the skin had been rubbed off, and other slight abrasions on the forehead and prominent parts of the cheeks. The palms, fingers, and feet were not corrugated (severely wrinkled), and he found no foreign material under the fingernails. The eyes: equal but dilated. Rigor mortis: present. The mouth open and fixed in rigor, but the tongue did not protrude between the lips. No lividity observed. The bruise, "a black and blue discoloration on the outer angle of the right eyebrow, the size of a quarter, superficial," had been inflicted, he thought, before death, most likely by means other than wave action. He couldn't say what type of implement might have caused it; in any case, it did not contribute to death. He dissected along the bruise and found some fluid blood under the skin. He pressed down on the chest with both hands, a whitish frothy mucous exuded from the mouth.

The doctor opened the body cavity and removed the internal organs. The stomach appeared normal and contained a small amount of water and semi-digested food. He sectioned the lungs and found a frothy mucous in the bronchial tubes and filling the alveoli but not the pleural cavities. The frothy mucous was not discolored with blood. He found no free water in the lungs, no sand or sea growth in the lungs or stomach. Shea incised the heart; it appeared normal. He found that "the right heart contained some blood—fine clots; the left heart was empty." The kidneys, bladder, and other internal organs appeared normal. He did not take organs or bodily fluid samples for chemical analysis.

Dr. Shea found "a decided enlargement of the uterus, which an examination showed to be a male fetus about four to four-and one-half months of inter-uterine life." As he would tell the press in the polite parlance of the day, the woman had died in a "delicate condition." All fetal membranes were intact—no operations had been performed. The young woman had not died from a botched abortion; she had drowned.

***

Deputy Sheriff Bludworth returned home and examined the contents of the handbag and vanity case. The handbag contained a blue night gown, a rouge box, a tube of toothpaste, a comb, and a box of *Naturelle* face powder. In the vanity case, he found a string of beads, a lipstick, a pair of glasses, a Gillette safety razor, a powder puff, a small pocketbook with a penny in it, a Kodak photograph of a dark-haired woman, three printed business cards, and the handwritten card with a woman's name and address. One of the business cards bore the name R.R. Remington, an employee of the Banker's Life Insurance Company, with a Long Beach, California, address. A second card bore the name H.F. Bittaker, an orchestra leader at "The Barn," a roadhouse in the out-country northeast of San Diego. The third card announced a "farewell performance" the previous October at The Barn for Miss Fritzie Mann.

Bludworth called Coroner Kelly.

"Deputy Sheriff John Bludworth telephoned me from Del Mar," Kelly said later, "stating that after I had taken the body to town, he had found the vanity case. He then gave several names which he found on the cards in the case. Among them was the name of Fritzie Mann. He did not tell me at the time that the card bore the words 'I am Fritzie Mann.' The telephone connection was extremely poor, and I had great difficulty in understanding him."

Kelly then called the Mann residence and asked the young man who answered to speak to Fritzie Mann. William Mann said he didn't know where his sister was, how to reach her, or when she might return. Later, facing criticism for his handling of the early stages of the case, the coroner would deem William's responses "evasive." William recommended he call back at eleven the next morning, then asked who he was speaking to.

"This is Kelly," the caller replied.

Kelly didn't mention that he was the county coroner holding an unidentified female body with a vanity case, presumed to belong to her, that contained a card with his sister's name on it.

"At the time I had no reason to believe that the body was hers," Kelly said later, responding to William's criticism, "but merely that she might be able to identify it."

When this peculiar conversation took place, William's little sister had been dead for twenty-four hours.

***

Chapter Three – That Damned Actor

The woman's body remained unidentified when the *San Diego Union* went to press the next morning, Tuesday, January 16: YOUNG WOMAN'S BODY FOUND ON BEACH, DRESS FOUND LYING NEAR, ABOVE TIDE-LINE, *Drowning Said Cause of Death, But Severe Bruise On Forehead Gives Rise to Suspicion of Murder.*

Twenty-four-year-old William Mann read the article with concern. When she left the house on Sunday evening, Fritzie had said she would call or be home by noon on Monday and here it was Tuesday morning and no sign of her. The description of the victim in the article seemed to match his sister. Similarities included size, age, teeth, and hair and eye color. And the dress found near the body, described as made of a "crepe material and fringed with beads," sounded similar to the dress she'd worn when she left for the "house party." But some things didn't fit. For one, the vanity case and handbag found nearby was said to contain "no clue as to her identity." William knew that Fritzie always carried a card with her name and address on it. Last summer he'd watched her write the card at their mother's request and knew she was to keep it with her at all times. Surely, if the authorities had found a card in the dead woman's vanity case that said "I am Fritzie Mann" they would've contacted the family by now, even though it listed their old address.

But if this line of reasoning gave William any solace, it was fleeting. The description of the dead woman sounded enough like Fritzie to make him "curious," as he later phrased it—curious enough to visit the undertaker. He may have noticed the coroner's name in the article and made the connection to the odd phone call he'd received the previous evening. As William said later, if the mysterious Kelly had informed him that he was the coroner with an unidentified woman's body, he would've hurried to the undertaking parlor the night before "and the unraveling of the case would have been set at least 12 hours ahead."

William Mann's photograph in "The Annual" of the East Denver High School graduating class of 1916 shows a handsome young man with closely cropped dark hair, piercing dark eyes, and an enigmatic half-smile who gives off a calm, self-assured air. Below the picture his memberships in the German Club, the Glee Club, and the student Congress are listed with a quote from Ferdinand, King of Navarre, in *Love's Labour's Lost*: "A man in all the world's new fashion planted, That hath a mint of phrases in his brain." If in high school William had fancied himself a witty, fashionable dresser like Shakespeare's Spanish courtier Armado, it didn't come across in his public statements seven years later. If anything, he sounded more like Ferdinand, who had renounced earthly pleasures in favor of scholarship. Or like an accountant, which he was, who lived with his mother and two sisters and worked as a civilian employee at the North Island Naval Air Station.

Amelia Mann's state of mind on the morning of the worst day of her life isn't recorded. Given her premonition on Sunday evening and with her daughter now overdue by a full day, she must've been insane with worry. Her reaction to the *Union* article also isn't recorded. What is recorded is that when the undertaker pulled back the sheet to reveal the embalmed and autopsied body of her daughter, Amelia Mann became hysterical. The papers quoted the coroner's account of Amelia's "hysteria" at seeing her dead daughter, as if hysteria were an unusual reaction of a parent at seeing her dead child.

Amelia knew at once who to blame: That damned actor.

"It was Rogers Clark!" she screamed. "Rogers Clark murdered my beautiful little girl!"

***

Chapter Four – The White Plague

The Mann family had endured tragedy before and would again. They had emigrated from Europe in 1910, near the end of the great wave of immigration between 1881 and 1914 during which almost two million Jews entered America to escape poverty, pogroms, or both. Fritzie's father, Isor, was Polish, her mother Hungarian. They settled in Sarajevo, Bosnia, where members of Amelia's family had settled and where she gave birth to their three children, the last—Fritzie—on May 27, 1902. In January 1910, the family departed Trieste, Italy, aboard the liner S.S. *Martha Washington*, bound for New York. They arrived in New York on the 12th of February, entering port after a blinding snowstorm passed through early in the morning. They are listed in Ellis Island records as Isidor, Amalia, Wilhelm, Helena, and Frieda.

The Manns were among the twenty-four first-class passengers onboard. This enabled them to avoid the misery of a winter North Atlantic Ocean transit crammed into the lower decks in third-class. More importantly, it meant that after the ship moored in New York, Public Health Service officers would give them only a cursory medical inspection. Travelling third-class would've subjected them to the lengthy registration process at Ellis Island, making it more likely that symptoms of Isor Mann's tuberculosis might be noticed. Under the Immigration Act of 1907, signed by President Theodore Roosevelt, he would've been barred from entering the country along with those deemed to be idiots, imbeciles, insane persons, polygamists, paupers, prostitutes, anarchists, and perpetrators of the crime of moral turpitude. The doctors did not discover Isor's illness.

The Mann family, with a total of $200 in their possession and who later struggled financially, made unlikely first-class passengers. Amelia's family almost certainly assisted them. Her father, sister, and two brothers had immigrated to America in the 1890s and settled in Nashville, Tennessee. Her brother, a jeweler who had become a leading Nashville citizen, met the Manns on the pier in New York.

After staying briefly with Amelia's family in Nashville, the Manns moved on to Denver. It wasn't a random choice. A disproportionate number of immigrant Jews settled in Denver around the turn of the century. Colorado, with its high altitudes, sunny skies, and dry air, was called "The World's Sanitarium," and Denver hosted two sanitariums for Jewish consumptives.

One of the leading causes of death in industrialized cities in the 19th and early 20th centuries and one of the most frequent causes of death in recorded history, people held tuberculosis in almost superstitious dread. But though horrific, the disease had attained a certain artistic cachet. So many noted 19th century writers, composers, and artists—Balzac, Keats, Shelley, Schubert, Stevenson, Poe, Shiller, Thoreau, Chekov, the Bronte sisters, Browning, Delacroix, Gauguin, Paganini, and Chopin to name a few—suffered from pulmonary tuberculosis that it came to be called the "Romantic Disease." Artists immortalized the disease in works of art from Verdi's opera *La Traviata* to Munch's painting "The Sick Child."

"It was the fashion to suffer from the lungs;" wrote Alexandre Dumas, "everybody was consumptive, poets especially; it was good form to spit blood after any emotion that was at all sensational, and to die before reaching the age of thirty."

Also known as the White Plague or the White Death, the disease inflicted fever, fatigue, bloody cough, and loss of appetite over a period of years, slowly "consuming" the victim. Public fear and ostracism added to the agony of the disease. When a person contracted consumption, the possibility that it would infect family members and visitors was ever-present. As a child, Fritzie could not invite friends to her house because of her father's consumption and later her sister's.

Despite his suffering, Isor Mann had brought some old-world bravado with him to America. In October 1911, he got into a ruckus with a Denver pawn shop owner named Heitler over a pawned watch. A dispute arose over the interest on the loan and the man slapped Isor. The honor code he had once followed as an officer of the Austrian army compelled him to avenge an insult or resign his commission, or so Isor claimed. He "forthwith sent a challenge to Heitler, but the latter declined to spill his blood in any such manner and then the Austrian swore out a warrant for his arrest on an assault and battery charge."

Thereafter, Isor's life grew less colorful. He sold insurance until 1916, then became unemployed as his health declined. He entered the Jewish Consumptives' Relief Society in February 1920. By then his suffering had neared its end; he died seven weeks later at the age of forty-nine.

In the fall of the following year, the fifty-two-year-old Amelia Mann and her children left Denver for San Diego. Consumption again prompted their move, this time for Helen's benefit. Denver's climate had failed to cure Amelia's husband. She hoped San Diego's sunny skies, desert-ocean air, and warm temperatures might save her daughter. The "Denver Society" section of the November 19, 1921 edition of the *Denver Post* noted their departure: "Mrs. A. Mann and Misses Helen and Fritzie Mann are leaving tonight for California to spend the winter." Like many who visit San

Diego, later to call itself America's Finest City, a winter's visit turned into a permanent move.

***

Chapter Five – Tangled Threads

The *Union* called the witnesses on Torrey Pines beach "actors in a weird scene," with a dead protagonist and an unknown antagonist, if one existed, and the supporting players scratching their heads. The manner of Fritzie Mann's death and the circumstances surrounding it hadn't been obvious, nor would they be the next day or later. On the first full day of the investigation, the police were chasing the mystery through "tangled threads" of conflicting evidence, some pointing to accidental death, some to suicide, some to murder.

A body washed up on a beach would normally be assumed an accidental drowning, common in San Diego County with its bays and beaches—in 1918, in a single incident, thirteen swimmers had drowned in a rip current off Ocean Beach. But an accident seemed the least likely scenario here. The waters off San Diego were chilly even at the height of summer, never mind in January, and the temperature had dropped into the mid-forties on Sunday night. Was Fritzie Mann the type of person to go for a frigid late-night swim on a desolate beach, perhaps inebriated, dressed to the nines? Her family, interviewed by reporters at their home, ruled this out.

"She certainly would not go in swimming in her 'teddies'," William Mann told reporters. "My sister wasn't a reckless girl and she didn't know what a drink was until she came to San Diego."

But the police couldn't take a bereaved brother's view of a dead woman's character as fact. She might've been wilder than her family knew or would admit. She performed as an *Oriental* dancer, after all, which members of polite society might consider disreputable, and that copper-beaded party dress looked like something a flapper would wear. She might've gotten tanked at that house party or a roadhouse and snuck off to a remote beach with a man for a late-night tryst. The advent of Prohibition following passage of the Volstead Act three years before hadn't stopped folks from drinking, to say the least, and people did stupid things when they drank bathtub gin. Maybe the girl had passed out on the sand and the tide had washed over her. But could it be that simple? Her personal effects, strewn over a five-hundred-yard stretch of beach, didn't seem to fit an accidental scenario.

Suicide seemed a better bet. An unmarried pregnant woman had obvious reasons to be despondent, perhaps to the point of wanting to end her life. It happened all the time. What were the circumstances of Fritzie Mann's pregnancy? Had a lout seduced her under the promise of marriage, a not uncommon ploy? Had her lover rejected her after he learned of her pregnancy, leaving her heartbroken, in a desperate financial situation, or both? Maybe the out-of-wedlock pregnancy constituted an unbearable scandal or shame in her family—it would have in most families. Maybe she ran onto the beach in despair, flung off her dress, and cast herself into the waves. But Amelia and William Mann had described her sanguine disposition and careful preparations for the party on Sunday afternoon; this did not suggest suicidal ideation in the hours leading up to her death. Her heartbroken mother ruled out suicide.

"I believe that my daughter was murdered!" Amelia Mann sobbed to reporters at her home. Fritzie loved life too much to kill herself. She was the victim of her blind faith in men. "I am positive that a man she loved too much was her slayer."

And that man was Rogers Clark, Amelia declared

Perhaps the age difference is what had so repelled her about Clark, as he was old enough to be Fritzie's father. Or maybe his profession, actor and director—almost certainly that. Tinseltown men bore watching. Over the past two years scarcely a week had passed without a scandal stinking up the front pages. The newspapers painted the film colony as a den of iniquity where booze, sex, and drugs flowed freely, where wild parties turned into orgies that might end in rape and murder, like the Fatty Arbuckle affair in San Francisco. Fritzie's suitor, tall, movie-star handsome and well-off, seemed to fit the Hollywood lady-killer mold—a *sheik* in current slang, so-called after the eponymous 1921 film that made flappers swoon and hurled Rudolph Valentino into the movie star stratosphere. Had this playboy ruined and then abandoned the poor girl, pushing her into despair, as her mother suggested? Possible, even probable.

But the bruise on the dead woman's forehead, apparently inflicted before death from an instrument or a fall, suggested a darker scenario, one District Attorney Chester Kempley already favored: A man stunned her with a blow and then carried her into the waves, hoping the cops would mistake it for a suicide or an accident. If her death were ruled a suicide, the killer would have executed a perfect crime. But the bruise alone didn't prove anything, because it may have been accidental or unrelated to her death. And although the papers said a severe blow had caused it, that was just one of their usual exaggerations. Dr. Shea described the wound as superficial and not a direct cause of Fritzie Mann's death.

But her scattered personal articles, apparently tossed out of a machine moving south toward La Jolla and San Diego, possibly in a panic, suggested the involvement of another person. And the woman's posture struck some people as odd. DA Kempley, in the job for one week when the case broke, found her posture suspicious and considered it evidence of foul play, even though he hadn't been one of the beach players. To the DA, Miss Mann seemed to have been posed, her legs stretched out, feet together, hands folded neatly across her breast in peaceful repose, as it were, frozen in rigor mortis. At least some of the witnesses described it that way. She would've looked almost peaceful if the situation hadn't been so tragic and her lifeless face such a ghastly sight, the combination a disturbing incongruity. Perhaps, as the *San Diego Evening Tribune* speculated, the hands had not landed that way by chance, "as ocean waves might have tossed them," but rather, "as human hands might have folded them."

But if someone had killed Fritzie Mann and hurriedly fled the scene, would they have taken time to position her body? Perhaps the killer had acted from shame, indicating an impulsive yet remorseful person who knew the victim, presumably the father of her unborn child or a rejected admirer. Some killers of this type, after their rage is spent and they realize with horror what they've done, cover the victim's face; maybe this reflected a similar motivation. Or, more unsettling, was the perpetrator a fiend without conscience who wished to mock the woman in death, taking warped pleasure in the knowledge that no Prince Charming would come to wake her? And considering her state of dress, a sex fiend?

The police also had to consider that the beach might be a secondary crime scene. The killer may have knocked her unconscious elsewhere, with a blow or a drug, then dumped her on the beach to make the crime mimic a suicide or simply to dispose of the body. If the killer carried her body into the surf, had she been merely unconscious, but he believed her dead? Dr. Shea had determined the cause of death as drowning, which meant only that she'd been breathing when her head became submerged. It didn't indicate how her head came to be submerged. Drowning was an uncommon method of homicide but also of suicide.

To San Diego Police Chief James Patrick, the factor most indicative of foul play was the location. Fritzie Mann did not get to that spot on her own, dressed for a party, carrying a handbag and a vanity case. Torrey Pines beach was too desolate, too far from public transportation, too improbable on a chilly, blustery Sunday night. The streetcar lines stopped before La Jolla, eight miles to the south, and the closest train station was two miles north at the Hotel Del Mar. If she'd somehow managed to walk from the train station—two miles on a hilly and winding road, down the jagged rocks of the embankment, and through the sand at night—it would've been evident by scarring to her delicate satin pumps, and it was not. Nor had she driven herself to that spot. Fritzie Mann did not own a car, and no one had reported an abandoned machine in the area. Whatever the manner of death, at least one other person was involved. Someone drove her to the beach.

***

Chapter Six – The Doctor

Deputy Sheriff Bludworth returned to Torrey Pines beach on Tuesday, January 16. Although the body had been discovered right on the line between city and county jurisdiction, the city cops had assumed responsibility for the investigation. But Bludworth considered the beach his turf and he knew it as well as anyone, a local knowledge that came in handy. With the sands shifting in the wind and tides ebbing and flowing, evidence might've been overlooked— no telling what might've been washed away or blown away or covered by the sand since Sunday night. He hunted up and down the beach, under the bridge, and along the road. His persistence paid off. On the hard ground just south of the slough bridge, where vehicles had parked and curiosity seekers had congregated the day before, Bludworth found a woman's gold bar pin. This was the only spot along Torrey Pines beach—the only spot within miles—where a car could pull off the road and gain quick access to the beach. Had the pin fallen to the ground as the victim stepped out of the car, or as her killer removed her body from the car? Amelia Mann later identified the pin as the one Fritzie had worn when she left home for the last time.

***

Police headquarters consisted of a two-story building with white clapboard siding attached to the city jail. From his second-floor office, San Diego Police Chief James

Patrick presided over an eighty-seven-man force comprised of a detective bureau, an identification bureau, and fifty-four patrolmen to cover a city of seventy-three square miles.

By most accounts, Chief Patrick performed his job well in challenging times. A tall, rugged native Alabaman and Spanish-American War veteran, he had a reputation as a self-effacing, quietly competent officer who ran a disciplined force. His low-profile approach, however, masked a shrewd politician. He had joined the force in 1912 and rose rapidly through the ranks, appointed to acting chief in five years and permanently appointed to chief two years later. But whether out of habit, conscientiousness, or necessity, he remained a hands-on cop. He kept tight control of the Fritzie Mann case and conducted most of the important interviews and interrogations personally.

On Tuesday at around 5:00 p.m., a suspect walked into the chief's office accompanied by a friend. The friend, Leo Greenbaum, a well-known produce merchant, introduced his companion as Dr. Louis L. Jacobs. A thirty-one-year-old physician who specialized in the treatment of tuberculosis, Jacobs held the rank of passed assistant surgeon (reserve) in the U.S. Public Health Service, the equivalent of an Army captain. Jacobs worked at the veteran's hospital at Camp Kearny, in the out country fifteen miles north of downtown on the Linda Vista Mesa.

Greenbaum recounted a conversation he'd had with the doctor earlier in the day. Dr. Jacobs had appeared in his store at 6th and Broadway holding the newspaper, having just read about the death of Miss Fritzie Mann., a mutual acquaintance of both men.

Jacobs had told Greenbaum, "I want to see my attorney, Mr. Wadham."

"Why see your attorney?" Greenbaum had replied. "Go down to the station and see Chief Patrick."

Greenbaum now said to the chief, "I steered him over to you."

Whether Jacobs had vacillated before he took his friend's advice to see Chief Patrick without his lawyer present isn't clear. But now the doctor found himself talking to Patrick, a large, intimidating man in an olive drab and khaki uniform, with a produce merchant instead of an attorney by his side.

"I am a friend of the dead girl," Jacobs said, speaking for the first time. "She recently confided in me and I want to do what I can to help you clear up the mystery surrounding her death."

Chief Patrick sized up Dr. Jacobs, a soft-spoken man of average height, a slim build, dark brown hair, a dark complexion, brown eyes, and a refined air.

Jacobs stated that he had first met Miss Mann around the first of July of the previous year. He last saw her on Friday, January 12 when they met for dinner at the Maryland Hotel. Afterward, at her suggestion, they went for a drive "to talk things over." They drove out east to La Mesa in Jacobs' Hudson, parked, and had a long conversation. Nervous and depressed, Miss Mann informed him of her delicate condition and asked him to perform an illegal operation. He refused. He dropped her off at her home around 10:00 p.m. Concerned about her state of mind, he phoned her the following day to check on her. He never saw or spoke to her again.

Where were you the next day, Sunday the 14th? Chief Patrick asked.

Jacobs said he had spent the day in Tijuana with Mrs. Ella Worthington, a widow who lived in Coronado. They returned from TJ via the Silver Strand, the narrow, sandy seven-mile-long isthmus that leads south from Coronado to Imperial Beach at the southern end of San Diego Bay. He dropped Mrs. Worthington at her home at around 6:00 p.m., took the ferry across to downtown, and drove to the Santa Fe Depot to meet people arriving on the 6:30 train.

Who did you meet? the chief asked.

I was supposed to meet two friends from Kalamazoo, Michigan, Jacobs said, but they never showed.

What were their names?

I don't know their names.

Then how did you know they were coming? How did you know when and where to meet them?

I received a postcard. When I realized they weren't coming, I got something to eat at Harvey's restaurant in the train depot. Then I drove "directly to Camp Kearny."

The chief didn't question Jacobs further about his no-named friends from Kalamazoo.

Leo Greenbaum meant well when he advised his friend to see the chief before consulting a lawyer, but it was a mistake. He made a bigger mistake when he told the chief the doctor's first thought had been to consult an attorney. Jacobs' impulse to lawyer up before the police even knew he existed made Chief Patrick suspicious, which he later admitted. So did the doctor's strange answers and squirrely behavior.

***

Chapter Seven – Pretty Little White Girls

Fritzie Mann's death instantly made the front pages in the San Diego papers and at least one major L.A. paper. A beautiful young exotic dancer found almost nude under confounding circumstances? Perfect recipe for a tabloid murder story. In the heyday of yellow journalism, you couldn't miss. Her pregnancy added a layer of scandal and there was more. Fritzie's public dance performances throughout 1922, often well-publicized and accompanied by articles and photographs, made her fairly recognizable in San Diego, even if she attained fame only in death. A photo of her in a cutesy pose, dressed in a frilly costume, on the front page of the January 16 *Union* lit a torch to the story. With more revelations to follow.

As the case grew into one of the most sensational news stories in southern California in recent memory, the papers in San Diego and L.A. would unleash a flurry of articles, many riddled with exaggeration, rumor, and speculation. Papers across the country repeated and sometimes embellished the inaccuracies, and as usual, the story got better and less accurate with each retelling.

The story stoked competition among the local daily papers, the *San Diego Union,* the *San Diego Evening Tribune* and the *San Diego Sun,* an already keen rivalry because of the acrimony between the owners. Both men permanently stamped their names on the city in the early part of the 20th century. John D. Spreckels, the wealthiest man in the area, owned the *Union* and the *Evening Tribune*. His other holdings included the San Diego-Coronado ferry, the city's streetcar system, the San Diego & Arizona Railway, Spreckels Theatre, and the Hotel Del Coronado. He helped fund the building program associated with the 1915 Panama-California Exposition in Balboa Park, a landmark event in the city's history, and with his brother had donated the park's famed Spreckels Organ Pavilion. Eccentric E.W. Scripps, along with his sister, Ellen Browning Scripps, owned the *Sun*, part of a family media empire that included twenty-five newspapers and the company that later became United Press International. Their philanthropic contributions included the Scripps Institution for Biological Research, the Scripps Memorial Hospital, the San Diego Natural History Museum, the San Diego Zoo, and the land for what became Torrey Pines State Park. With opposing ideas about how best to serve the city, Spreckels and Scripps sometimes used their newspapers as vehicles to attack the other's pet projects.

But competition among the local papers was nothing compared to the big-city papers. William Randolph Hearst had invented the modern version of sensationalized, fact-challenged reporting dubbed "yellow journalism" around the turn of the century. His *New York Journal* competed with other city papers for readership, most notably Joseph Pulitzer's *New York World*, by hyping and sometimes creating the news. The prime catalysts to the onset of yellow journalism had been the Goldensuppe Long Island dismemberment case of 1897-1898 and efforts to ignite the Spanish-American War.

Yellow journalism still reigned in the early 1920s, typified by Hearst's coverage of a series of infamous Hollywood scandals. In the sixteen months preceding Fritzie Mann's death, Hearst's papers, led by the *Los Angeles Examiner* and the *San Francisco Examiner*, had shattered the careers of three major silver screen players—Roscoe "Fatty" Arbuckle, Mabel Normand, and Mary Miles Minter—with stories filled with innuendo, exaggeration, and fabrication. The lurid coverage of these scandals paved the way for the success of the Fritzie Mann story.

The journalistic sins of the San Diego papers were innocuous compared to Hearst's, the exaggerations more subtle. For instance, all three daily papers went out of their way to portray Fritzie as small and meek, referring to her as "petite" or "little" or "dainty" whenever "pretty" didn't suffice. Though pretty, Fritzie wasn't a particularly small woman for her time. According to Dr. Shea, the most reliable source, Fritzie Mann stood approximately 5 feet 4 inches tall and weighed about 130 pounds—average size or better for a Caucasian-American woman of her day, even allowing for normal weight gain four months into her pregnancy. Nor, with her confident manner and athletic dancer's physique, was there anything meek about her character or dainty about her appearance. This inaccuracy owed much to the photographs of Fritzie in her dance costumes plastered on the front pages, some of which did make her appear dainty or petite. But accurate or not, those terms endeared her to newspaper readers. Then, as always, pretty little white girls made the best-selling corpses.

***

Chapter Eight – Butterfly Girl

Fritzie had held odd jobs in Denver. In 1921 she worked briefly as a dental nurse and later in a music store but spent much of her time dancing or training for it. Her first recorded performance, in the role of Dame Trot, came at age thirteen in a production of "The Mother Goose Convention" on December 5, 1915, part of the Chanukah celebration at the Temple Emanuel School in Denver. She developed a passion for the art of dance, often called "Terpsichore" in homage to the ancient Greek Muse of Dance.

In newspaper advertisements and articles on her 1922 San Diego area performances, Fritzie boasted of an illustrious dance pedigree. She claimed indirect linkages to the most famous Russian ballet companies of the early 20th century, that of Anna Pavlova, one of the most renowned and influential ballerinas in history; and Theodore Kosloff, a noted dancer and silent film star. Pavlova and Kosloff had performed together for Sergei Diaghilev, the legendary impresario of the Ballets Russes, often considered the greatest dance company of the 20th Century. The claim about Pavlova's company, at least, was true.

As a teenager, Fritzie had trained and performed under Domina Marini, a former premier danseuse of Pavlova's Imperial Russian Ballet Company. Known for a time but now forgotten, the Italian Marini had grown up partly in England and studied dance there. She joined Pavlova's company in 1910 and performed as an apprentice before the

British royal family. Over the next five years she performed with Pavlova all over the world. Marini was accomplished enough to fill in on at least two occasions for an injured Pavlova, performing her mentor's signature ballet, "Dying Swan," to a mournful Saint-Saëns cello melody. Later Marini divided her time between Pavlova's company and the Orpheum vaudeville circuit. She settled in Denver in 1915. She opened the "Marini School of Classical Dancing" and performed locally on occasion as well as teaching for periods in neighboring states.

Most *Denver Post* articles about Marini's performances don't mention the names of her students. One performance in which Frieda Mann is listed by name took place at the Denver Automotive Show between the first and fifth of April 1919 at the Stockyards Stadium, shortly before her seventeenth birthday. The dancers performed on a large stage with an elaborate garden scene built for the production. Fritzie took part in both dances Marini directed. The first dance, *Daphne et Chloe* (presumably after *Daphnis et Chloe*, the famed Ravel impressionistic ballet commissioned by Diaghilev), featured fifteen performers, including Fritzie and her sister, Helen. In the other dance, *Pas de Trois*, Fritzie was one of four girls who, suspended on wires, glided above the stage wearing huge, simulated butterfly wings. After her death, the papers occasionally referred to Fritzie as the "Butterfly Girl" or the "Butterfly Dancer." As she apparently never performed another butterfly dance or went by that name while alive, the automotive show performance appears to be the source of the posthumous moniker.

***

Chapter Nine – Victim Of Her Own Popularity

Dr. Jacobs and Rogers Clark weren't Fritzie's only suitors. An attractive and gregarious dancer frequently in the public eye, she'd inspired more than her share of male admirers. As the police began to track down the men she'd associated with recently, the focus of the investigation shifted to the north.

She'd spent most of her last two months in the L.A. area, the cops learned from her family. She knew a number of men there, including the actor Rogers Clark and a stockbroker named Richards, and may have met others while performing at various venues. She'd left San Diego in mid-November 1922 to fill dancing engagements in L.A. and then planned to move on to San Francisco. She'd spent short periods at the beginning and end of her trip in Long Beach, a suburb south of L.A. known for its oil fields and seaport. There she visited an old friend named Bernice Edwards. Fritzie had reportedly met several men through Miss Edwards, one of whom may have visited her in San Diego the day before her death. Fritzie left Bernice's house on the midnight train on Sunday, January 7, one week before her death, arriving home on the morning of the 8th.

Chief Patrick wired his Long Beach counterpart with this information. He asked him to interview Bernice and to forward any belongings the victim may have left behind at the Edwards residence.

As Chief Patrick and his detectives sifted through conflicting reports of Fritzie's activities during her L.A. sojourn and final week in San Diego, some of the promising early leads fizzled. The business card of Mr. R.R. Remington, found in Fritzie's vanity case, listed a Long Beach address. The police quickly cleared Remington, a Mann family friend. They also cleared another man whose card they'd found in the vanity case, H.F. Bittaker of San Diego, leader of an orchestra at The Barn when Fritzie performed there in the summer and fall of 1922. They were looking for another man whose card was in her vanity case and whose name Amelia Mann had screamed at the morgue: Rogers Clark.

***

The *Union* and the *Tribune* had their moments, but of the three daily local papers, the *Sun* had the strongest tendency toward speculative and often strange-sounding journalism. One of their top reporters and a soon-to-be Pulitzer Prize winner, twenty-eight-year-old Magner White, became the *Sun*'s main reporter on the Fritzie Mann case.

It's not clear if White wrote a January 16, 1923, front-page *Sun* article, but it's not atypical of the articles the paper produced about Fritzie's death. The "pretty dancing feet of little Fritzie Mann, favorite at many San Diego social entertainments, are stilled forever," the article announced. For Fritzie, "the mystery of life, with its cross purposes, its frequent injustices, has been solved in death…for Fritzie locked her secret within the depths of her broken heart." If she had killed herself, then something drove her to her death, "something so vital to her continued existence that she preferred the balm of the grave to the bitterness of life, for life must have seemed bitter to her once gay little spirit when she faced the ocean and strode in to end it all." But a more sinister possibility loomed. She may have been "lured by false promises that made her trusting heart happy." When she headed to the seashore that night, she may not have known that the ocean would be her tomb. Perhaps "the other player in the drama sought the most desperate way out."

This article, though strange to modern ears, hints at important questions, questions the press sought to underscore but that propriety forced them to address in whispers. The papers used the sheltering euphemism "delicate condition," or simply "her condition," when referring to Fritzie's pregnancy, never acknowledging her out-of-wedlock pregnancy in plain terms. Rather, she was a "victim of her own popularity" who had "loved someone not wisely but too well." Superficially, such language reflected a Victorian squeamishness about all matters sexual, but it contained a subtext about an unwritten moral code and the status of women in a changing—and unchanging—society.

Societal change had come at a dizzying pace in the four years since war's end, on the surface at least. It was a frivolous age, the time of speakeasies and petting parties, flappers and sheiks, an era F. Scott Fitzgerald had already dubbed the Jazz Age. But despite the apparent wave of liberalism and sexual freedom, the Victorian era moral code and associated laws lingered. News of a single pregnant woman remained no small scandal. The unwritten code designated women as the arbiters of morality, placing upon them a disproportionate share of the burden to prevent premarital sex. Until married, a woman could not allow a man to kiss her, let alone seduce her. Men, the code recognized, cursed by a natural weakness of the flesh and an unfortunate tendency toward profligacy, might succumb to temptation from time to time, but this could happen only with "low-class women," the sort a respectable man would never marry anyway. Respectable women, of course, did not suffer libidinous temptations—women weren't considered sexual beings—and because desire wasn't an issue, their obligation under the code wasn't difficult. The only contraception a woman needed was to squeeze an aspirin tablet between her knees. If the flapper and the New Woman now claimed their right to enjoy casual sex, and if activists like Margaret Sanger demanded access to effective birth control, it didn't change the law. Contraceptives and abortion remained illegal, risky, and difficult to obtain. When an unmarried woman got pregnant, the code required the man to "do the honorable thing," but when he didn't, the wronged woman had no good options. And the dichotomy between what was said and what was done created motives for desperate acts.

Thinly disguised phrases in the *Sun* commentary such as life's "cross purposes" and "frequent injustices," and that Fritzie had "locked her secret within the depths of her broken heart," spoke to these moral quandaries and unspoken truths. They also pointed to Fritzie's pregnancy as a likely factor in her death, whether by suicide or murder. The *Sun* rightly asked whether the "other player in the drama," seeking a way out of a messy dilemma, had murdered Fritzie Mann; or, if despondent and desperate, she had preferred the balm of the grave to the bitterness of life and sought a desperate way out for herself.

***

Chapter Ten – Oriental Dancer

On Wednesday, January 17, 1923, two days into the investigation, Chief Patrick interviewed Dorothy Armstrong, Fritzie's fellow interpretive dancer. Dorothy, one of Fritzie's closest "chums," as the papers referred to her friends, was not yet eighteen. She had emigrated as a child from Hastings, England, with her widowed mother, who now worked as a solicitor at the *Sun*.

Fritzie had once described an article about a "betrayed woman," Dorothy reported to Chief Patrick. If she ever found herself in a similar predicament, Fritzie had said, she intended to commit suicide.

This seemed to echo what Dr. Jacobs had told the chief the day before about Fritzie's depressed demeanor in the last few days of her life. But Dorothy went on to describe her friend's relationship with the doctor as a "longstanding love affair," contrary to what Jacobs had told the chief, that Fritzie was just a good chum.

As evidence of the ardor between dancer and doctor, Dorothy described five occasions she'd seen the couple together in recent months. A few of these piqued the chief's interest. She'd seen them most recently in the lobby of the U.S. Grant Hotel on the afternoon of January 8, 1923, the day Fritzie returned from L.A. Dorothy left the hotel with the couple in Jacobs' Hudson. They dropped her off at her home, saying they were going for a drive south to National City. Fritzie didn't mention any upcoming plans to attend a house party in Del Mar. That was the last time Dorothy saw her.

The previous September, Dorothy had accompanied Fritzie to visit Jacobs at Camp Kearny, at the time a patient in his own hospital recovering from an appendectomy. During the half-hour visit, Fritzie had kissed Jacobs. A proper woman of a previous generation would've considered such a public display of affection as unseemly, even immoral, whereas a modern woman might consider it a mark of liberation. Dorothy saw the kiss as proof of Fritzie's strong feelings for the doctor.

Rumors going around about Fritzie seeing other men in San Diego or having "ardent admirers" in Long Beach or San Pedro, Dorothy said, were nonsense. Fritzie loved Dr. Jacobs and only Dr. Jacobs.

Dorothy also described one occasion during the previous summer or fall, she wasn't sure of the month. She'd accompanied the couple to The Barn, a rustic dance hall and café on the El Cajon road in Grossmont. This name had already come up more than once.

The Barn might have been a converted barn, probably as common in Grossmont as houses. Located a dozen miles from downtown, the area was so rugged and sparsely populated that director Alan Dwan had used it in 1911 to film about a hundred single-reel westerns. The Barn, though isolated from the downtown show business center, advertised in the entertainment pages alongside the major theaters, touting its "famous" chicken dinners and H.F. Bittaker's six-piece orchestra. It held dances three or four times a week and periodically offered comedy, musical, and artistic dance acts.

Fritzie had performed at The Barn at least twice, in July and October 1922, and probably on other occasions in between. A *Union* article announcing her July engagement stated that "her repertoire of dances had attracted considerable favorable comment all over the Pacific coast" and named her mentors as "Madame Domina Marini of Pavlova's company" and Russian ballet dancer and actor Theodore Kosloff. An advertisement in the *Union* called her last performance at The Barn, on October 18, a "farewell program of this celebrated Polish dancer." A *Union* article embellished her background and future plans. A talented young dancer, Miss Mann "expects to leave shortly to fill a number of engagements in Los Angeles, San Francisco and other points...Born in Turkey of Polish-Hungarian parentage, Miss Mann's personality has the color of her ancestry and upbringing in foreign countries." She also expected to travel to Europe in the early spring to continue her training at one of the "famous Alexander Rinstsky schools of dancing" in Germany or Poland.

Fritzie practiced a form of modern dance that suited Jazz Age sensibilities as much as it outraged traditional ones. Interpretive dance had developed beginning in the 1890s by dancers such as Loie Fuller and Isadora Duncan who sought a freer style than ballet allowed but wanted to be taken more seriously as artists than accorded vaudeville performers. Their exotic and skimpy costumes, flamboyant presentations, and sinuous movements tended to create an erotic effect even when the dancer didn't intend to. The objective was to physically translate traditional ethnic stories and emotions, especially from the Middle East and Asia, into expressive movement. The more exotic the presentation the better.

Other than Isadora Duncan, who performed mostly in Europe, the quintessential interpretive dancer in America during Fritzie's formative years was Ruth St. Denis. An innovator and something of a mystic, St. Denis specialized in eastern cultures and myths, including her signature "Hindoo" dance, *Radha*. Fritzie most likely saw her perform. St. Denis frequented the Orpheum in Denver when Fritzie lived and danced there, and in San Diego during the early 1920s at places like the Spreckels Theatre, the Hotel Del Coronado, and the Colonial Theater. Fritzie's style fit the St. Denisian mold. She specialized in "Oriental and Hindoo dances" and other "impersonations of national types."

Fritzie's first San Diego performance and perhaps the first solo performance of her career, occurred on January 7, 1922, at the Colonial Theater, a year to the week before her death. The engagement ran for a week, ending exactly one year before her death. With its Romanesque façade and opulent interior—frescoed walls, ivory and gold drapery, and ornamental brass rails surrounding three tiers of boxes—the Colonial stood with the Spreckels, the Lyceum, and the Savoy in the top tier of local theaters. It had hosted many celebrities before, Sarah Bernhardt and Ruth St. Denis among them. A new manager with Hollywood connections had recently converted the Colonial into a movie house to capitalize on the growing demand for motion pictures. The program format used live musical-dramatic performances to introduce major films.

On the night of Fritzie's opening performance, patrons taxed the theater's 1400-seat capacity. The orchestra began the program with an overture. Then came a film, "The Skipper's Flirtation," followed by the main live feature, a prologue that included a pantomime routine and specialty numbers with tenor solos. Fritzie performed the solo finale, described as "an enticing 'Dance of Destiny'." After her dance, they screened the featured film, a Bert Lytell comedy called "A Trip to Paradise."

That the Colonial management had hired Fritzie to perform the finale of a week-long production only six weeks after she arrived in San Diego may be a testament to her talent and fortuitous timing; it also suggests connections in the local dance community. Fritzie had brought with her a letter of recommendation from a Denver mentor, presumably Domina Marini, addressed to an unnamed prominent member of the San Diego dance community. This likely opened the door to the Colonial job. One of the best-known local dancers at the time, who may have been in a position to facilitate her entry onto the Colonial show, was Gladys Escher, a pupil of Ruth St. Denis. She also taught and worked as studio manager at her mentor's renowned Los Angeles school, Denishawn. Escher had recently opened what she billed as San Diego's "first real school of the interpretative arts." She had relocated her school to the Colonial shortly before Fritzie arrived in town.

Fritzie followed the Colonial gig with a series of themed performances in February 1922 at the Point Loma Golf Club, then home to the San Diego Country Club. The members "were treated to a special interpretive dance of a Circassian slave girl by Miss Fritzie Mann, who was born and educated in Turkey." She depicted the "wild, Oriental dance of Zuelka, a slave girl who had escaped from the harem of the sultan and fled to a mission." The sultan and his men follow. Seeing him, "she utters a wild shriek and stabs herself."

Two nights later, "re-engaged by popular request," Fritzie performed a Spanish-themed dance. She repeated it the following week, the audience calling her out to perform several encores. She performed again as the main feature on Valentine's Day, this time a barefoot French dance, "Mon Amour." On Washington's Birthday, with decorations that included a real cherry tree, Fritzie delighted the audience "with her nimble feet and shapely form. Miss Mann is one of those dancers who never gets to the end of her list of dances—she always has something new and generally something startling."

A more consequential event for Fritzie's budding career came in mid-May 1922 in Balboa Park. She performed at the Shriner's Circus and Mardis Gras celebration, an elaborate, raucous affair put on by the local Al Bahr Temple, Nobles of the Mystic Shrine, the biggest event of its kind in the city's history. Parking lots overflowed and the streetcar line became jammed with people trying to reach the park. The celebration kicked off with a sunset concert at the Spreckels Organ Pavilion and a parade ending at the Civic Auditorium, one of the largest and most beautiful of the buildings left over from the 1915 Panama-California Exposition. Some 20,000 people passed through the auditorium on opening night. Befitting their Middle Eastern theme, the Shriners had festooned the Civic Auditorium with multi-colored wall paintings of the Egyptian pyramids, the Sphinx, and camel caravans. The timing was perfect. Middle Eastern themes were in vogue following Rudolph Valentino's blockbuster movie, *The Sheik*, from the year before.

A stage featured singers, jazz ensembles, vaudeville acts, and interpretive dances by Fritzie and Dorothy Armstrong. Like Fritzie, Dorothy performed St. Denisian routines at venues around town. Dorothy's high cheek bones, aquiline nose and dark, vaguely exotic good looks enhanced her on-stage allure. She enhanced it further by claiming to have studied in Egypt, a claim no more real than Fritzie's Turkish origins. The newspapers singled out the pair for praise, calling them "two of the cleverest terpsichorean artists in the business." One article declared Fritzie's "novel dances and impersonations" to be the "real class" of the event.

Fritzie performed in a series of semi-professional and social engagements in the San Diego area through the balance of 1922. She paid her dues at venues large and small, prominent and obscure, from the Shriner's celebration to a sailor stag party in November just before departing for Los Angeles. She had genuine talent and the makings of a career as a serious artist. Few places offered better opportunities in the entertainment business than L.A.

***

Chapter Eleven – The Hollywood Connection

Fritzie had modeled outfits at a fashion show at Coronado Tent City in June 1922 representing the Star Cloak and Suit House. In a large photograph on the front page of the Wednesday edition of the *Evening Tribune*, Fritzie stands next to her chum Dorothy Armstrong, who also worked the show. Fritzie appears confident and older than twenty in a longish dress, a cloak with tassels, a scarf, a wide-brimmed knit hat, and oxfords. Above the photo, a banner headline announced BARE SECRET MARRIAGE OF SLAIN S.D. GIRL, *Police Learn Dead Dancer Was Wife of Actor in Hollywood*. This development instantly launched the investigation into new directions and intensified public interest.

"The gay life of the Hollywood film colony was linked today with the mystery surrounding the death of Fritzie Mann, beautiful exhibition dancer," when Chief Patrick learned that she'd been "secretly married to a motion picture actor in Los Angeles." A doctor, whose name the police withheld, had told the chief that she'd "confided her troubles to him, and told of her desertion by her husband, who is alleged to have treated her brutally..." The doctor "also stated that Miss Mann had a contract with the Famous Players Film company and was to have taken part in their productions."

The unnamed doctor, Dr. Louis Jacobs, had told Chief Patrick about Fritzie's secret marriage, but claimed she'd refused to reveal her husband's name. Was this Rogers Clark? So far, the police had been unable to locate Clark, said to be an actor although no one had heard of him. Everyone, though, had heard of Famous Players

The number one studio in the fledgling movie industry, the Famous Players-Lasky Corporation had formed in 1916. Adolph Zukor's Famous Players Film Company had merged with Jesse Lasky's Feature Play Company and other firms, including Paramount Pictures. Pioneering director Cecil B. DeMille was another partner. In the early 1920s the studio held many of the biggest stars under contract. Rudolph Valentino, Roscoe "Fatty" Arbuckle, Pola Negri, Wallace Reid, and Gloria Swanson were Famous Players. The studio churned out hits like Valentino's *The Sheik*. The film was so popular that it added a word to the lexicon, inspired an eponymous brand of condoms, inspired the most famous song of the 1920s, *The Sheik of Araby,* and spawned a film sub-genre about Arab men (portrayed by white actors slathered in henna) who seduced or raped adventurous white women in desert tents. A Famous Players contract was the fantasy of many a young woman, a fantasy that ended in disappointment or ruin for all but a fraction, and ended for Fritzie on a desolate beach.

The recent series of Hollywood scandals had mostly involved Famous Player stars and directors. Mention of the studio's name in the same breath as the headline-making murder of Fritzie Mann no doubt alarmed scandal-weary executives. The news came at the worst possible time, when outrage over perceived Tinseltown debauchery and calls for censorship had reached critical mass. The first major scandal of the bunch, the drug overdose death of archetypal movie flapper Olive Thomas in Paris in October 1920, had excited the yellow press and shocked the public. But it was a minor prelude to what came next.

Next came the Arbuckle Affair. In September 1921, Roscoe "Fatty" Arbuckle, the rotund, ruddy-faced king of farce comedy, a Famous Players mega-star who rivaled Charlie Chaplin in popularity, was charged with manslaughter. During a Labor Day weekend bash at the posh St. Francis Hotel in San Francisco, the actor allegedly raped a struggling actress named Virginia Rappe, causing her death by peritonitis. What actually happened depends upon which version of the story a person believes. There are many from which to choose. The full truth is lost to history in boozy memories, self-serving lies and half-truths, false statements made under duress, and yellow newspaper fiction. Hearst's papers led the frenzy with screaming headlines and front-page articles riddled with fabrication and speculation. The Arbuckle affair "sold more newspapers than any event since the sinking of the *Lusitania,*" Hearst once boasted. The media circus dragged on for eight months and three trials. Though ultimately acquitted, the affair turned Arbuckle into the public face of Hollywood debauchery and a film colony pariah overnight.

At the height of Arbuckle mania, news broke on what became an even bigger scandal, the most notorious Hollywood mystery of all, the baffling and still unsolved murder of William Desmond Taylor, a noted Famous Players director. One morning in February 1922, Taylor's valet arrived at the director's bungalow to find him shot to death. Hoping to forestall another public relations fiasco, the studio's general manager rushed to the scene with a small team. Under the nose of a detective, and with his tacit approval, he tried to sanitize the bungalow of embarrassing materials. He missed a few items including love letters and a filmy nightgown. The mystifying murder of a high-profile director and a list of colorful suspects provided excuse enough for another media extravaganza. But the involvement of two movie stars, comedy queen Mabel Normand and screen ingénue Mary Miles Minter, a Famous Player, put it over the top. The press coverage was even more incendiary than Arbuckle's. Reporters for the yellow papers contrived a sex scandal and various lurid theories, ruining the careers of Minter and Normand.

Just as the Taylor scandal finally began to subside, the ordeal of another A-list Famous Player rocked Tinseltown and unleashed a fresh firestorm of publicity. Wallace Reid epitomized the All-American image the studios sought to project, the antithesis of an Arbuckle, an image shattered when the public learned of his morphine habit. The studio tried to keep the actor's struggles out of the papers, but then Reid's wife checked him into a sanitarium and went public. He died on January 18, 1923, from complications of his addiction. News of Reid's death appeared on front pages alongside that of Fritzie Mann.

The scandals made Hollywood the epicenter of the brewing culture war. Members of congress and religious groups denounced the film colony in fiery speeches and threatened to censor its films. At a time when half of the population saw movies every week, one senator said, movie men exercised outsized influence on young minds and wielded their power irresponsibly for profit. In Hollywood, he said, "debauchery, drunkenness, ribaldry, dissipation and free love seem to be conspicuous."

Spooked by the attention and desperate to thwart outside scrutiny, the studio heads, led by Adolph Zukor of Famous Players-Lasky, took action. They hired former Postmaster General Will Hays as a morality czar, inserted moral turpitude clauses into stars' contracts, and tried to discourage depiction of objectional material. This included sexual perversion, white slavery, and miscegenation—the exact sins of *The Sheik* that so offended conservatives. The studios declared their intention to expel "undesirables" from the film colony. Undesirables included young women like Fritzie who flocked to Tinseltown seeking Famous Players contracts and the studio men who took advantage of them.

None of this stemmed the tide of young women arriving in LA every day, nor did it prevent studio men from exploiting them.

After fourteen months of non-stop scandals, no one, least of all Famous Players executives, would've been shocked if the death of an aspiring starlet turned into another scandal. The studio denied any knowledge of Fritzie Mann. But whether they knew it or not, they had reason to worry because she had a connection to one of their stars.

***

Fritzie claimed to be a protégé of Theodore Kosloff. Although now forgotten except by ballet historians and silent film buffs, he achieved considerable fame in his day as a dancer for Diaghilev and later as an actor and choreographer for Cecil B. DeMille. He played a key role in the use of dance in silent pictures and foreshadowed the musicals of the 1930s. He appeared in more than two dozen films for Famous Players, contributing to almost all of DeMille's films until the talkies arrived and ended his acting career. When not making movies, Kosloff performed with his own dance company and ran a ballet school where he trained dancers, mostly young women, for his studio's productions. Kosloff trained De Mille's niece, Agnes, later an acclaimed dancer on Broadway, as well as film stars Joan Crawford, Pola Negri, Gloria Swanson, and May McAvoy. He also helped to stage the huge crowd scenes common in De Mille's films, often supplying extras from his school.

The nature of Fritzie's association with Kosloff is unclear. She may have taken lessons at his downtown L.A. studio after she arrived in San Diego in late 1921. More likely they met in Denver through Domina Marini, who would've known Kosloff either from Pavlova's company or the Orpheum circuit. Kosloff had performed in Denver, then a small city, at least twice while Fritzie was training under Marini. He performed in a week-long program called "Russian Melodies" at the Orpheum Theater in May 1919. Fritzie had danced with Marini at the Denver auto show the previous month and probably at another performance, the Denver Press Club Frolic, on 19 May, the last day of Kosloff's engagement. Or Fritzie may have met him through another Denver dance instructor, recently returned from working with Kosloff in L.A. Or she might have answered one of Kosloff's ads soliciting dancers for DeMille's films such as *Forbidden Fruit*, released in February 1921, that featured scores of dancers in extravagant ballroom scenes. Or Kosloff stopped by Marini's school and gave an impromptu lesson and that was the extent of Fritzie's association with him, and she exaggerated the connection. In one San Diego article she claimed only to have "danced under the supervision of Theodore Kosloff," which could mean anything. But more than once she claimed to be his protégé, implying a stronger link than a brief meeting or a few lessons. Hitching her name to Kosloff's star would've been the best career move Fritzie could've made. No better path existed for a dancer who wanted to be in movies.

Based on their public stances, Will Hays and Famous Players-Lasky executives should have considered Kosloff an "undesirable," as he was the kind of womanizer they ostensibly wanted to purge. The Russian had offered many of his young pupils a chance to break into pictures, a chance that may have come with a price. He is said to have seduced numerous of his students, some of them underage, a famous example being dancer and set designer Natacha Rambova, who later married Rudolph Valentino. When Rambova tried to leave Kosloff, he shot her in the leg.

Chief Patrick took reports of Fritzie's Hollywood connections seriously. But other than her relationship with unknown actor Rogers Clark, he could not confirm them. Records in L.A. and San Diego held no evidence of Fritzie's marriage to Clark or anyone else. She never mentioned a marriage to her closest chums and her family dismissed it outright. Where did this idea come from?

Had Fritzie lied to Jacobs about her Hollywood connections, or had Jacobs made it all up and lied to the cops? One of them had lied. Had Fritzie conjured up a fictitious husband and a Famous Players contract for her own reasons, or was Jacobs trying to muck up the investigation? Jacobs knew of Fritzie's relationship with Rogers Clark and knew that Amelia Mann despised the actor, so the man made a perfect scapegoat. And like everyone else, Jacobs knew about the Hollywood scandals. Linking Fritzie to the film colony, whether true or not, would excite the press and might point the cops in a new direction. It did both.

Whoever was lying, was it a coincidence that Jacobs had named Famous Players as Fritzie's studio? It was the best-known studio and the one most associated with the scandals. It also happened to be Theodore Kosloff's studio. Jacobs knew of her connection to the dancer-actor or at least knew she claimed to be his protégé. The Russian would've made a much better scapegoat because it would've created a new Hollywood scandal. Kosloff's name hadn't come up related to the case, at least publicly, but this was just the start of the Hollywood rumors.

***

Chapter Twelve – Fritzie's Injury

Bernice Edwards, another of Fritzie's good chums, lived in Long Beach, California. They had lived around the block from one another growing up in Denver. Bernice's family had moved to Long Beach around the time the Mann family moved to San Diego, and they had kept in touch. Bernice, a tall, strawberry blonde not yet eighteen, danced recreationally but not professionally. According to family lore, she once won first-prize in a Charleston dance contest. Her prize: a silver loving cup, from which she shared a sip of champagne with Rudolph Valentino.

The Long Beach police conducted the initial interview with Bernice at Chief Patrick's behest on Wednesday. She helped fill in the timeline of Fritzie's L.A. period. Fritzie had stayed with her and her family at their home on Loma Avenue for about a week beginning in mid-November 1922. On November 22, she took the train to L.A.

Fritzie checked into the Rosslyn Hotel, located at 100 5th Avenue in downtown L.A., on the same day. Bernice visited her there on December 1. She stayed at the Rosslyn, known for its attractive décor and amenities at an affordable price, until December 17, when Bernice visited her again.

This time Bernice found Fritzie in bed, ill and morose. Bernice insisted on taking her back to Long Beach. Fritzie didn't have enough money to pay her bill, so the hotel held her luggage. She returned two days later and paid with a $75 check, signed by a man, and drawn on a San Diego bank.

Fritzie stayed at Bernice's house until she boarded the train to San Diego on the night of Sunday, January 7.

"When she left here she said she was going to cancel her contract with her employers in San Diego and return to Los Angeles at once to accept an engagement with a café or with a film company," Bernice said.

Fritzie left a suitcase and personal articles behind at Bernice's house, and borrowed Bernice's beaded brown party dress and brown hat for the trip to San Diego. The next time Bernice saw her dress it was a tattered courtroom exhibit.

***

Many men admired Fritzie, Bernice told reporters, but she only cared about one, a San Diego man.

"If the officers would question him closely they would learn why Frieda died," Bernice said. "Frieda never attempted to hide from me the fact she was infatuated with this man and during her stay of three weeks at my home she exchanged several letters with this person. Of course, she never confided to me the exact status of their relationship or whether they were engaged to be married, but I am convinced there was a lovers quarrel."

They had quarreled over Fritzie's plan to return to L.A. for work, Bernice said, but soon made up.

"One day while visiting here she appeared blue and despondent. Later a telegram came and after reading it she became cheerful again. I never learned the contents of the message, but it made her very happy and she exclaimed to me, 'That's the way, tell them to go to the devil and they'll come around all right'."

Bernice had received a letter from Fritzie a few days before she died.

"It was just a note and I do not recall all of its contents," she said, "but I do remember she said she was coming to

Long Beach and urged me not to write her because she would not be at San Diego to receive the letter. I hardly can believe she is dead and it seems impossible that what they say regarding her condition as revealed at the inquest can be true. [By inquest, Bernice meant the autopsy.] Frieda was not a bad girl nor one who could be misled easily. If what they say is true then she loved the man very deeply whoever he is…she may have been married secretly but of course I don't know."

The Long Beach police took possession of some of the dead woman's personal effects. In a suitcase, the cops found newspaper clippings about Fritzie's performances, a photograph of a young man, and a number of letters and telegrams. Some of the letters, addressed "Dearest Girl," bore the initials "L.L.J." Bernice identified the man as an Army surgeon at Camp Kearny.

***

According to Bernice, Fritzie mentioned that she had injured herself dancing. It's not clear when this injury occurred because the date and location of Fritzie's last performances are uncertain.

Her last San Diego engagement was a stag party at the Navy Chief Petty Officer Club at 4th and A Streets on November 10, 1922. In a Navy town the words "Navy CPO stag party" might evoke images of drunken debauchery and semi-pornographic entertainment, which the vaguely sleazy Oriental dancer image fit all too well. But there was nothing salacious about the program. A female jazz pianist, a male Oriental dancer, and a woman who whistled popular songs and bird calls also performed for one hundred boisterous chiefs. But, as described in the *Union*, "The treat of the evening was two interpretive dances, 'The Bat,' in a specially designed costume, and 'Lure of Jade,' both by Miss Fritzie Mann…a dancer of fine artistry and grace and her efforts were so pleasing that she was required to respond to several encores."

Fritzie left for L.A. about five days later. In late November and early December, Bernice informed police, Fritzie had performed at the Café Royal in Culver City, west of downtown L.A., where nightclubs and speakeasies abounded. Fritzie might've sustained an injury while performing there, or it may have been a lingering injury from the CPO stag party. But the "injury" was almost certainly a veiled reference to morning sickness. Although to reporters Bernice expressed surprise at learning of Fritzie's pregnancy only after her death, she already knew about it, as she admitted to police. And to reporters she described Fritzie's condition as "ill," an odd word for a dancing injury. By the time she arrived back at Bernice's house on December 17, 1922, Fritzie was over three months pregnant. Bernice described the "injury" differently to reporters from the *Los Angeles Examiner*.

"She told me a slight operation would be necessary before she could resume dancing."

***

Chapter Thirteen – Murdered Beyond Doubt

Chief Patrick interviewed another of Fritzie's chums, Helen Whitney, a stenographer for a law firm, on Wednesday. The two had met early the previous year, becoming closer in the last four months of Fritzie's life. In June 1922, Helen had appeared with Fritzie and Dorothy Armstrong in the fashion show at the Coronado Tent City, a sprawling collection of shops and bathing facilities along the Silver Strand south of the Hotel del Coronado. Helen, a cute woman of twenty with a rounded chin and cheeks, short hair, and a wide, toothy grin, had represented Holzwasser's Department Store, where she worked then.

Fritzie had stayed over in her room at the Sanford Hotel on the night of Saturday the thirteenth, Helen stated. She arrived about 5:00 p.m. in good spirits.

"That night Fritzie told me she had received a telegram from a man in Los Angeles asking her to meet him in San Diego on the train arriving Sunday night at 6:30," Helen said. "But I did not see the message."

Fritzie said that some Hollywood friends were to accompany the man.

"Some of my moving picture friends are coming down for a house party Sunday night," Fritzie told Helen. "We are going to have some fun."

Fritzie also mentioned their plans to attend a party in Del Mar that night.

Later Helen later expressed confusion about the order of events and corrected her initial statement. The conversation about Hollywood people had actually taken place on a previous occasion, she said, and wasn't related to Fritzie's meeting at the Santa Fe depot on the evening of January 14. That night, Fritzie didn't tell her who she was meeting, just that it was a man and some friends.

Fritzie left the Sanford Hotel on Sunday around noon and went home. Helen never saw her again.

***

Helen Whitney had written some of the correspondence Fritzie left behind at Bernice's house. The newspapers published excerpts. Most of it was prosaic and of little interest to Chief Patrick, such as when Helen complains about her low wages at Holzwasser's department store. Or when she expresses her opinion of sailors, a ubiquitous presence in San Diego since the Navy opened the U.S. Destroyer Base in February 1922. Sailors turned downtown into a sea of blue or white crackerjacks on paydays.

"They're cheap skates, most of them," Helen wrote. "Don't think I'll run around with them anymore."

Another time she describes her ride back to San Diego after visiting Fritzie at the Rosslyn Hotel in L.A. She rode with a junior Navy officer named Eddie who was "a nice fellow and seems to think a lot of me. He's all right, even if he is only an ensign."

In the same letter, she says, "Gee! I guess I made an impression with the cigarette, but I thought it was the regular thing there."

Until recently, a woman who smoked in public risked arrest. But like driving cars and kissing in public and the other audacious acts flappers committed on the silver screen and in real life, smoking was a symbol of liberation for Jazz Age women. To go with the short, beaded, or fringed dress, rolled stockings, modish cloche hat and bobbed hair, the flapper image included a waif-thin, androgynous look and a cigarette in a long holder. Tobacco companies helped create and then capitalized on this image by advertising smoking as a weight loss method and a mark of sophistication for women. Conservatives, even in the big city, viewed these behaviors as rebellious. Despite its size—ten times larger than San Diego—and co-location with Hollywood, L.A. retained puritanical sensibilities.

Other excerpts from Helen's letters to Fritzie contained personal snippets that delighted the town gossips. The gossips must've been ecstatic—and Helen mortified—when the *Sun* published this one:

"There's an old fellow wants to go out with me. He wants to buy me clothes and pay my room rent. The rent is $15, but I told him it was $20. He only wants to go with me twice a week. Don't think I will get into trouble because he's too old."

But Helen may not have been so embarrassed by these and other revelations in the papers. In some ways, she seems to have been a young woman of her times, perhaps liberated enough to not worry so much about her reputation.

While excerpts from Helen's chummy letters amused the public, a single passage among them stood out to Chief Patrick.

"I saw your Dr. Jacobs today. He sure looked fine in his Hudson sedan. I'd like to go out with him if it could be arranged. I wouldn't let him treat me rough as he did you. I'm pretty strong."

The chief was even more intrigued by a series of letters and telegrams found in Fritzie's suitcase at Bernice's house, from Dr. Louis Jacobs to his "Dearest Girl," Fritzie.

***

The police had been trying to find Rogers Clark ever since Amelia Mann had screamed his name at the funeral parlor. They finally located him, or thought they had, in San Pedro, a community on the Port of Los Angeles near Long Beach. Chief Patrick asked the LAPD to question him, but reporters got there first.

"I am at a loss to understand how my name became connected with this case," the man told the *San Pedro Pilot*. "I had no acquaintanceship with the girl; am sure I never met her and if it is true one of my cards was found in her vanity case I do not know how it came to be there unless it was a regular business card which she may have had."

"It has been two months since I was last in San Diego," he told the *Los Angeles Examiner*, "although I have many friends in that city."

It took another day to sort it out, but the police had located—and reporters had hounded—the wrong man. This wasn't Rogers Clark, actor-director, but *Roger Clarke*, part owner of Clarke & Bentley Electrical Supplies, San Pedro.

***

As public interest intensified, seemingly by the hour, pressure mounted on Chief Patrick to solve the case. He and his detectives worked feverishly to verify the information flowing from Fritzie's friends and family, much of which proved to be dead ends or red herrings. The manager of the Café Royal in Culver City said he'd never heard of Fritzie Mann. Detectives checked telegraph offices but couldn't find a telegram to confirm that Fritzie had met friends from L.A. or anywhere else on Sunday night. And they found no evidence of a house party in Del Mar.

Manner of death still seemed uncertain—suicide or homicide could be argued with equal conviction. Despite her mother's protestations, had Fritzie been melancholy, as Dr. Jacobs and Bernice Edwards described her? If so, enough to commit suicide? A possible indication of her recent state of mind emerged from an unconventional source, as published in the *Evening Tribune*: "Saturday afternoon the dancer visited a Mme. Hands, who terms herself a research specialist. She asked the medium about a man keeping a promise, and when she was told the man's initials she began to weep excitedly." She told Madame Hands that she had agreed to meet the man in San Diego and spoke of a trip to Los Angeles.

Advertisements for soothsayers such as Madame Hands Sutherland occupied considerable space in the papers. Tens of millions of deaths during the war and the 1918 influenza pandemic had sparked a Renaissance in spiritualism in the U.S. and Europe as bereaved people sought to contact deceased loved ones.

No one witnessed Fritzie's meeting with Madame Hands, but it did not require paranormal means to conjure up the initials she claimed she'd revealed to Fritzie. By the time police spoke to her, two persons of interest had been mentioned in the papers. Were the initials "L.J." for Dr. Louis Jacobs or "R.C.," for actor Rogers Clark, Amelia's prime suspect? Or could it have been someone else? A more important question for Chief Patrick: Was a visit to a medium in character for Fritzie or a rare event prompted by an agitated or melancholy state of mind?

Yet despite indications of suicidal ideation, by Wednesday the chief seemed convinced of foul play—convinced enough to tell reporters that Fritzie had been "murdered beyond doubt."

***

Chapter Fourteen – The Blue Sea Cottage

Historians debate the origin of the name La Jolla. Many assume it's Spanish but there's no such word in the Spanish language. The Spanish *La Joya,* though, means "the jewel"—an apt name for this beautiful little place—so the name may stem from an early spelling error. Or it may derive from the Native American term *Woholle,* meaning "hole in the mountains," referring to the caves and rocks along the shoreline there. Nestled on a hilly point between Mount Soledad and the ocean twelve miles northwest of downtown San Diego, La Jolla was not yet the affluent enclave it would become, but a lazy village of cottages, beach bungalows, and unpaved streets with a population of 2500.

Chief Patrick focused the search for clues on La Jolla. If the killer had headed south on the coast highway from Torrey Pines toward San Diego, as seemed likely, he almost certainly would've passed through La Jolla, eight miles to the south. He may have turned onto a dirt road that ran east toward Camp Kearny, but the road was rough and little used. Some clues also pointed to La Jolla. Fritzie had mentioned a change of venue to La Jolla for the "house party" in the phone call to her mother. And veteran patrolman George Churchman, one of two officers posted at the La Jolla sub-station, reported seeing a woman who resembled Fritzie Mann on a La Jolla street the night of her death. Churchman remembered her because the woman wasn't wearing a coat or hat in the chilly weather, and she appeared to be waiting for someone. This prompted a search on the coast highway between the crime scene and La Jolla, in case the articles had been tossed out of a car like the handbag and vanity case. But the search for the missing brown hat and electric blue coat—the latter presumably hard to miss—failed. Chief Patrick also had officers canvassing the hotels and rental cottages in and around La Jolla.

At mid-morning on Wednesday, George Churchman turned from the coast highway onto Bonair Street, south of the village in an area called Neptunia, in his flat black Model T, recently purchased at his own expense in accordance with police department policy but which he used on the job. The unpaved street sloped gently downhill for four hundred yards, dropping more sharply toward the end above Windansea Beach. The beach is one of the more stunning spots on the southern California coast, where sandstone boulders, eroded smooth by the surf, divide the beach into sections of sandy nooks and crevices beneath short cliffs. A strong offshore break makes the area treacherous for swimmers, but also made it a surfing hot spot starting in the 1940s and later immortalized by Tom Wolfe in *The PumpHouse Gang*. Houses were sprouting in a nearby development, but the lots on Bonair and nearby streets remained mostly undeveloped, giving Churchman an unobstructed view of the ocean. Halfway down to the beach his machine rumbled to a stop at 371 Bonair. Churchman, tall and slim with dark hair, an angular face, close-set eyes, and prominent ears, stepped out of his vehicle. The sea breeze blew a tangy fragrance of sea salt and sea life up from Windansea Beach.

The Blue Sea Cottages, built between 1909 and 1915, consisted of twenty-seven rustic cottages arranged in rows, some painted white, others left unpainted. Most of the cottages were stand-alone units, the rest double units. The cottages catered to the growing tourist industry but also hosted local events.

About a year before Fritzie's death, the owner of the Blue Sea Cottages, businessman Willis H.P. Shelton, had hosted the La Jolla Cinderella Club there over a period of several days. Shelton was a de-facto leader of the group of well-to-do bachelors. One of the activities was a mock wedding on Windansea Beach. The stated purpose of the event was to attract old-fashioned brides for the conservative club members, men who lamented the changing times and pined for a return to traditional mores, especially gender roles. Shelton had invited "Cinderellas," defined as old-fashioned women who eschewed parties and drinking and other Jazz Age frivolities—no flappers or New Women allowed. Many women showed up. But Shelton also used the event to attract tourists to La Jolla and his Blue Sea Cottages. He published photographs of the wedding party on the beach wearing bathing suits in mid-winter. Apart from tourists, locals often rented the cottages for parties or trysts.

Churchman walked into a double cottage that served as office and living quarters for Albert and Mary Kern, who managed the Blue Sea Cottages.

The patrolman asked Albert Kern if a man named Jacobs or Clark had checked in on Sunday evening, possibly accompanied by a young woman.

With his bland features and long, straight nose, wire-rim glasses, oversized driver's hat and tweed jacket, Albert Kern, a native of Switzerland, looked more like a college professor than a beach resort manager.

Kern checked the register. No Jacobs or Clarks, he told the cop. But a young couple had checked in that evening.

Churchman examined the signature in the register. *Alvin Johnston and wife, L.A.* Or something like that. The first name was an illegible scrawl—instead of Alvin, it might've been "Wm," "William," or even "Wise" and the last name could've been Johnstone. Churchman asked Kern to describe Mr. and Mrs. Johnston and their visit.

He and his wife were hosting dinner guests, Kern said. Around 6:30 p.m. he heard a machine pull up outside and sound its horn. He stepped outside into the darkness. An arc light mounted above the office door, the Blue Sea Cottage trademark, illuminated the area in stark blue light. Kern saw a closed car parked nearby on the side of the road with the headlights off and two people inside. The shiny machine appeared new. Kern recognized the make as either a Velie or a Hudson Essex based on what he described as the distinctive sharp corners of the hood peculiar to those two-door, closed-body coupes.

Kern approached the driver's side window. He put his foot on the running board and rested his arm on the open driver's window and greeted the couple. Mr. Johnston, about twenty-eight years old, seemed nervous, almost to the point of trembling. He appeared "dissipated" and "sallow" like a consumptive or a dope fiend—thin, sunken cheeks, dark circles under the eyes, and a rather sharp nose. He had a dark complexion. Kern noticed a mark on Mr. Johnston's left cheek, near his mouth, possibly a cold sore. Mrs. Johnston was dark-haired, pretty, and younger than the man. In contrast to her husband, she seemed in good spirits, as if she'd consumed a drink or two.

Mr. Johnston asked Kern if he had any cottages for rent, and if so, how they rented. Yes, he had cottages, Kern said, and they rented by the day, the week, or the month—anyway Johnston wanted.

"I want a cottage with running water in it," Johnston said.

"All right, I can give you a cottage with bath," Kern said. "If you will step out of the car, I will show you."

Johnston stepped out of the car. About five feet eight inches tall, Kern estimated, the man was dressed in dark clothing—dark overcoat, dark suit, dark tie, black slouch hat.

Kern led the way down a sidewalk between the cottages of the first and second rows. He stopped at the last cottage on the right, number thirty-three. It had a small front porch, a simple pitched roof, and a combination of redwood slat and shake siding, giving it a rough-hewn look. Inside, Kern switched on the lights and led Johnston through the front room, the kitchenette, and the bathroom in back.

Mr. Johnston took a cursory look. "This will do," he said, and walked out. As they walked back to the office, he said, "I might as well pay you right now. How much is it?"

"Two and a half," Kern said.

"I might want it for a day or two days or three days."

In the office, Mr. Johnston signed the register and paid. "We are going out for a little drive," he said, "a half an hour or three-quarters of an hour; we will be back."

Kern returned to his dinner guests. About an hour later he went outside to switch on the hot water heater for cottage thirty-three. He noticed the light burning in the front room but saw no movement behind the drawn shades. Johnston had parked his machine nearby in the dirt alley that ran behind the cottages parallel to Bonair Street. Kern walked around cottage thirty-three and entered cottage twenty-six, an identical cabin that faced in the opposite direction onto the adjacent row; it shared the bathroom with cottage thirty-three. Kern started the hot water heater and returned to his quarters.

Per his usual practice, Kern made his rounds between 10:00 and 10:30 p.m. to turn off the exterior lights around the premises. When he passed cottage thirty-three it was dark and quiet. Johnston's car was gone. He didn't see the car or the couple again.

Unfortunately, Kern didn't write down the automobile's license plate number.

After listening to Kern, Churchman checked out cottage thirty-three. Belying the rough exterior, the inside was pleasant and well-tended. It had obviously been cleaned since the Johnstons' visit three nights before. A made-up queen-sized bed stood near the front door with the headboard positioned beneath the front window. To the left was a recessed window. Right of the window, on a little ledge, Churchman spotted a red hair net, a brown barrette, and a dozen or so bobby pins, which looked out of place in the otherwise neat room. He picked these up. He walked through the kitchenette and into the bathroom and saw nothing else out of order.

***

A swarm of law enforcement officials descended upon the Blue Sea Cottages. Churchman turned over custody of the articles he'd found to Detective Sergeant Dick Chadwick. Chief Patrick had assigned Chadwick and his partner, Det. Sgt. George Sears, to the case. Chester Kempley, the county's new DA, becoming more interested in the case as publicity increased, paid a visit. So did County Detective Frank Wisler, who the DA had ordered assigned to the case. A reporter arrived with the cops.

The relationship between the police and the press, although acrimonious at times, was generally cordial and mutually beneficial—the cops gave reporters inside scoop, reporters gave the cops favorable press. When the police made an arrest, they often invited reporters to ride along, allowing them to interview suspects on the way to the station. They gave them liberal access to suspects in jail as well. And at a time when police procedure didn't always include securing crime scenes or systematically collecting evidence, reporters often accompanied police to the scene in high-interest cases and might even help search for clues. But at the moment, the police department's largess towards the press was not divided evenly among the San Diego dailies. At the time of the Fritzie Mann case, they favored the *Sun* over its rivals because of that paper's vocal support for

Chief Patrick and the administration of Mayor John Bacon, especially with a mayoral election beginning to heat up.

Intrepid *Sun* reporter Magner White searched cottage thirty-three with Det. Sgt. Sears. White found a promising piece of evidence—a pint liquor bottle—in a closet. The bottle contained a small amount of a liquid the detectives assumed to be alcohol but had a peculiar, unrecognizable odor.

"On the bottle were finger prints which may knot a noose around the neck of the guilty party or parties," the *Union* reported.

The detectives questioned the Kerns. Prior to the Johnston couple's brief stay on the evening of January 14, they said, cottage thirty-three had been unoccupied since New Year's Eve, when someone rented it for a party. Mary Kern stated that she had cleaned the cottage a day or two after the party.

Albert Kern said he had checked inside cottage thirty-three at about 7:00 a.m. on the morning after the Johnstons' stay. He noted the hairnet and barrette by the window in the front room but left the items there. The bed appeared to have been used, but he saw nothing amiss in the kitchen. The bathroom also appeared to have been used and he saw two wet bath towels on the floor.

Mrs. E.V. Spencer, who worked for Mary Kern and lived in one of the cottages, had cleaned cottage thirty-three on Tuesday morning. She hadn't noticed anything out of the ordinary; it looked like it had barely been used. The bedsheet was turned back, and the bottom sheet wrinkled as though someone had lain or sat there briefly but hadn't slept in it overnight. While changing the linen she noticed a spot of blood the size of her thumbnail in the center of the bottom sheet but didn't think much of it. She found the hair net, barrette, and bobby pins on the dressing table by the window. She moved them aside, dusted the table, then returned them to the same spot. The kitchenette appeared pristine except for a wet hand towel in the sink. She noticed a small, thin pool of water at the bottom of the white porcelain tub. The water appeared slightly discolored, a dark brown or iron rust color, around the edges. Two towels, one unused, one wet, hung on a wire stretched across a corner over the tub that served as a towel rack.

***

Later that day, Chief Patrick drove an anxious Albert Kern to the Smith, Goodbody & Dunn funeral home, showed him Fritzie Mann's body, and asked if it was "Mrs. Johnston."

Kern said he couldn't tell "because of all that stuff on her face."

Preparing the body for funeral, the undertaker had completely covered the face with filling compound. The next day, after he had cleaned up the face, Kern had another look.

That's Mrs. Johnston from Sunday night—no doubt in my mind, Kern said.

A remarkable identification, it seemed to Chief Patrick. Kern had barely glimpsed the woman inside of a darkened automobile and yet instantly recognized the body of Fritzie Mann, three days dead. Detectives confirmed the identification when Amelia Mann recognized the items found in the cottage as her daughter's. An encouraging sign. The sharp-eyed Kern had seen the man for a longer time, in lighted rooms, had conversed with him. It was reasonable to assume he'd be able to identify Mr. Johnston.

George Churchman's discovery of the Blue Sea Cottages was a major break in the case. Without question, the victim and "Mr. Johnston" had been there shortly before her death. With an observant eyewitness, fingerprints on the liquor bottle and the register signature as evidence, Chief Patrick had reason to be optimistic about swiftly solving the crime.

***

Det. Sgts. Dick Chadwick and George Sears, the principal members of the city's "purity squad," spent much of their time rousting bootleggers and disorderly house madams. Their names appeared in the papers frequently, usually together, making them the most recognizable police officers to the public aside from Chief Patrick. They made most of their busts downtown; speakeasies and gambling joints abounded there, tucked into the back rooms of restaurants, cafés and stores, and rooming houses served as fronts for brothels. These establishments, wanting to keep a low profile, usually employed a surreptitious entry method even though most people, including the cops, knew about them. The typical procedure required the customer to whisper a code word to gain entry. On one occasion, Sears and Chadwick discovered a "tap easy," gaining entry to the place by tapping out a secret code on the door. Another time they gained entrance into the back room of a cigar store by pressing a buzzer behind the counter. Inside they arrested twenty gamblers. They also raided private residences, once discovering three hundred gallons of grape brandy and a distilling outfit inside of a house. They busted dope fiends and dealers as well. The previous November they had dealt a blow to a Tijuana drug ring by confiscating 2700 bindles of morphine and a cache of weapons. When it came to enforcing vice laws in San Diego, Chadwick and Sears, who one paper had dubbed the "Gold Dust Twins," were the experts. The feds had even qualified Sears as an "expert whisky smeller."

Chief Patrick had assigned the pair as the lead detectives on the Fritzie Mann case, so they weren't on the prowl for speakeasies right now. They visited Torrey Pines beach on Thursday, January 18. Neither had been there on Monday. On the way they stopped at Rannells Oil Station on the coast highway above the Scripps Biological Institute. They asked the station owner, David Rannells, to accompany them. He had been on the beach after the body was found and was one of the men who'd found Fritzie's vanity case and handbag. Others had combed the beach in the past three days, so it seemed unlikely they'd find new evidence. But approximately three hundred yards south of the slough bridge, just over the highway guard rail, Sears and Chadwick found an olive drab army blanket lying on the rocks on the embankment. The Kerns later identified the blanket as belonging to the Blue Sea Cottages. One like it appeared to be missing from cottage thirty-three.

***

Other than vague allusions in the *Evening Tribune* and the *Sun* on Thursday about police activity and "important discoveries" in La Jolla, Chief Patrick managed to keep the discovery of the Blue Sea Cottages out of the papers for two days. This was an impressive feat given the public interest in the case and that Magner White had been present. The Blue Sea Cottages revelations would not break big until Friday. Meanwhile, the hunt was on for the mysterious "Mr. Johnston."

***

Part II – The Mysterious Mr. Johnston

Chapter Fifteen – A Dirty Murder

The law required the coroner to inquire into and determine the cause, manner, and circumstances of violent, sudden, unusual, or unattended deaths. The ambiguous manner of death and circumstances surrounding Fritzie Mann's death justified a formal inquest. The coroner conducted his inquests at the funeral home, where the jury viewed the body together and was sworn in its presence. The inquest was thus held "over the body" of the deceased.

The coroner's inquest over the body of Fritzie Mann commenced at 2:00 p.m. on Thursday in the funeral chapel of Smith, Goodbody & Dunn's mortuary. Coroner Schuyler Kelly and DA Chester Kempley took turns questioning witnesses before a jury of six men and six women. Kelly called Deputy Sheriff Bludworth, autopsy surgeon Shea, and Amelia and William Mann. Det. Sgts. Chadwick and Sears, though present, did not testify. "Five pretty girls," presumably including Fritzie's chums Bernice Edwards, Helen Whitney, and Dorothy Armstrong, attended but weren't called.

Helen Mann did not attend. Her family had checked her into a sanitarium in rural Alpine, thirty miles east of San Diego. Apparently, they hadn't yet informed Helen of Fritzie's death. She was so frail from consumption and an associated heart condition, doctors feared, that hearing of her little sister's death might prove fatal.

"Why doesn't Fritzie come to see me?" Helen, who adored her sister, kept asking her nurses.

Deputy Sheriff Bludworth described the crime scene, emphasizing the aspects indicative of foul play: The inaccessibility of the location except by machine at the only spot within miles where an automobile could park adjacent to the beach, and the position of the vanity case and overnight bag, apparently tossed from a moving vehicle.

Dr. Shea testified to the key autopsy findings: Drowning as the cause of death, the decedent's pregnancy, the bruise over the right eye, most likely caused prior to death and though superficial, perhaps sufficient to render unconsciousness.

Amelia Mann leaned on William Mann's arm as she walked slowly to the witness chair. In a broken voice, on the verge of a breakdown, she described the last time she'd seen her daughter alive at the Redwood Street trolley stop. She also described Fritzie's odd phone call twenty minutes later.

The DA showed her Fritzie's gold bar pin and barrette.

"Oh, my little girl, my darling!" Amelia sobbed. "I know it's a dirty murder! Roger Clark killed my poor little girl!" During an extended outburst, Amelia sometimes lapsed into Hungarian and frequently shouted Clark's name. "That man Roger Clark! He's the man! Oh, my child! Mother's heart is broken forever! I came to San Diego to be happy and my innocent child was murdered!"

Amelia's anguish was so palpable, so heartrending that nearly every person in the chapel teared up or wept. Kelly, Kempley, and her son tried to console her. With considerable effort, she managed to regain her composure enough for her son to escort her to a seat at the rear of the chapel. Fritzie's friends attended to her while her son testified.

William Mann, the final witness, described the weird phone call he'd received on Monday night, apparently from the coroner but wasn't sure.

Kelly acknowledged this with a nod.

William described reading the *Union* article about the discovery of a woman's body, how it had alarmed him, and how he'd later identified his sister's body at the funeral parlor. Much of his testimony dealt with accusations against Rogers Clark.

"Clark frequently visited my sister, but as far as I remember never came into the house," William said. "He would come up outside and honk his horn." Fritzie seemed to be very attracted to Clark, he said, but his mother tried to discourage the friendship. "I believe Clark to have been responsible for her condition and so does my mother."

Fritzie's condition had become evident soon after Clark drove her down to Tijuana on the first of November, confirming his and their mother's fears about the man. He described his understanding of how the actor had contrived to meet Fritzie.

"It was in the Grant hotel when Fritzie was selling tickets to a performance at the Barn. I am not positive as to the exact date. Clark saw her in the hotel and I am informed remarked that he would give $1000 to know my sister. Some friends introduced the two."

"Fritzie was a good girl, I know," William said, responding to a question from a jury member. "She had many friends, but none I know of who would prevail upon her to give herself to them. I am almost willing to swear that she was taken advantage of in some manner, probably when not in her right mind. When we first became aware of her condition she said she did not know exactly what was the matter. This leads me to believe she was not conscious when the thing happened."

In truth, William had limited insight into Fritzie's activities and relationships outside of their home and took his cues regarding Rogers Clark from his mother. They had no evidence against the actor, just suspicion and loathing. William, grieving and angry, sought to protect his dead sister's reputation through his testimony and in statements to reporters.

William caused a stir when he challenged Dr. Shea's testimony, pointing to what he viewed as the doctor's conflicting statements about the state of Fritzie's pregnancy.

"I don't question Dr. Shea's veracity," William said, "but what just has been said does not correspond with a statement made to me just after the autopsy. I'd like to have another examination made to give two angles."

"You could have done so at the time the autopsy was made," the coroner replied, apparently meaning at the funeral parlor when William had identified Fritzie's body, not the autopsy the prior evening.

"At the time the statement given me corresponded with information already in my possession. Now there is a difference." He added that he had been too upset then, unable to think clearly.

"We'll be glad to permit you to make such an examination."

When he'd identified Fritzie's body, William told Shea that he and his mother had known about his sister's condition, that she hadn't "come around" on schedule in mid-October. This was consistent with Shea's four-month gestation estimate, but now William thought the timing didn't work.

At the end of the inquest, the coroner's jury reached an open verdict, meaning they couldn't determine the circumstances or manner of her death. By the time the coroner signed the official record this had changed slightly. It stated that Fritzie Mann "...came to her death on the 14th day of January, A.D. 1923, in San Diego County, California, by drowning in the Pacific Ocean near Torrey Pines under circumstances unknown to jury. (homicide)"

As soon as the inquest had ended, Amelia and William had Fritzie's body moved to Johnson & Saum's funeral parlor.

"I am convinced she was murdered," William Mann stated to reporters following the inquest, "but I no longer feel inclined to murder the man, as I did when I first learned of her death. I am willing to let the law take its course, and am sure justice will be done…Fritzie was a good girl and was, no doubt, deceived. I am confident that she brought death to herself by insisting that the man in the case make her his wife."

***

Dr. Harold Thompson performed the second autopsy in the morgue of Johnson & Saum's, at 4th and Ash, shortly after the body arrived. Dr. Shea observed the procedure. Thompson had formerly held Shea's job, performing three to four hundred autopsies as the coroner's autopsy surgeon. He now conducted forensic analyses for the coroner and the police at the city laboratory.

Dr. Thompson had two main tasks, to form an opinion as to the state of Fritzie's pregnancy, and to remove the stomach, kidneys, uterus, and fetus for chemical analysis. The undertaker had covered the body with so much powder that Dr. Thompson couldn't make an adequate external examination. The only relevant feature he could discern was the bruise over the right eye. He re-opened the body. All the internal organs had been incised during the first autopsy, he noted. The heart had been cut entirely loose. He couldn't express an opinion about the state of the heart because of the organ's poor condition four days after the victim's death. The lungs had been incised and sliced to reveal the bronchi. He found a gritty substance he referred to as hardening compound, which the undertaker had used to firm up and temporarily preserve the tissues, throughout the chest cavity, the stomach, and the rest of the abdomen.

Dr. Thompson corroborated his colleague's finding about the state of pregnancy. Fetal development and uterus size were consistent with at least four months gestation, perhaps a bit longer.

***

Chapter Sixteen – The Sheik

Just past noon on Thursday, January 18, 1923, a warm, cloudy Los Angeles day, LAPD Detectives Jack Trainor and Tom O'Brien waited outside of the fashionable La Casa de Flores Hotel on West Adams at Grand. A *Los Angeles Times* reporter, hoping for an exclusive on an arrest in the Fritzie Mann investigation, waited with them. An anonymous informer had phoned police earlier and said that Rogers Clark might be planning to flee, possibly to his home state of New York. Clark had endorsed a large check and engaged in an "agitated" phone conversation that morning. Learning of this, Chief Patrick asked the LAPD to arrest Clark on suspicion of murder.

A short time later the detectives observed an upscale automobile motoring down the street. It parked in front of a private residence a block and a half from the hotel. A man fitting Clark's description got out of the car and walked toward the house. They'd never heard of an actor by that name, but this man had a movie player's looks—six-foot-three, slim, blue eyes, dark hair and complexion, square jaw, and chiseled features. They intercepted him before he reached the door. He confirmed his identity.

Why did you park here and not at the hotel? the detectives asked him.

A lady friend of mine lives here, Clark said. She's been ill and I'm checking on her.

You're wanted downtown in connection with the Fritzie Mann case.

Clark did not act surprised.

The detectives inspected Clark's 1919 Marmon Model 34A touring car, a large, beautiful machine, the kind an honest cop could never afford. The name Marmon oozed cachet: soon after he'd published *This Side of Paradise* and married Zelda Sayre, a style-conscious but broke F. Scott Fitzgerald bought a second-hand Marmon. The sporty Model 34 was the company's flagship model. It was one of the fastest cars on the road, capable of sustained speeds of over eighty m.p.h., making it popular with playboys and bootleggers, some of whom outfitted their machines with secret compartments to conceal cargoes of hooch. Clark's car had cost about $3500 new. It sported black fenders, spoke wheels and a canvas top, plus expensive optional features: a front bumper, a spare tire mounted behind the right front fender, and a spotlight mounted near the driver's window.

Clark had driven Fritzie to Tijuana and back in this car. Had he also transported her body from the Blue Sea Cottages to Torrey Pines beach in it? By the looks of the car, maybe so. The last number on the license plate had been ripped off and the rear body bore a dent with grayish marks, indicating an impact, possibly with a sandy rock or cliff. The glass covers of the speedometer and clock were smashed. And there were bloodspots on the dashboard and a fresh stain on the back-seat cushion—which someone had tried to clean up.

The detectives drove him to the central station and booked him on suspicion of murder. They found two San Diego hotel keys in his pocket, one for the Maryland Hotel, the other for the U.S. Grant. Clark gave the latter hotel as his current address. During the afternoon, Clark conferred with two attorneys and talked freely to detectives and reporters in his cell.

In Clark's La Casa de Flores room, LAPD detectives found two trunks, one bearing the initials "W.G.R," the other the initials "M.E.E." They also found a letter from Clark's mother, inquiring about his current living arrangements. Detectives canvassed businesses near the La Casa de Flores. The only thing they learned was that Clark apparently had trouble sleeping since the case broke in the news. According to a drug store proprietor, Clark had purchased sleeping powder several times in recent days.

Detectives interviewed the La Casa de Flores manager. Clark had checked in and out of the hotel several times over the past two and a half months, the manager said. Clark had first arrived on November 4, then came and went several times that month and the next. He last checked out on Friday, January 12, returning on the afternoon of Monday, January 15. Clark cashed a $250 check at the hotel, announcing his intention to check out on Tuesday and depart for a two-week trip to New York. But Clark didn't check out and had since stated his intention to postpone his departure for two or three days.

Clark told the police he'd delayed his trip because he expected to be arrested any time in connection with Fritzie Mann's death. A suspicious cop might interpret the situation another way. Clark had intended to flee and someone, perhaps his lawyers, talked him out of it. This might explain the "agitated" phone call the informer, mostly likely the La Casa de Flores manager or another employee, overheard. Clark had good reason to be agitated—his name had been all over the news for two days. He knew the police wanted to talk to him, yet he had waited for them to find him, also suspicious.

Notified of the day's developments, Chief Patrick asked the LAPD to hold Clark, and boarded a train for L.A.

***

Chief Patrick, accompanied by San Diego County Detective Frank Wisler, arrived in L.A. around 7:00 p.m.

The chief interrogated Clark for hours. Clark vigorously protested his innocence and denied any knowledge of Fritzie Mann's death. He admitted knowing her, but only as a casual acquaintance. He had met her in September at the Grant Hotel, he said, while she was selling tickets for a benefit performance at The Barn to raise money for her invalid sister. He described their Tijuana trip, how he had dropped Mrs. Mann off at the Paradise Hills sanitarium on the way. The last time he saw Fritzie, he claimed, was on November 7 when she asked to borrow $75 to help pay for her sister's medical bills. He refused to loan her the money and hadn't seen or heard from her since.

Clark said he came from a wealthy New York family and had been head buyer of print paper for a newspaper there. He currently made and promoted agricultural motion pictures in Mexico. His ex-wife, Henrietta Clark, lived on B Street in San Diego with their eight-year-old son.

Were you in San Diego last weekend? Chief Patrick asked Clark.

Yes, Clark said, but I didn't see Fritzie Mann. And I have a rock-solid alibi for the night of Sunday the 14th.

On Saturday he had motored down to Ensenada, Mexico, Clark said, with two men, William Heltzen, head of the film company, and another man who worked for Heltzen. They made an educational film. They returned to San Diego that evening and registered at the Maryland Hotel.

On Sunday evening he visited the home of a prominent San Diego citizen, Mr. Albert Flowers. He picked up Mr. Flowers' stepdaughter, Miss Gladys Taylor, around 8:00 or 8:30 p.m. They ate supper at the Golden Lion Tavern and then returned to the Flowers' residence, where he remained until about one o'clock on Monday morning. After that he returned to the Maryland Hotel and didn't leave his room until the next morning. Mr. Heltzen could corroborate this as he had awakened when Clark walked into the room. Moreover, hotel records should confirm his presence during the night because he'd called down twice to order ice water. He and Heltzen left San Diego at 11:40 a.m. on Monday, arriving in L.A. around 4:30 p.m.

Chief Patrick asked about the blood stains in his Marmon.

They had picked up an injured motorist on Whittier Boulevard and drove him to the hospital, Clark said. Heltzen could verify this as well.

***

William Heltzen had lived an adventurous life. During the war he served as an Army Signal Corps pilot at Rockwell Field on Coronado, a hazardous occupation. ("If you expect to be married soon, or are in love," prospective student pilots were warned, "don't take up aviation.") Flying in formation over San Diego Bay in October 1918, Heltzen collided with another plane, shearing off his own plane's tailpiece. He landed the disabled plane in the bay and swam ashore. After the war he worked as a cameraman for the Fox News Service. He spent most of 1921 and 1922 filming in Mexico with the support of the Mexican government, documenting the land and its undeveloped resources. In what was regarded as one of the greatest feats of photographic derring-do to date, Heltzen captured the first air footage of an active volcano, Mount Popocatépetl, as a crack Mexican pilot made a death-defying dash into the bubbling crater. Heltzen's footage of spewing lava, billowing sulfur clouds, and ash plumes made a dramatic newsreel in movie houses across America.

Heltzen employed non-movie men in his fledgling Fellows Motion Picture Corporation. The other man on the Ensenada filming trip, presumably the camera operator, worked as a car dealer in Pasadena. Rogers Clark had joined Fellows in October 1922, accompanying Heltzen on several trips to Mexico over the next three months. The Mexican Navy had delivered Heltzen (and presumably Rogers Clark) to San Diego in a patrol boat in December after one filming trip. Clark apparently appeared in, helped direct, and promoted the company's films.

Heltzen corroborated Clark's claim that he had left the Maryland Hotel around 8:30 p.m. on Sunday. But he said he didn't see him again until the next morning, when he woke to find Clark in bed.

"From 8:30 p.m. Sunday until 7:00 a.m. Monday I cannot give any information as to Clark's whereabouts," Heltzen told police.

To Clark's relief, Heltzen did verify his account about the blood in his car.

"On our return trip from San Diego we found a man by the road who had been injured in an accident," Heltzen stated. "We took him in the car and left him at the Receiving Hospital. He had suffered a cut about the head and the wound was bleeding. This explains the bloodstains, I think."

***

Detectives contacted Al Flowers to check out the rest of Clark's alibi. A publisher by trade and the exalted ruler of the San Diego Elks Lodge, Flowers had just announced his candidacy for city council.

"Clark's statement that he spent the night at my home is not true," Flowers told reporters. "He called the house by telephone about 7:45 p.m. Sunday and asked my step-daughter, Miss Gladys Taylor, to take dinner with him. She accepted and Clark called for her about 8 p.m., bringing her home at 11 o'clock. I understand they dined at the Maryland Hotel. Immediately after bringing my daughter home Clark departed."

Al Flowers, also the parent of a twenty-year-old woman, shared Amelia Mann's disdain for the skirt-chasing Rogers Clark.

"I tried to discourage the friendship," said Flowers, "but I never seemed to make much progress. Clark has made frequent week-end trips to the city, to see my step-daughter, I presumed."

***

Chapter Seventeen – Rogers Clark

Rogers Van Buren Clark was born in East Orange, New Jersey, on November 21, 1885, the scion of a wealthy New York family. His father died four months after his birth. He grew up in the small town of Queensbury, north of Albany, in upstate New York, with his mother and older sister. As a young adult he listed his occupation as "paper expert." He may have worked for the International Paper Company, which owned a pulp and paper company near his hometown.

He turned up in San Diego in the early 1910s. His son, Rogers Van Buren Clark, Jr., was born in 1915. He married the boy's mother, Henrietta, a year later. He maintained various addresses in the San Diego area during the late 1910s and early 1920s. His World War I draft registration card listed him as a self-employed rancher in Palm City, then a rural community three miles north of the border. Henrietta Clark filed for divorce in August 1921 alleging her husband's "attentions to 'another woman,' cruelty and drunkenness" among her justifications. She requested custody of their son and alimony payments of $150 per month. Her husband, she claimed, received a $4,000 annuity from a relative.

It's not clear how Clark became involved with the Fellows Motion Picture Corporation, a company lost to movie history along with William Heltzen and his films. It may have been part investment, part hobby for Clark, a man with disposable income. He owned a ranch near the border and frequently travelled south into Baja California; perhaps he met Heltzen in Mexico during one of the latter's filming trips. There's no record of Clark having film or acting experience before or after he briefly worked for Heltzen.

The newspapers had trouble pinning Rogers Clark down. They usually reported his age as thirty-three or thirty-five; he was thirty-seven. They labeled him at different times an actor, a director, an assistant director, a film promoter, and a film producer. At other times they called him a car dealer, a broker and a merchant, apparent references to Roger Clarke, the San Pedro automobile electric shop owner the police and reporters mistook for him.

The papers used Clark to reinforce the Hollywood angle. He could hardly have been called a movie player, at best a wannabe. But he otherwise made an ideal tabloid murder suspect, a handsome, wealthy sheik in a bloody Marmon, the kind of man parents tried to keep away from their young daughters.

***

Chief Patrick had reasons to be suspicious of Rogers Clark beyond the condition of his car, discrepancies in his alibi, and statements inconsistent with those of key witnesses. For one, the chief noted a strong resemblance between Clark's handwriting and that of Mr. Johnston. For another, the LAPD had found a gray overcoat and dark hat in a trunk in Clark's room similar to Albert Kern's description of Mr. Johnston's attire.

Did the actor have a motive to kill Fritzie Mann? If he had fathered her unborn child, yes, a compelling one. He was already paying child support to his ex-wife. Given the state of Fritzie's pregnancy, could he have been the father? Based on Clark's statements to police, yes. The conception had occurred in early- to mid-September—the same month he had met Fritzie. But he denied being the father.

Throughout the hours-long grilling at LAPD headquarters, Clark denied any involvement.

"I am innocent of any connection with her death and will be able to prove positively that I am not the person wanted for this crime," he told reporters.

***

Chief Patrick wanted to clarify Clark's conflicting alibi statements and to let Albert Kern have a look at him. Clark agreed to accompany the chief to San Diego, in custody, "to clear up this mystery." Police chief and murder suspect left L.A. on the 1:30 a.m. train, arriving in San Diego around 7:30 the next morning.

***

Chapter Eighteen – The Ultimatum

Why did Fritzie tell her friends that you had treated her roughly? Chief Patrick asked Dr. Jacobs. That you had bruised her legs?

"I may have stepped on her feet while we were dancing," Jacobs said.

The interrogation began at 11:00 a.m. on Thursday. The tone in the chief's office was altogether different from the meeting on Tuesday when Leo Greenbaum walked in with a reluctant Jacobs in tow. No friendly faces greeted the doctor this time, only grim ones, those of over-worked detectives, a coroner being criticized for his handling of the case, and a police chief under escalating pressure to solve a crime that had taken on a life of its own. This was an interrogation, not a voluntary interview.

Much had happened in two days. The cops couldn't verify the doctor's alibi for the night of the murder between 6:15 p.m., when he left Mrs. Worthington's house in Coronado following their Tijuana visit, and 9:00 or 9:30 p.m., when multiple witnesses saw him at the Camp Kearny hospital. This coincided with the general time frame of Mr. and Mrs. Johnston's visit to the Blue Sea Cottages. Moreover, according to Fritzie's chums, Jacobs had lied to the chief about the nature of their relationship. But the key development was the discovery of the correspondence among Fritzie's belongings at Bernice Edwards' house.

Jacobs and Fritzie had exchanged at least eight letters and seven telegrams between December 5, 1922, and January 5, 1923, during her stay in the L.A. area. A few of the letters had mysteriously vanished from Bernice's house soon after the Long Beach cops had discovered them. The rest had arrived from Long Beach that morning. During the interrogation, the chief handed the correspondence to the doctor one piece at a time.

Jacobs had mailed the first letter special delivery to "Miss F. Mann, Hotel Rosslyn, Los Angeles, California," post marked December 5, 1922.

> *Do you know Mrs. Minor who used to trot around with Leo Greenbaum and is the soul of discretion and a good sport? How would you like her to take you to a specialist she knows in L.A.? Of course I mentioned no names but the best way to accomplish results rapidly is to go with her. I am sure she can be trusted. Above all avoid mentioning that a doctor sent you because they will absolutely turn down anything if you say that. I am learning lots of things but then that's the way things go. Let me know immediately and I will forward full instructions.*

The vague terms, "specialist" and "accomplish results," didn't fool anyone. Illegal and spoken of in hushed tones, abortion and birth control had previously been legal in America. During the eighteenth and early nineteenth centuries, common law allowed a woman to terminate a pregnancy at any time prior to "quickening," the point at which she could first feel the fetus move, usually around the eighteen- to twenty-week mark in a first pregnancy. A series of events in the latter half of the nineteenth century, championed by Dr. Jacobs' profession, led to the criminalization of abortion and birth control. The American

Medical Association launched a campaign against abortion in 1857. Next came the "Comstock Law" of 1873, which linked abortion to existing anti-obscenity laws. Then one state after another passed anti-abortion laws between 1860 and 1880. The law granted one exception. If pregnancy or childbirth endangered the mother's life, a "therapeutic" abortion could be performed, or an abortifacient—a drug or herb used to induce a miscarriage—administered. This was the law in California in December 1922.

Jacobs' next letter, written on U.S. Grant Hotel Stationary, was post marked the following day, December 6, 1922.

Sorry - but I think the whole thing was engineered wrongly. Of course - a delay – while inconvenient - should not worry you. It may be all the better for you. Will inform you as soon as I can definitely determine how to go about it. You see physicians like to keep their business to themselves - and not allow anyone to get anything on them. Which of course is perfectly businesslike but sometimes inconvenient. The enclosed notice please return as I have to forward it to my attorneys. In the meantime keep a stiff upper lip -- and your courage high. I am sure everything will turn out OK. Should anyone you go to question you -- you may tell them that you are an arrested case of pulmonary tuberculosis in 1916 and are worried that if carried all the way thru it will re-activate the disease--and above all that you are a married woman!

What had the doctor "engineered wrongly?" Apparently, a consultation with an L.A. physician. The doctor had probably turned Fritzie down because she failed to provide sufficient justification for a therapeutic abortion, admitted to being single, or both.

Jacob's advice to use tuberculosis as justification made sense, whether or not Fritzie had ever developed an active case of the disease. Tuberculosis was the most common justification for a therapeutic abortion and Fritzie had a family history of the disease. And Jacobs specialized in treating tubercular veterans. His exhortation to conceal her unwed status also made sense because doctors were less inclined to perform an abortion on a single woman. More often they pressured her to get married. One Tennessee physician in the 1890s had advised women to "take a revolver with them, and if the young man refuses to marry, to kill him on the spot." But marriage wasn't always an option and murder hardly a good one.

The "enclosed notice," Jacobs mentions, presumably designed to protect him in case he got caught arranging an illegal abortion, is puzzling. How did he hope to escape responsibility for conspiring to commit a criminal act, with or without a signed waiver? If an abortion would've been medically justified, all the subterfuge would've been unnecessary anyway. And if Jacobs was the father, as Chief Patrick suspected, how could he in good conscience ask Fritzie, the woman he had wronged, to sign a waiver? More outrageous still, he urged her to "keep a stiff upper lip?"

The next letter, again on U.S. Grant Hotel stationary, was undated though Jacobs had mailed it between the 6th and the 13th of December.

Now read carefully - Go to see Dr. F.P. Young, - Black Building. Tell him you were sent by Miss Minor (if he asks you) of San Diego - who saw him a few months ago with a friend and who recommends him most highly. Be diplomatic – tell him that they have stopped for two months and that you are feeling terrible – intense nausea- much vomiting – dizziness – unable to hold your job if things are not remedied – etc. He is a good man–

so don't worry – and write me the results. Don't
call up – because I am moving and don't know
where I'll be. Above all <u>don't tell him you were sent</u>
<u>by a doctor</u>! Best luck.

Doctors considered excessive vomiting during pregnancy, another common justification for a therapeutic abortion, a medical emergency. But why did Jacobs implore her to keep a doctor's—his—involvement secret? A doctor who performed legitimate therapeutic abortions would presumably prefer a referral to come from another physician because it validated medical need and kept them on the right side of the law. Jacobs knew Fritzie's case didn't meet the therapeutic criteria; he just wanted to keep his name out of the illegal arrangement.

For some reason, Fritzie did not see Dr. Young.

Jacobs probably mailed the following undated letters on December 13 and 16 respectively.

The lady in question has just informed me that she
will be glad to go up – and will let me know when.
I told her as instructed that you were secretly
married and that your hubby left and that you were
feeling frightfully on account of the whole thing.
I mentioned no names. Will let you know when to
meet her. Hope you are feeling better.

I shall know definitely by Monday when Bill can
come up. She is surprised that you cannot get in
touch with Young – as someone else shared his
office and would know of his whereabouts. In the
meantime have moved and they have disconnected
my phone – I do not intend to have one at the
hospital as I don't know how long I'll stay. So if
you need anything in a hurry wire me. Hope you
are well and taking good care of yourself.

Jacobs mailed the next letter on December 18. He addressed it to the Rosslyn, unaware that Fritzie had already left for Long Beach with Bernice the previous day: *Expect reply to my letter which was written last Tuesday any minute. My man must be out of town. If I do not hear today will call up and as soon as I hear will let you know. Hope you're getting along O.K.*

Jacobs sent a telegram, again addressed to the Rosslyn, on December 20. By then Fritzie had been at Bernice's house for three days. *Will call you up at six thirty today. Billy.*

Jacobs explained to Chief Patrick that he absentmindedly signed this telegram "Billy" as he'd just been on the telephone with an acquaintance, Wilma Minor, who he often called "Bill" or "Billy."

Fritzie sent her first known communication in the chain, a telegram, to Jacobs at the Camp Kearny hospital. Undated, she sent if from the Long Beach Western Union telegraph station sometime after Jacobs' "Billy" telegram of December 20: *Write me in care of 505 Loma Avenue, Long Beach, immediately. Mark all letters personal. Fritzie Mann.*

There was a gap in the correspondence for twelve days. On January 2, Fritzie sent this telegram:

> *Have gone through enough these last two weeks on account of you to embitter me more than ever. If I do not hear from you in the next two days will come to San Diego immediately and stop at nothing.*

***

Chapter Nineteen – Whole Matter Looks Very Funny To Me

Why the sudden ominous tone in Fritzie's telegram of January 2? Had she endured more failed consultations or was she was fed up with Jacobs' apparent inaction or failure to contact her for days at a time? Had her distress and frustration, building over the past month as the clock continued to tick, finally reached a breaking point? When Bernice had visited her at the Rosslyn on December 17, she found Fritzie in bed, ill and depressed, most likely from morning sickness exacerbated by stress. Had her mental state finally reached a breaking point?

A flurry of communications came over the next few days. On January 3, Jacobs sent a telegram asking her to *Wire immediately if you can meet her Thursday and all details.*

Fritzie responded via telegram the same day: *Received your wire at six p.m. cannot see Miner til, Friday. Wire at once where she will be, so I can meet her.*

Jacobs mailed a letter the same day.

> *Just returned to the hospital and found your telegram. Wrote you to tell me all particulars but have not heard one word. Am just recuperating from an attack of influenza and am pretty low in every way. Let me know what happened. Hope that you are recovering rapidly. Thank Mrs. Bond for writing.*

"Mrs. Bond" was Bernice Edwards, who had eloped at age fifteen with an older man with that surname back in Denver. Her father had quickly tracked them down, brought her back home, and had the marriage annulled. Apparently, she hadn't yet changed back to her maiden name, or so Jacobs thought.

Jacobs sent this telegram on Thursday, January 4: *Meet Miss Minor Hotel Lankershim Friday at noon. She's registered there.*

He finally responded to Fritzie's threatening telegram in a letter, also on January 4:

> *Tho I was shocked at your outburst I can scarce blame you--for I realize your point of view far better than one usually does. However I hope you will soon be well and recognize many things that you have failed hitherto. Miss Minor will meet you at the Hotel Lankershim at <u>noon on Friday</u>. She's registered there. She will make all arrangements. You wired me something about returning one hundred dollars. Please don't do that - but use it to cover incidental expenses. In the meantime I shall wire you to make sure that you will get the right steer. Of course I told her that you were secretly married and that he has left you or you left him – I did not know which, that I was interested in you– professionally–I hope everything will turn out O K – because Miss minor is a peach – and she'll help you as much as she can. Lots of luck!*

Fritzie failed to meet Minor on Friday, January 5, and again the following day, then sent this telegram: *This is the second time I have tried to get Miner and have failed. Cannot understand the whole thing. Things are getting on my nerves. Whole matter looks very funny to me.*

This was the last known piece of correspondence in the series. Fritzie left Long Beach dressed in Bernice's fancy outfit two days later at midnight on Sunday, with one week to live.

***

Chapter Twenty – Wilma

The papers continued to refer to Wilma Minor as a nurse even after she denied being one. Reporters apparently assumed her profession because Dr. Jacobs had engaged her to assist Fritzie with a medical matter. Once in print, as often happens, the misinformation stuck. Wilma had been many things, but never a nurse.

Apparently born in Azusa, a suburb northeast of L.A.—"apparently" because little about Wilma or her family is certain—she'd worked as a touring actress in vaudeville dramas and musical comedies during much of the 1910s. She also wrote movie scenarios and supposedly appeared in a few films. Her acting troupe included her husband, Frank Minor, and her mother, Cora. Wilma was unusually close to Cora and had travelled with her on the vaudeville circuit. An eccentric shapeshifter, Cora had at various times called herself an actress, a writer, a poet, a medium, publisher of a magazine called *The Thinker's World*, and founder of the Society of Natural Science, a free-love cult based in Chicago, of which Wilma and her husband were members.

Wilma settled in San Diego in early 1922, aged thirty-five although if asked she would've given a younger age. With each ten-year census, Wilma's rate of aging appeared to slow. She is listed as twenty-one years old in 1910 when she was twenty-four; twenty-seven in 1920 when she was thirty-four; and thirty-one in 1930, when she was forty-four. In 1922, she ran a short-lived dress design company called

My Lady's Dressmakers from her residence. Around this time, she reinvented herself as a writer and associate editor for *Southwest Magazine*, a now-defunct San Diego monthly magazine. She later wrote a human interest column for the *Union* called "Sidelights on Life" and became known for her distinctive purple prose. She once described a book as "so full of fresh air and high zest of living that it plays on jaded senses pleasantly like the muted strings of a violin."

Five years after her role in the Fritzie Mann case, Wilma's writing skills, along with her voluptuous figure and seductive charm, would combine to launch her overnight from obscurity to nation-wide notoriety. With help from her allegedly clairvoyant mother, she would perpetrate one of the most audacious literary hoaxes of the 20th century involving fake letters from Abraham Lincoln. But in January 1923, Wilma was an unknown former vaudeville player and fledgling writer who Dr. Louis Jacobs regarded as a peach and a good sport.

How well they knew each other isn't clear. Wilma told reporters that Jacobs was "practically a stranger to me," but she had reason to downplay their association. They'd met the previous summer at his friend Leo Greenbaum's house. Wilma told him about a friend of hers who had recently undergone an abortion in L.A. Several months later, when Jacobs began trying to make arrangements for Fritzie, he contacted Minor for the doctor's name.

Wilma told Chief Patrick that she'd spoken with Jacobs on the telephone on several occasions. At first, he avoided names.

"She is a girl of a very nice family, a nice young girl," Jacobs said according to Wilma. "She has been secretly married and deserted, and she is in ill health, and she says she has a great career ahead of her as a dancer, and can go to a position in San Francisco. She has appealed to me, and I am very sorry for her, and I would like to help her out."

Wilma gave Jacobs the name of Dr. F.P. Young, who had an office in the Black Building in downtown L.A.

Jacobs called Wilma a few days later, informing her that his woman friend "cannot find him or anybody like that there at the address you gave," so Wilma must have given him the wrong address.

Wilma insisted that her information was correct. After more phone conversations over the next two weeks, Wilma offered to travel to L.A. to assist the woman. During their last conversation, on the 3rd or 4th of January, she asked the woman's name.

"Her name is Miss Mann," Jacobs said.

"Not Fritzie Mann?"

"Yes. What made you think of that?"

"Because you had spoken at length about her promising dancing career, and everything. I met the little lady last summer, and knew she was a dancer. Why, I will remember her when I see her. Tell her to meet me in the lobby of the Lankershim Hotel between 12 and 1."

According to Wilma, she and Jacobs never openly discussed Fritzie's pregnancy or the nature of the operation she sought; it was inferred from the context. Jacobs offered to defray her expenses for the trip. Wilma declined to accept payment, but later Jacobs mailed her a thirty-five-dollar check. After Fritzie failed to meet her at the Lankershim, Wilma wired Jacobs. She had spoken to Dr. Young and his office was still in the Black Building. The L.A. city directory listed a F.P. Young with an office in the Black Building, thought it did not list him as a physician.

By the time of her scheduled meeting with Wilma in L.A., Fritzie had been at Bernice Edwards' house in Long Beach for over two weeks. But she knew the Lankershim's location—four blocks from the Rosslyn—and could easily have traveled there by train or streetcar. Wilma would've recognized her on sight. So how did Fritzie manage to miss the meeting, twice? Bad luck? A miscommunication that isn't obvious in the correspondence or in Wilma's and Jacobs' later statements? By this time, was Fritzie so erratic from stress and illness that she showed up at the wrong place or at the wrong time? Or did she miss the meetings on purpose, having changed her mind or afraid of going through with the abortion despite her seeming urgency for Jacobs to arrange one?

***

According to Bernice Edwards, Fritzie had meant her final trip to San Diego to be a quick visit, implying that her friend had moved to L.A. permanently. She must have re-located for career reasons, both to move her dancing career to the next level and to increase her income to help pay for her dying sister's medical treatment. Fritzie and people close to her had mentioned forthcoming dance engagements in L.A. and San Francisco. According to Bernice, Fritzie had performed at the Café Royal in Culver City but the manager there told police he'd never heard of her. Fritzie apparently had performed in Culver City clubs because people sometimes referred to her as the "Darling of the Cafes" there. But Bernice, it seems, had confused the Café Royal with the Palais Royal Café, located in downtown L.A. After her death, several papers reported recent performances there. Three weeks before, according to the *Sun*, Fritzie "was the toast of the diners at the Palais Royal, a bright light café and cabaret on Spring Street. She was a favorite there—as she was at San Diego. She had a host of admirers who feted her and entertained her. Fritzie was popular."

The *Sun* had the date wrong—three weeks before her death would've been near the end of December, when Fritzie was three-and-a-half or four months pregnant, ill, and staying in Long Beach with Bernice. More likely this article referred to her activities in late November or early December, before she became too ill and depressed to perform. The Palais Royal, owned by a syndicate that also owned the better-known Palais Royal in San Francisco, was located near Pershing Square, four blocks from the Rosslyn Hotel. Performing there could have set Fritzie up for bigger and better things in L.A. and San Francisco. She apparently intended to sign a contract with them when she returned to Los Angeles and told others she hoped to travel to San Francisco next.

L.A. was also the place to be for a young woman trying to break into the film business. She may have also hoped to reconnect with Theodore Kosloff, whose studio was downtown in the Trinity Auditorium. From there it would have been one step to the Famous Players-Lasky studio at Sunset and Vine. But first she had to deal with her condition.

***

Chapter Twenty-One – Damn Fool Altruism

"Why did you furnish Fritzie money?" Chief Patrick demanded of the doctor. "Why did you send money to Miss Minor or assist Fritzie when you say you never had intimate relations with Miss Mann?"

"Call it damn fool altruism, if you want to," Jacobs replied.

Fritzie, "was up against it" with her pregnancy, the doctor said, and he was particularly sympathetic because they were both Jewish. But in getting involved with her, he now realized, he made the worst mistake of his life.

Chief Patrick didn't buy the friend story—no way would Jacobs have gone to such lengths, taken such risks, and spent so much money if he didn't have more at stake personally. Jacobs had given Fritzie at least $100, that they knew of, for "incidental expenses" and paid her $75 Rosslyn bill. And he had risked criminal charges and losing his medical license for his attempts to arrange an illegal abortion.

Embitter me more than ever, she said in her ultimatum.

For the chief, only one scenario now made sense: Jacobs had gotten Fritzie pregnant and then refused to marry her. Fritzie had mentioned to Dorothy Armstrong that she would kill herself if she were in that situation. But because abortion was illegal and an out-of-wedlock pregnancy scandalous, it made an equally good motive for murder.

I will come to San Diego immediately and stop at nothing.

Assuming Fritzie didn't mean to take that Tennessee doctor's advice and shoot Jacobs, this could only mean one thing: She would expose his betrayal, to anyone and everyone if need be—to her family and friends, to his family and friends, to his superiors at the Camp Kearny hospital. The only card she had left to play, it would ruin the doctor personally and professionally. It would've put him in trouble with his Public Health Service superiors, placed his medical license in jeopardy, and possibly landed him in jail. Did the prospect of these consequences so alarm Jacobs that he decided to lure Fritzie back to San Diego and kill her? To Chief Patrick, this was more than plausible. Twelve days after she threatened him, Fritzie washed up on Torrey Pines beach.

Jacobs admitted to writing the letters and trying to arrange an illegal abortion. He also admitted that he'd known about Fritzie's pregnancy since October, when she'd first missed her period. At his first interview he said he'd first learned of her pregnancy on the Friday evening before her death. But he still insisted he wasn't the father. He had no personal stake in her pregnancy. He acted out of friendship and damn fool altruism.

Why had you tried to arrange an abortion in L.A.? Chief Patrick asked. Why not in San Diego?

Because an acquaintance, Miss Wilma Minor, knew two L.A. physicians who did that kind of work, Jacobs said.

Who was going to pay for the operation?

I offered to pay half. As to who was to pay for the other half, "I give you my word, I don't know."

Chief Patrick made Jacobs re-tell his story about the evening ride to La Mesa on Friday, January 12, and what Fritzie had told him. He modified aspects of his original story and offered new details. Fritzie, he said, despondent and anxious, had pressed him about when and where the operation would happen. He replied that Wilma Minor would accompany her back to L.A. for the operation.

Jacobs agreed to provide a handwriting sample. At Chief Patrick's direction he wrote "Awin Johnston & wife L.A.," which was how the chief interpreted Mr. Johnston's scrawl. Jacobs omitted the "T" in Johnston and instead of printing a capital "A," as it appeared in the Blue Sea register, wrote the letter in cursive. Chief Patrick specified precisely how he wanted it written and made him do it again.

The interrogation lasted almost three hours. In addition to the admitted lies, Chief Patrick found many of Jacobs' responses noncommittal, evasive, or odd. The doctor had done as little as possible to fill in the blanks in the correspondence and claimed to have disposed of Fritzie's letters and telegrams. At the end of the interrogation, Chief Patrick said he was dissatisfied and arrested Jacobs on suspicion of murder. By coincidence the LAPD detectives arrested Rogers Clark at almost the same instant.

Jacobs maintained a calm demeanor as the cops took him into custody. To reporters, he expressed regret at signing the jail register under his own name, saying, "If my mother hears of it, it will kill her." He declined to make a statement to the press regarding the case, but reporters waited around in case he changed his mind. Later he complained that his jail cot made him feel like a waffle.

***

Chapter Twenty-Two – Doctor Jacobs

Louis Llewelyn Jacobs was born on August 20, 1891, in either Baltimore, Maryland, or Lithuania, from where his parents had emigrated around the time of his birth. Jacobs had one sibling, a younger sister. At some point the family moved to Norfolk, Virginia, and Jacobs attended high school there in the 1900s. Although the family struggled financially after his father's death, he managed to graduate from Johns Hopkins University in 1913 with a Bachelor of Arts, and then from Johns Hopkins Medical School, in 1917. His extended family had pitched in to make this possible.

His Johns Hopkins classmates described him as congenial, sociable, and active in athletics. He participated in football, baseball, track, and swimming. He was a member of the glee club, the instrumental club and the Woodrow Wilson Club, and served as assistant business manager of the *Johns Hopkins News Letter*, a weekly university newspaper. Friends and former Johns Hopkins classmates in Baltimore were said to be "shocked" at his arrest.

After medical school, Jacobs interned at the Hebrew Hospital and Asylum in Baltimore. His time there included intensive work in the genito-urinary department. Later commissioned as a first lieutenant in the Army Medical Corps, he spent his war-time service at a series of military hospitals around the country, to include Walter Reed in Washington, D.C., and Fort Bayard, New Mexico. Along the way he developed a specialty in the treatment of tuberculosis, a specialty much in demand among veterans. In 1919, with the war coming to an end, he applied for appointment in the Public Health Service Reserve. The PHS commissioned him as an assistant surgeon, the equivalent of an Army first lieutenant, in February 1920.

His first assignment, at a hospital in New Haven, Connecticut, proved a good start to his PHS career. In a fitness report covering the period October through December 1919, the surgeon in charge rated Jacobs' professional ability and devotion to duty as excellent and predicted a bright future as a "diagnostician of diseases of the chest." The surgeon noted that although Jacobs "occasionally allows his youth to affect his better judgement," it did not affect his value as an officer and described his character as "very temperate in all things." The PHS promoted him to the rank of passed assistant surgeon (reserve), the equivalent of an Army captain, in November 1920.

Jacobs transferred to Veteran's Hospital 64 at Camp Kearny in March 1922. Those who knew him at this time and later described him as soft spoken. But he was an active player in the local social scene and had many friends, including those in the upper crust of San Diego society. He frequented popular nightspots such as the Golden Lion Tavern and the U.S. Grant Hotel and often made trips down to the Tijuana race tracks, where he owned a small string of horses.

Perhaps distracted by his social activities and love life, Jacobs' professional performance declined during the latter half of 1922 in the opinion of his superior. In an efficiency report for the period July 1 to December 31, 1922, Surgeon Henry Cohn wrote that although Jacobs was a capable diagnostician as ward surgeon, "his work requires more than ordinary supervision." Jacobs "has the confidence of most of his patients," Cohn said, but is "inclined to be argumentative with patients." Cohn rated Jacobs as average in six of eleven performance categories. He considered him above average in general professional knowledge, proficiency in specialty, and neatness and personal appearance. He rated him below average in physical energy, endurance, and tact. For the question "Especially desire to have him?" Cohn marked "no." To the question "Be satisfied to have him?" he marked "yes." He called Jacobs "a valuable officer while serving under those who understand him." Jacobs was "inclined to be rather irresponsible, but who is a good ward surgeon while under strict supervision." In the military and elsewhere, Cohn had "damned him with faint praise," but it may have been worse than that. Jacobs received this fitness report sometime in the two weeks before Fritzie's death.

**

Chapter Twenty-Three – Suppositious Immoralities

Newspapers in the Jazz Age tended to dwell on bad news, the more salacious and violent the better, a tendency not confined to the big-city yellow papers. And if not salacious or violent, then weird. They blasted out pithy headlines of murder, mayhem, and weirdness in bold and all-caps without respite. On Thursday, January 18, a banner headline in the *Evening Tribune* shrieked S.D. MAN FORCED TO DIG OWN GRAVE; TORTURED, SHOT AND BURIED ON SPOT. Another headline announced, GIRL BRANDED, *FIERY CROSS SEARED IN ARM BY MAN*. Other front-page stories included SMUGGLERS ACCUSED OF MIDNIGHT MURDER, WOMAN STABBED TO DEATH AT 'PARTY', THREE KILLED WHEN SEWER CAVES IN, and 123-POUND HUBBY SAYS 200-POUND WIFE IMPAIRS HIS HEALTH. The biggest headline, from an Associated Press dispatch with a Los Angeles dateline, read, NAB S.D. MURDER SUSPECT, *DETAIN MAN FRIEND OF GIRL SLAIN ON BEACH:* "Roger V.B. Clark, motion picture actor and assistant director, was arrested here today at the request of the San Diego police and booked at the central police station on a charge of suspicion of murder in connection with the mysterious death of Fritzie Mann at Torrey Pines."

By Thursday the story was appearing on the front pages, often as the lead, of the major papers in San Francisco and L.A. and had begun to spread outside of California, as far east as Pittsburgh. Most of the major eastern and mid-western papers hadn't picked it up yet but the story was sprinting east. On Friday, after the arrest of two suspects the day before, both photogenic and urbane men from the east, each with a motive, a shaky alibi and circumstantial evidence against him, the case zoomed into a full-fledged national story. It spread to all of the major east coast papers, making the front pages of *The Washington Post* and the *Baltimore Sun*, and even across the Atlantic.

Though San Diego was a backwater and Fritzie Mann wasn't famous, stories that appealed to base human instincts were always ripe for top billing and achieved disproportionate coverage. This story had it all or could be made to seem that way. It was a murder mystery with the right kind of victim, not just a young white woman, but a beautiful exotic dancer washed up dead in her teddies, who cavorted with Hollywood players and enjoyed assignations at beach cottages and got pregnant out of wedlock.

The San Diego dailies generally refrained from moralizing or maligning the victim, but often implied scandal and sometimes more than implied it. On Friday, the *Union* ran a big headline referring to the Blue Sea cottage as a "love cottage." The article did not call the Johnstons' Blue Sea sojourn a tryst, but the headline stimulated scandalous thoughts even if people didn't read the article beneath. The *Sun* went farther. It blamed Fritzie's sexy appearance and ambitions in the entertainment world for her death, publishing a picture in one of her more provocative poses with an inset titled *She Pays, Always---A Lesson*. She'd studied interpretive dancing with a great artist and hoped for a career, it said. She'd performed at resorts and gone round and round in the "Hollywood maelstrom." Fritzie "had a pretty face, which always charms, and a beautiful form, for display of which a certain element is always ready to pay… Her mother, horror-stricken, weeps…Suicide or murder, IT IS THE WAGES!"

In an editorial the following week in the *San Diego Herald*, a small weekly paper, editor Abraham Sauer would take the daily papers to task. Sauer, the city's resident muckraker, accused them of hyping sales with lurid innuendo at the expense of a dead woman's reputation and a mother's broken heart. He called them "journalistic sensation-mongers" that should be punished for spewing "suppositious immoralities that may be false."

The tragic death of Fritzie Mann is a crime which demands the severest punishment for the brute who took her life, if it was murder, and even a worse punishment for someone if it was a case of suicide to shield herself from the ostracism of her friends, because her betrayer was not man enough to give her and her unborn babe the father's name. From all that can be learned of her, Fritzie was a loving and lovable girl, endowed by Nature with unusual charms and artistic accomplishments, with a strong passion and a weak will. Responsive to the impulses planted in her by the forces of nature, she must have rightly felt that there could be no immorality in true nature or true art. Nothing that now is said about her can do her either good or harm. But she had a mother who loved Fritzie and to that mother is due every solace and cheer which can aid in comforting her. Instead the daily papers are printing sensational details and allusions which make a loving mother wonder if her dear girl was really a bad and evil thing, instead of the loving daughter she thought she knew. Then, to give more effect to their stories the sensational papers publish pictures, which in life would be considered artistic poses, but under the circumstances make Nature and beauty seem immoral.

Sauer, a blunt, perpetually outraged gadfly in his early seventies whose little weekly has itself been called yellow, was making suppositions of his own about Fritzie's will and her views on the morality of nature and art. But he made a valid point: The photos spoke volumes to the public and the editors of the daily papers knew it.

But people saw in those pictures what they wanted to see. A conservative might see a sleazy Oriental dancer in an indecent costume, a flapper thumbing her nose at conventional morality, intentionally inflaming male passions by writhing seductively for randy sailors at CPO stag parties. A progressive might see a talented, confident New Woman pursuing a legitimate artistic career, who flaunted her "sex appeal"—a recently-coined term much in vogue—without shame in the service of her art and the spirit of sexual freedom. Whatever lies and half-truths about Fritzie readers perceived in the photos, they wondered what role her profession and lifestyle might have played in her death.

***

Chapter Twenty-Four – He Is Not The Man

Dr. Jacobs' attorney, James "Jimmy" Wadham, had arrived in San Diego as a five-year-old in 1870. It was then a pioneer village of 1500 people centered in the area later called Old Town. He told stories of hunting rabbits and trapping quail where downtown now stood. A Harvard Law School graduate, Wadham had served as San Diego mayor between 1911 and 1913, then resumed his law practice. He ran for mayor again in the next election, losing by eighty-two votes to John L. Bacon.

As his first act on Jacobs' behalf, Wadham filed a writ of *habeas corpus* to compel the police chief to release Dr. Jacobs. The writ was returnable in superior court on the following Monday when Chief Patrick would have to provide justification for continuing to hold Jacobs. The chief announced his intention to contest the writ. Even if the court freed the prisoner, he said, he would re-arrest Jacobs on a definite charge preferred by Fritzie's mother.

Outraged that Jacobs would have to spend the weekend in jail, the Camp Kearny hospital commanding officer demanded the doctor's immediate release. The welfare of numerous tubercular veterans depended upon it, he said. Informed of this, Chief Patrick replied dryly that as far as he knew, "the city was not yet under martial law."

***

With Jacobs in jail, DA Chester Kempley and Det. Sgt. Chadwick visited Camp Kearny to check out his alibi. They verified reports of several people who saw the doctor at the hospital between 9:00 and 10:00 p.m. on the night of the crime. Flushed with the excitement of his first big case, Kempley came off as brash and disrespectful. This generated sympathy for the doctor and animosity towards the DA among the hospital staff. Some thought the DA was trying to frame Jacobs.

After questioning the hospital staff, Kempley spoke to reporters. Even if the doctor had made it back to the base as early as nine o'clock, he said, it did not establish a viable alibi. Jacobs could have murdered Fritzie Mann as early as 7:30 p.m., giving him ample time to wrap the body in an Army blanket, drive it eight miles up the coast, dump it on the beach, and make it to the hospital by nine. Most people had overlooked this key detail, but there was a shortcut. About halfway back to La Jolla from the beach, a little-used dirt road ran east from the coast highway directly to Camp Kearny.

***

Albert Kern, Blue Sea Cottages manager, sat in Chief Patrick's office.

"This man is in an army uniform," Patrick said. "Take a good look at him and let me know if he is the man that was out there at your cottages."

The chief stepped outside. He returned a minute later with Dr. Louis Jacobs.

Patrick asked Jacobs if he'd ever seen Albert Kern.

"No sir," Jacobs replied. "I have never seen him before."

Leaving Jacobs in the office, the chief pulled Kern into the hall and asked him if Jacobs was the mysterious Mr. Johnston.

No, Kern said.

This took the chief aback. He'd been confident—it *had* to be Jacobs. Jacobs, whose first thought had been to consult a lawyer. Who gave odd answers to straightforward questions. Who lied about his relationship with the victim and tried to arrange an illegal abortion. Who had a motive for murder and a three-hour gap in his alibi. Patrick, now convinced that Jacobs was somehow involved in Fritzie's death, refused to let Kern off the hook so easily. He asked him several variations of the same question. Each time Kern replied, "No, it's not him."

Dumfounded, Chief Patrick finally asked if Jacobs at least *resembled* Mr. Johnston.

Now Kern prevaricated.

Maybe, he said. There was some resemblance as far as complexion and size. "I might possibly be mistaken and I think it would help matters if you would bring the man out and let him go through the motions and stand in the same place and do the same things all over again…but I do not think that he is the man."

***

Chapter Twenty-Five – Clear Me Up, Boys

On the morning of Friday, January 19, newsboys waived copies of the *Union* and shouted out headlines from downtown street corners: OWNER OF 'LOVE COTTAGE' SEES PHOTO OF CLARK; SAYS HE RESEMBLES FRITZIE MANN'S COMPANION.

"There is a remarkable resemblance between this man and the man to whom I rented a cottage Sunday night," Kern said, but added that he'd have to see Clark in person to be sure. Looking at a photograph of Clark taken in L.A. the day before, he said, "I believe I can see a scar on his left cheek, near his mouth, where the man to whom I rented the cottage had a bad cold sore, the size of a dime. This sore, however, has had ample time to heal since Sunday night."

To readers of the *Evening Tribune* and the *Sun*, Clark's situation had seemed dire on Thursday evening. When arrested, he'd seemed ready to flee out of state. The partially cleaned up blood spots and broken gauge glass appeared to be the aftermath of a violent struggle. Witnesses he named declined to vouch for him. William Mann and Al Flowers had publicly assailed his character. Kern's statement on Friday morning made his guilt seem *fait accompli*. But behind the scenes, things had changed.

Police had learned that on Friday, January 12, before Clark and his Fellows Motion Pictures buddies departed L.A. for Ensenada, the actor had stopped by the Pacific Title Card Company in Hollywood, presumably to pick up title cards—

cards used to show dialogue and narrative description in silent films—for the shoot. While there, a printer at the shop stepped outside to admire Clark's Marmon. The man noticed the shattered gauge glass.

"How did that happen?" he asked.

"Oh, a chicken did it," Clark said.

According to Clark, the "chicken" had smashed the gauge glass with her French heels. But those heels couldn't have belonged to Fritzie Mann since the gauge glass incident had occurred sometime before the 12th in an incident unrelated to her death on the 14th.

Clark's alibi had also tightened up. Al Flowers may have let his animosity towards Clark color his initial statements to the police and press. Flowers had initially claimed that Clark had left his house around 11:00 p.m. He now admitted that, although he didn't actually *see* Clark after eleven, he knew the actor was still at his house for another two hours.

"I heard his voice and knew it was late, and Mrs. Flowers looked at the clock and said it was 1 o'clock," Flowers said, sounding like it pained him to admit it.

And Clark's date that evening, Flowers' stepdaughter Gladys Taylor, confirmed his alibi for the entire evening. Police also verified that the couple ate dinner at the Golden Lion Tavern, as both claimed.

Satisfied with the alibi, Chief Patrick didn't bother to let Albert Kern have a look at Clark and his possible cold sore. He cleared Rogers Clark on Friday afternoon and let him go. When his cell door swung open, a relieved Clark broke into a big smile, laughed, and shook hands with everyone within reach. Outside he spoke to reporters.

"Clear me up, boys. Give me my good name again," he said, hoping the reporters might grant him an honor he seemed unlikely to get from Amelia Mann and Al Flowers.

Asked if he had immediate plans, Clark said, "No, I don't know what I will do, just go on as before, I guess, and try to forget that I was ever in such a situation." He would probably head back to L.A. in a few days, he added. Clark thanked Chief Patrick for the courtesy the police had shown him and left.

The change in Clark's status from assumed guilt to exoneration overnight caught reporters and their readers by surprise. Friday's *Evening Tribune* announced in stark headlines MANN SUSPECT HAS ALIBI. The story covered most of the front page. It featured a number of photos, including a new one of Fritzie, most likely taken backstage during her Colonial "Dance of Destiny" performances a year before. In the photo she wears a shear split skirt over a tasseled silk one-piece and an ornate feathered headdress. She is posed on one knee, the other muscular leg stretched out, her torso bent back at a severe angle, eyes skyward, arms crossed over her breast in a way eerily redolent of her death pose. Of the photos published after her death, this may have been the most provocative pose in her most risqué costume.

The *Los Angeles Examiner*, which had treated Clark's guilt as axiomatic the day before, gave his release top billing under a screaming headline: BARS SUSPECT IN DANCER'S DEATH. The *Los Angeles Evening Express* screamed louder: HUNT NEW MAN IN GIRL KILLING, *DANCER MURDER MYSTERY DEEPENS AS FILM MAN CLAIMS 'CAST IRON' ALIBI.* The latter article featured a photo of two LAPD detectives gesturing towards the Marmon's broken license plate and another of a grinning Clark being released from jail in San Diego. The article dwarfed one about Wallace Reid, one of the most famous film actors on the planet, even though his death had reportedly sparked a new Hollywood dope war.

As a prime suspect, Rogers Clark had been too good to be true. The press would miss him and his Hollywood connections, however tenuous those may have been. But as if to compensate for his loss, the police were investigating another movie man Fritzie had reportedly met at an L.A. club.

***

Chapter Twenty-Six – It Has To Be Him

Saturday afternoon was cloudy and cool, temperature in the mid-fifties, a light breeze blowing up from Windansea beach. Chief Patrick stood outside the Blue Sea Cottages office with Dr. Jacobs, Albert Kern, other cops, and reporters. At Kern's suggestion, Patrick planned to re-enact the night of the murder. Dr. Jacobs, wearing the brown suit and hat he claimed he wore that night, played the starring role as the mysterious Mr. Johnston.

The group walked down the paved path between the cottages. Kern pointed out Mr. Johnston's tire tracks in the alley near cottage thirty-three, still visible in the mud. It didn't matter because a forensic technique for analyzing tire tread impressions hadn't been invented.

The group entered cottage thirty-three.

"Have you ever been here before?" Chief Patrick asked Jacobs.

"I have not," Jacobs said.

The chief along with Det. Sgts. Chadwick and Sears, County Detective Wisler, and others began peppering Jacobs with questions. Soon flustered, the doctor refused to answer more questions without first speaking to Jimmie Wadham.

Back outside, Chief Patrick asked Kern about Jacobs. Kern nervously scrutinized the doctor.

"I am not absolutely sure that Dr. Jacobs is the man," he said. Jacobs resembled Mr. Johnston, but quickly added "I am not sure! I am not sure!"

The frustrated cops now harangued Kern. Dr. Jacobs had to be the man, they insisted—no way could it be anyone else! It's not Clark, who you just said resembled Mr. Johnston! It has to be Jacobs!

It might help, Kern said, if they brought Jacobs back after dark dressed in a long black coat and a black slouch hat, to duplicate the conditions that night.

Kern's equivocation irritated Chief Patrick. How could the man instantly recognize the woman's corpse, powdered and embalmed and dead for three days, yet be unable to say whether the live man standing in front of him was her companion? And now Kern refused to commit either way. He might be Johnston; he might not be.

Many more people would interview Albert Kern over the days and weeks to come. Thrust unwittingly into a starring role in a tabloid murder case, his every utterance repeated in papers across the country, the sudden attention overwhelmed the unassuming Kern. Other than his positive identification of Fritzie, he vacillated on almost every detail of what happened on the night of January 14, 1923. Nitpicked and harassed by the police, the DA and his men, reporters, curiosity seekers, lawyers and private investigators, Kern's uncertainty would grow as he told the story time and again. It reached the point where he could no longer be sure of what he'd seen and unable to distinguish his memories from other people's suggestions. People with their own agendas. People not always interested in the truth.

***

Chapter Twenty-Seven – Veil Of Mystery

Chief Patrick needed to regroup. On Saturday, January 20, he and DA Kempley tried to part the "thick veil of mystery that now enshrouds the investigation," as the *Union* phrased it. They co-chaired an evidence review to see if they'd missed anything.

Dr. Thompson had analyzed the tissues he'd collected during the second autopsy and found no poisons or drugs in Fritzie's system. He'd also analyzed the contents of the whiskey bottle found in cottage thirty-three. The discovery had led to an early theory, that Fritzie had attended a party at the cottage. After a bad reaction to bootleg whisky, her companions had believed her dead and, in a panic, dumped her body in the ocean. But Dr. Thompson, unable to identify the substance, concluded only that it wasn't alcohol. After eliminating the fingerprints of *Sun* reporter Magner White, made when he'd found the bottle in cottage thirty-three, the lab had compared the prints to the suspects; none matched, and the prints were never identified. The police had concluded that the last renters of the cottage prior to the Johnston's visit, New Year's Eve revelers, must have left it behind. In any case, it had no connection to the case. The olive drab Army blanket from cottage thirty-three Sears and Chadwick had found on the embankment provided circumstantial evidence of how the crime might have occurred, but it would not help to identify Mr. Johnston. The chief and DA had carefully examined the blanket and found a greasy imprint near the edge. They speculated that a woman's French-heeled slipper might have caused it; if so, they couldn't prove that one of Fritzie's pumps had caused it. Further, the coarse fabric of the blanket didn't lend itself to fingerprint impressions and forensic hair and fiber analysis was in its early infancy.

Unless a new witness came forward, the only evidence left that might help identify Mr. Johnston was the Blue Sea Cottages register signature. Chief Patrick had compared the register with Jacobs' exemplars and samples from his letters and noted a "startling" resemblance. He'd also asked two local bank officials to compare the register signature with those on Jacobs' cancelled checks. They, too, noted a striking similarity. They singled out the uncommon way Jacobs and Johnston both formed their capital "J's." Instead of making the upper loop first in the customary way—the way schoolchildren learned via copybooks—they made the bottom loop first. But the chief and bank clerks weren't qualified document examiners, and no experts were available locally. They'd have to get back to that.

The chief and the DA also waded through the numerous eyewitness accounts, most of dubious veracity. Bogus reports had been filling the chief's inbox since the case broke. Typical of high-profile cases, people wanted to involve themselves in the excitement. Consciously or unconsciously, they tended to exaggerate the significance of their observations and to mentally connect unrelated events. Once Fritzie's photograph had appeared on the front pages on Tuesday, people "remembered" seeing her all over. Many of the reports could be judged spurious at a glance, but no matter how strange the detectives still had to check them out.

Some plausible-sounding results wilted under scrutiny. A promising report came from the conductor of the 6:30 p.m. Sunday train from L.A.—the train Fritzie and Jacobs told friends they were meeting. The conductor claimed he saw Fritzie meet two men from the train. One of the men, the conductor stated, appeared "very nervous." This tantalizing lead went nowhere.

Another report sounded good at first. Three people reported they'd seen a couple arguing on Torrey Pines beach at around sundown the night Fritzie died. They described the man as five feet nine inches tall, one hundred fifty pounds, smooth shaven, and wearing a light-colored suit and hat. The woman wore a dark beaded dress, black pumps and stockings, a tan coat, and a light-colored hat. One witness identified Fritzie from a photograph. All three said they could identify the man if they saw him again. Chief Patrick also dismissed this report. Among other problems, the timing didn't work: Fritzie had left her mother's house around 5:15 p.m.—ten minutes after sundown—and thus could not have been on Torrey Pines beach, some fifteen miles away, at the same time. And certainly not the spot the witnesses pointed out, a relatively inaccessible area beneath the 350-foot Torrey Pines cliffs, two miles south of where the body was found. By the time Fritzie could've arrived there it would've been long past dark.

The DA thought enough of one report that he announced it to reporters following the Saturday conference. An owner and operator of an express line reported that at about 8:00 p.m. on the night of the crime, he and his wife were driving south on the coast highway. At the top of the Torrey Pines Grade, approximately one mile south of the slough bridge, they saw a man and woman quarreling violently inside of an automobile. His truck's old-fashioned acetylene lights threw a wide arc of light, he said, illuminating the car long enough for them to see what was going on inside.

"It appeared to be a closed car, with the front glass dropped," he said, "and while I did not see them actually struggling together, it was perfectly apparent that a quarrel was in progress."

Someone combined this account with a check of the tides that night and proposed a new scenario. The killer had quarreled with Fritzie in the car instead of at the cottage. He knocked her out with a blow, drove the short distance down the grade, and dumped her body over the side of the slough bridge. High tide that night had occurred at 8:32 p.m., close to the time the killer would've dumped the body. According to this conjecture, the body would've remained relatively stationary until the tide began to ebb. During a flood tide, water streamed into Soledad Lagoon for a couple of miles inland, filling the lagoon. When the tide ebbed and the current accelerated, water rushed through the estuary entrance "like a mill race." The current carried the body the short distance—one hundred yards or so—to the surf. The next ebb tide left it stranded on the beach. The body had been found just south of the slough entrance.

Plausible? Maybe. But few bought the new theory, including the DA and Chief Patrick, at least the part about the killer throwing her body off the bridge. It didn't explain the presence of the army blanket, or the dress stretched out on the beach or the bar pin near the scene, nor did it account for the position of the girl's arms and hands—the strongest indicator of foul play to some, especially the DA. In his working theory, the killer tried to stage the scene to look like a suicide but gave himself away by laying the body out in a tranquil posture, unconsciously folding Fritzie's hands over her breast and placing her feet close together. The DA believed that physicians routinely folded the hands of patients when they died, one reason he was so suspicious of Dr. Jacobs.

The DA and the chief ultimately judged another eyewitness report the most credible. It came from Oscar Sachs, who worked as a mechanic with his brother Harley at the Torrey Pines Garage, and lived nearby, one of the few people who lived near the beach. He reported seeing a suspicious automobile at about 7:45 p.m. on the night in question. Sachs, his wife, and his sister were on their way to church in La Jolla when they spotted a closed car parked at the southern end of the slough bridge, pointed south. The car was dark and appeared unoccupied. The witnesses recalled how odd it had seemed at the time—people rarely visited that desolate beach after dark, less so on a chilly January night. The DA imagined Mr. Johnston on the beach folding Fritzie's hands over her breast at the moment Sachs' vehicle passed by. The 7:45 sighting, which the witnesses insisted was accurate, seemed a bit early to fit the DA's timeline, but not by much, and eyewitness reports can be wildly inaccurate, even when the witness is "sure." And if Fritzie had met Mr. Johnston downtown at 6:30, he could've driven the twenty-two miles from the Santa Fe depot to the beach via the Blue Sea Cottages by 7:45, provided the couple spent little time at the cottage and Johnston drove at a relatively high rate of speed—35 mph or higher.

Around this time an alternative theory of the killer's movements emerged. He hadn't fled north to L.A. but south across the border. This came from a tip to the San Diego Sheriff's Office. It made some sense considering that both suspects had ties to Mexico, and both had been there during the weekend of Fritzie's death—Jacobs at clubs and the horse races in Tijuana with Mrs. Worthington, Clark on a film shoot in Ensenada. A deputy sheriff rushed to Ensenada to investigate the hot tip, perhaps hoping to break the case before the city cops.

While in Ensenada, the deputy sheriff checked out a report concerning Clara Phillips, the "hammer murderess." Someone had recently spotted her there. In a bizarre case with nation-wide notoriety, Clara had bludgeoned her husband's alleged mistress to death in L.A. She later bribed or seduced her jailer and escaped. Whether the witness had actually seen Clara in Ensenada is doubtful. As in the Fritzie Mann case, people were "seeing" Clara all over the place. The deputy didn't find Clara in Ensenada—she would be arrested in Honduras three months later—nor did he find evidence related to the Fritzie Mann case.

In addition to spurious eyewitness accounts, Chief Patrick had to waste time responding to requests from colleagues outside of San Diego. A strange one came in a letter from Nashville, Tennessee. The chief of detectives of that city's police department wrote to Patrick on behalf of Aaron Bergeda, Fritzie's maternal uncle.

The letter informed Chief Patrick that Mr. Bergeda wanted his niece's murder investigated and the guilty parties punished. The chief must leave no stone unturned and bring everyone connected to this heinous crime to justice. He made this request as a favor to Mr. Bergeda, a personal friend and a leading Nashville citizen.

Another peculiar one came in a telegram from L.A. DA Thomas Lee Woolwine: *Please write me details of death of Freida Mann, as far as known, and wire me condition of her mother, Mrs. Amelia Mann, address XXXX Spruce Street, San Diego.*

Woolwine had a legitimate interest in the case given the Los Angeles and Hollywood connections and Kempley would later seek his help. A controversial and colorful man, then in the last of his eight years as DA, Woolwine was already suffering from the liver disease that would force his resignation a few months later and kill him in two years. A bombastic attention-seeker, he was known for being tough on corruption, vice, and the KKK and for his dealings with the Hollywood elite. He played a key role in the William Desmond Taylor investigation and once tried to have Rudolph Valentino jailed for bigamy.

Chief Patrick responded to Woolwine with a terse telegram: *Mrs. Mann grieved over daughter's death, mental and physical condition considered normal.* He followed up with a short letter, stating that Amelia Mann was "very much grieved," adding, "As to details surrounding the case, we cannot furnish them at the present time."

Photos

Interpretive dancer Fritzie Mann posing in costume backstage, most likely at the Colonial Theater in January 1922, when she was nineteen. Fritzie performed the solo finale, called "Dance of Destiny," before a sold-out audience of 1400. The program ended on January 14, 1922, exactly one year before Fritzie's death.
New York Daily News Archive/Getty Images

Fritzie in a different pose, same costume. ABCDVDVIDEO

View of Torrey Pines Beach and the coast highway
looking north from the Torrey Pines Grade,
circa1910. The Soledad Lagoon (now called the Los
Peñasquitos Lagoon) is on the right. Fritzie's body
was discovered a few hundred feet from where the
highway curves to the right across the slough. At the
top right is Del Mar. San Diego History Center

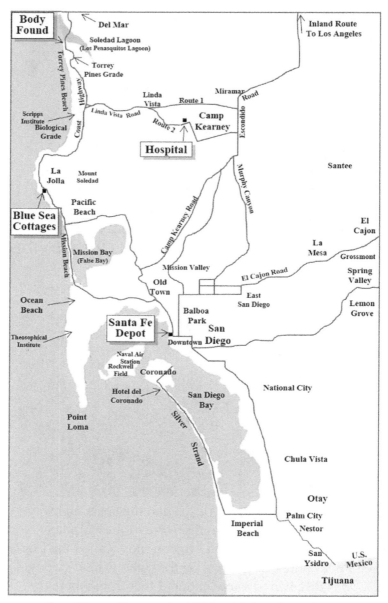

San Diego County in 1923 with key locations
indicated. Illustration by author

Front page of the January 19, 1923, *San Diego Union*. Photos of Fritzie, cottage number thirty-three, and the Blue Sea Cottages register with the signature of the mysterious "Mr. Johnston." A smaller article announces the death of Famous Player movie star Wallace Reid. *San Diego Union*

Dr. Louis L. Jacobs, U.S. Public Health Service
physician specializing in the treatment of
tuberculosis at the Veterans Administration hospital,
Camp Kearny. San Diego History Center

Front page of the January 19, 1923, *Los Angeles Evening Express*. Photos of Rogers Van Buren Clark, actor for the Fellow Motion Pictures Corporation, and his 1919 Marmon Model 34A touring car. Two LAPD detectives examine the car's damaged license plate. *Los Angeles Evening Express*

Cottage thirty-three at the Blue Sea Cottages in La Jolla, where Fritzie died. This view is from the alley where "Mr. Johnston" parked his car on the night of January 14, 1923. San Diego History Center

Fritzie's best chums, Bernice Edwards (left) and Dorothy Armstrong, dressed to the nines in the courtroom. San Diego History Center

Handwriting expert testifying about "Mr. Johnston's" signature in the Blue Sea Cottages register. San Diego History Center

Trial participants visiting Torrey Pines Beach, about to descend the embankment. In a straw boater hat at the extreme left is District Attorney Chester Kempley. The man in the light-colored suit and hat is lead defense attorney Paul Schenck. The man in the center of the picture in glasses with a cigarette between his lips is the defendant. The man next to him in the straw boater is Judge Spencer Marsh. San Diego History Center

Trial participants visiting the Blue Sea Cottages. Cottage thirty-three is to the right. Schenck and the defendant are partially visible at the extreme right. Judge Marsh is in the center, gesturing. Members of the jury are seated in the "auto stage" behind him. San Diego History Center

Chapter Twenty-Eight – Hollywood Again

On Sunday, January 21, one week after Fritzie's death, Chief Patrick gave Dr. Jacobs another chance to fill in the three-hour gap in his alibi. During the visit to the Blue Sea Cottages the day before, Jacobs had clammed up and asked for his lawyer when the police fired questions at him, but he agreed to speak with the chief alone in his cell.

"Doctor, where did you go from there?" the chief asked, "there" meaning the train depot.

"I went to the Grant Hotel."

"Who did you see at the Grant Hotel?"

Jacobs replied that he visited a friend and patient. But he claimed he couldn't remember the man's name, only that he worked as the chief dispatcher for the Owl Taxi Company. He stayed at the Grant for about two and a half hours.

"Where did you go to from there?"

"I went direct to Camp Kearny."

Interviewed by reporters in jail, Jacobs threw more confusion into the mix.

"Fritzie Mann had been married twice," he declared. "She came to me as a friend and professionally. She told me things about herself. She did not tell me the names of her husbands, but said that she had kept her marriages secret because of opposition of her family."

Fritzie had been engaged for a time in Denver in 1920 but had never married as far as anyone close to her knew. Certainly not *twice*.

***

Nobody could accuse Chief Patrick of having tunnel vision. Suspicious of Jacobs from the start, he had grown more so with the revelations in the correspondence and the doctor's evolving alibi. But although certain Jacobs knew more about Fritzie's death than he'd admit, he wasn't convinced the doctor had killed her. Maybe he had arranged for Fritzie to meet a doctor at the train station or in La Jolla and that man was Mr. Johnston. He hoped Jacobs would say more by Monday or he'd be forced to release him on the *habeas corpus* writ.

Meanwhile, Patrick had his detectives out pursuing other leads. On Sunday, the focus of the investigation abruptly shifted north again, as reported in the *Los Angeles Examiner* under the headline ACTOR SOUGHT AS SLAYER OF FRITZIE MANN, *Finding of Noted Star Here May Solve Mystery of San Diego Murder, Say Police.* Two unidentified girlfriends of Fritzie's had apparently reported to the San Diego police that they saw the well-known actor with Fritzie late in the afternoon on the day of her death driving to La Jolla in a closed car matching Mr. Johnston's car. The girlfriends had "worked in the various Hollywood studios and claimed that they were positive in their identification of the actor." The police were now combing Hollywood for the man, "prominent in film circles," and expected to take him into custody in the next twenty-four hours. "Other information which lends credence to this theory is that Fritzie was for some time a scintillating figure in the gay night life of the picture colony and attended several dinners given by various motion picture men at a Los Angeles café" shortly before her death.

Chief Patrick could've dismissed this as *Examiner* yellow fiction if the other papers weren't also reporting fresh Hollywood leads and if LAPD detectives weren't pursuing those leads. A captain at the LAPD Hollywood station had grilled a "well-known motion-picture star and a photoplay producer" for two hours about their knowledge of Fritzie's final days. L.A. County sheriff deputies arrested a movie scenario writer named J.N. Rios at the request of San Diego authorities, although this later turned out to be unrelated to the Fritzie Mann case. The San Diego sheriff's office and the San Diego DA also had officers chasing down clues in the L.A. area. A San Diego County deputy sheriff, who had accompanied Chief Patrick to L.A. for the Rogers Clark interrogation, had stayed behind to investigate clues about "a man in the film industry," reportedly once married to Fritzie.

Chief Patrick sent the Gold Dust Twins north with instructions to interview Bernice Edwards and track down Fritzie's "motion picture people." They were also to take custody of letters that *Examiner* reporters, posing as detectives, had allegedly stolen from Bernice's house. With the assistance of LAPD detectives, Sears and Chadwick sifted through and checked out various sketchy reports: That a "member of the Hollywood film colony" had escorted Fritzie to parties at a roadhouse near L.A.; that she'd met a man "connected with the motion picture industry" while performing at a cabaret in Culver City; that a "prominent film actor" frequently took Fritzie to resorts along the coast; and that a "well-known figure in Hollywood movie circles" had hosted a party at the Blue Sea Cottages the night she died, information apparently submitted to Chief Patrick by two unnamed friends of Fritzie's. But despite intense investigation, not one Hollywood man the police interviewed was publicly named except for Rios the scenario writer after his arrest, likely due to pressure from the besieged studios. Because of the film colony's importance to L.A., city officials and the police looked out for studio interests, especially after the scandals and congressional scrutiny had become an existential threat in the past two years, a threat the Wally Reid scandal had amplified.

DA Kempley also travelled to L.A. to solicit DA Woolwine's assistance and to investigate leads unrelated to Hollywood, including reports about "a prominent San Diego man." During Fritzie's stay at the Rosslyn Hotel in late November, the house detective had reportedly ordered the man out of her room after he caused a disturbance. The unnamed married man admitted knowing Fritzie and visiting her at the Rosslyn but denied that the detective had ordered him to leave.

***

Chapter Twenty-Nine – Sodom And Gomorrah

Although the Los Angeles authorities had good reason to downplay the Hollywood angle, the newspapers certainly didn't. Yet for all the Tinseltown talk, the southern California papers didn't take the next step and link the case to the scandals. There was no shortage of fodder.

They could've used a dope angle and the timely drug-related death of Wallace Reid. Dope and Hollywood in the same breath always made good copy and articles about Reid and Fritzie were appearing side-by-side on the front pages. One paper hinted at drug involvement in her death: "The sinister shadow of dope today hovers over the cloudy web of circumstances surrounding the death of Fritzie Mann...Detectives are searching for a woman known to be a drug addict who they assert is in possession of valuable information..." They were extending the search for the "mysterious woman addict" to the small towns and beach resorts around San Diego.

According to Det. Sgt. Dick Chadwick, while he didn't believe Fritzie was a dope addict, she moved in those circles. But if this dope fiend friend existed, the police never identified her. The *Los Angeles Examiner*—king of the yellow papers, the big player in the Hollywood scandals— reported this drug angle. But even the *Examiner* didn't try to tie the Fritzie Mann case, tailor made for it, to the Hollywood scandals.

Papers outside of southern California showed how easily it could be done. You just had to play a little loose with the facts and Hollywood's reputation as a den of Godless heathens did the rest. The Friday, January 19, 1923, edition of *The Buffalo Enquirer*, Buffalo, New York, among other papers, had run a front-page story alongside one about Wallace Reid's death under the title NEW HOLLYWOOD MYSTERY. "The world of screendom" received another shock when "motion picture actor and assistant director" Rogers Clark had been arrested. Already mourning the death of Wallace Reid a few hours earlier, Clark's arrest stirred Hollywood to its foundations. "More stories of 'wild parties,' similar to those which stirred the moving picture colony after the death of Virginia Rappe and the arrest of Roscoe (Fatty) Arbuckle a few months ago, are gaining circulation following the reported statement of the owner of a cottage at La Jolla that Miss Mann and a male escort stopped there on Sunday night."

The *Peoria Star* published an editorial captioned "Hollywood Again": "The tragic death of Wally Reid, a universal favorite of the moving picture going public and Fritzi Mann, a beautiful twenty-year-old dancer, call fresh attention to the excesses and frivolities of the moving picture colony in Hollywood." Calling Clark "a well-known moving picture director and attaché," the writer declared that Fritzie Mann's death "appears to be in some respects another Arbuckle case…Despite all the apologies that have been made for it we fear that Hollywood is still deserving of its title of the modern Sodom and Gomorrah."

These writers and others like them had no qualms about inflating Rogers Clark's meager film colony credentials, drawing inaccurate comparisons of Fritzie's death to the Arbuckle affair, or using Wallace Reid's death as an excuse to use the tragedy as more evidence of Hollywood debauchery.

These themes, true or not, played well in places like Peoria and Buffalo, and their readers didn't know true from fake facts when it came to hyped Hollywood stories.

*****

Movie Weekly, a New York-based film fan magazine, would later far surpass the papers in linking the case to the scandals. In a series of articles beginning on March 24, 1923, the magazine stitched together an elaborate tale of conspiracy and intrigue involving the deaths of Fritzie Mann and William Desmond Taylor, using the best possible villain: Was there an "invisible power" in the film colony that "shrouded in all of the foreboding secrecy of the Ku Klux Klan juggles with the lives and fates of picture folks to accomplish revenge and blackmail by striking in the dark?" A sinister force lurked in the studios "ready to mark any person for punishment who incurs its hostility." The evidence? Somebody murdered William Desmond Taylor, for one. And "pretty Fritzie Mann, a movie player, was found on a lonely spot…Her slim young body, scantily clad in one silk garment, clearly indicated she was the victim of foul play…an invisible power in the films could have committed this crime and drawn over it the impenetrable shadow of mystery that still baffles the police."

The Klan apparently worked in cahoots with a "secret movie Black Hand," an allusion to the wicked Italian extortion gangs of the early 20th century, known to extort money from the rich and famous, perhaps the best-known example being renowned tenor Enrico Caruso. Around Hollywood, the gang shadowed movie people and manipulated situations to exact revenge or bring about scandals for blackmail, according to the article.

In a follow-up article, the writer described with horror how the KKK had threatened him, by letter and telephone, following publication of the first article. He would "go the way of William Desmond Taylor and Fritzi Mann," if he didn't back off, he was told. The same fate awaited movie players who continued their debauchery.

The Pittsburgh Klan No. 1 responded to the *Movie Weekly* articles in an official letter, which the magazine printed. The Klan denied the threats but reiterated its opposition "to the mixture of white women and Sheiks" and the display of indecency in films. It objected to the insulting portrayal of "low ideals of womanhood" in movies such as "Bella Donna," and the "bigoted, sacrilegious, untrue and disgraceful portrayal of the Protestant Church AS ISSHOWN IN 'The Pilgrim'."

Of course, the KKK would scorn Hollywood's recent offerings. *Bella Donna*, a Famous Players-Lasky production starring Pola Negri in her American film debut, was a blatant rip off of *The Sheik*. Negri portrays an American vamp who runs off to Egypt. Conway Tearle, an Anglo actor transformed into a Valentino clone with henna-face, pomaded hair, turban, and striped pantaloons, plays her suave "Arab" seducer. In the Charlie Chaplin-Edna Purviance film *The Pilgrim*, Chaplain plays an escaped convict posing as a preacher who is forced to perform a religious service in a rural Texas church. These films no doubt triggered the loose morals of the younger set, the Klan letter stated. Instead of such trash, movies should teach high morals, clean living, and respect for religion, patriotism, and law and order. This would help grow "he-men and patriotic womanly women, not cigarette smoking devils who love poodle dogs more than they do babies."

The Klan, then in the midst of a massive resurgence thanks in part to D.W. Griffith's landmark 1915 film *The Birth of a Nation* and approaching peak membership, made the perfect villain. Newspapers nation-wide featured front-page articles about the Klan's acts of intimidation and persecution of those who didn't meet its moral standards. People often suspected KKK involvement in well-known crimes, especially those cases of perceived moral turpitude such as the 1922 Halls-Mills affair, one of the most sensationalized murder cases in a decade full of those. It involved a steamy affair between an Episcopalian priest and a member of his congregation, both married to others, who were found shot to death under a crab apple tree near an abandoned New Jersey farm, their bodies posed with love letters scattered nearby. The Klan, although probably not involved in that case, would no doubt have cheered the deaths of the sinners as just punishment. Likewise, they would've had nothing but contempt for William Desmond Taylor, a Hollywood insider portrayed in the press as either a womanizer or gay, or Fritzie Mann, an immigrant Jew and a modern woman who sought a career in a sleazy profession and got pregnant out of wedlock.

Movie Weekly invented the story out of whole cloth, seizing the opportunity the Fritzie Mann case offered to resurrect the specter of William Desmond Taylor. A known scandalmonger that lasted but a few years, it had been about the only major film fan magazine to blatantly exploit Taylor's death the year before. But some did suspect the KKK in the director's death and recent high-profile blackmail schemes had occurred in the film colony. Taylor's death could've easily fit this scenario and maybe it did. Although *Movie Weekly* didn't mention it, Taylor and Fritzie's purported dance mentor, Theodore Kosloff, had had a recent brush with the Black Hand. It happened on the set of *The Green Temptation,* Taylor's second to last film in which Kosloff played a major role.

"I was walking with Taylor, discussing what he wanted me to do in my role," Theodore Kosloff recounted. "Suddenly from behind a clump of bushes, a stranger sprang up and glared at us. Taylor reacted with a suddenness almost as surprising, leaping to one side and facing the stranger. For a brief minute, the unknown man and Taylor stood without speaking, looking each other straight in the eye. The stranger turned and walked away."

After Taylor's murder, Kosloff said he thought the encounter might be a drug kingpin's attempt to intimidate the director to make him stop trying to help Mabel Normand kick her cocaine habit. But the incident may have been directed at the Russian, not Taylor.

Two months after the murder, in an incident covered in the newspapers, Kosloff received a "Black Hand" letter. The letter demanded $10,000 under the threat of death. Frightened, Kosloff bought a gun and enlisted the help of Cecil B. DeMille, who brought in the Pinkertons. The money exchange played out like something in a movie: Kosloff dropped off a leather bag containing the cash at the designated spot; the crooks came out of hiding and grabbed the bag; the Pinkertons shot at the crooks and gave chase, but the crooks made a clean getaway.

Had *Movie Weekly* put this together it would've been a more tangible link between Fritzie and Taylor through Kosloff and the Black Hand. It would've added credibility to their conspiracy theory and created another scandal involving a Famous Player star.

***

Chapter Thirty – Secrets To Her Grave

At 10:00 a.m. on Monday, January 22, Dr. Louis Jacobs stood with Jimmy Wadham under the high frescoed ceilings of the Department One courtroom for his *habeas corpus* hearing, Judge Spencer Marsh presiding.

Chief Patrick stood and addressed Jacobs. "I am not satisfied at all that you have told us all you know about this case." He turned to the judge. "The police are unable to get any evidence to connect Dr. Jacobs with the probable murder of Fritzie Mann."

The DA moved for the prisoner to be dismissed and Judge Marsh ordered Jacobs released.

***

Three hours later they buried Fritzie. A *Los Angeles Times* article said, "Fritzi Mann carried the secret of her tragic death to her grave this afternoon. The girl who had made her way into the hearts of San Diego's society was buried in the Home of Peace Cemetery." Shortly afterward, authorities released Dr. Jacobs after three days in jail.

The family kept it small. About twenty people gathered for the private service in the Johnson-Saum Mortuary chapel. These included Amelia and William Mann, several of Fritzie's close friends, the rabbi, reporters, and detectives. Helen Mann was too ill to attend her sister's funeral. Amelia Mann, having lost one daughter, was about to lose the other and she knew it.

Brief and simple in accordance with Jewish custom, the service was non-traditional in that Fritzie's plain wooden coffin sat upon a flower-laden dais. The handling of her body, desecrated through autopsy and embalming, had already violated religious edicts, including the requisite quick burial.

Fritzie lay all in white. She wore a simple white dress and bridal veil with a wreath of white, sweetly fragrant orange blossoms, a popular bridal adornment but sometimes used to adorn the dead. In Greek and Roman mythology, orange blossoms symbolized innocence, purity, fertility, and everlasting love. Her face showed no hint of her horrible death and two autopsies and bore a faint smile. Until recently, as one paper pointed out, a smile had been ever-present in life and had endeared her to many people.

Rabbi Maxwell Dubin of the Temple Beth Israel, one of the oldest synagogues in the West, gave the eulogy. He extolled Fritzie's virtues in simple words and read from the Psalms. Music was not played during the ceremony; other than when the rabbi spoke, the room was quiet except for the sobs of family and friends.

At one point, Amelia stood beside her daughter's coffin. "The girl's mother, irreconcilable," a reporter for the *Riverside Daily Press* observed, "broods over the untimely death of the dainty creature who was her pride, her life. Sobs that have been her portion for many days shook her as she named a man's name and said: 'He has done this.' And so they buried Fritzi." Whose name she uttered is not known but Chief Patrick had cleared Clark days ago. Because renewed investigative interest began around this time, perhaps Amelia mentioned Kosloff or some other actor she knew.

The pallbearers carried the coffin to the waiting hearse. The funeral cortege made its way slowly a few miles to the Home of Peace cemetery, the only active Jewish cemetery in the city and located within the grounds of the large Mount Hope cemetery. After the coffin was lowered into the grave, the rabbi read the traditional Kaddish prayer, and the ritual ended.

"So all hope of solving the mystery of the girl's death seems to have accompanied her to the grave," reported the *Los Angeles Times*, reflecting the general mood one week after Russell Chase found Fritzie Mann embedded in the sand.

***

Chapter Thirty-One – Conspiracy

"CONSPIRACY IS HINTED! *Authorities Say Someone Being Protected In Fritzie Case*," read the headline in the Tuesday, January 23, 1923 *Sun.*

According to Chief Patrick, certain witnesses had withheld information, purposely garbled their stories, and covered up aspects of the case that "if exposed would unveil a series of scandals in San Diego." He seemed to be referring to Jacobs but perhaps to Fritzie's chums as well. Some believed that Helen Whitney hadn't told all she knew about Fritzie's "Hollywood friends," so with the investigation now focused on the film colony, he likely had her in mind. And Bernice Edwards had been more than a little circumspect during her initial interviews, feigning surprise when told of Fritzie's pregnancy and fibbing about the reason for Fritzie's San Diego trip. Only with great reluctance did Bernice finally admit that she had known all along about the pregnancy and abortion. If Fritzie's chums were withholding information, it had nothing to do with protecting suspects— least of all Louis Jacobs—but modesty on a delicate topic and loyalty to their friend's posthumous reputation. The young women were under nerve-racking pressure, forced to deal with their friend's death while seasoned cops and rabid reporters grilled them in the glare of a media spotlight the likes of which San Diego had rarely if ever seen. The chief mentioned no names. Under pressure, without enough evidence to charge or even hold the man he believed at least partially responsible, he may've been trying to shake things up.

But if the pressure on Chief Patrick hadn't subsided, press interest had. A big national story only two days before, with Jacobs' release the papers seemed to lose interest, although they made attempts to revive it. The *Sun* offered a $100 reward for information about the identity of Fritzie's companion at the Blue Sea Cottages. The *Union* announced that it expected "sensational developments" upon Sears' and Chadwick's return from L.A., but their expectations couldn't have been high as the brief, easily missed article appeared on page two. The papers heralded new developments on the 24th of January: Chadwick and Sears had found a box of "powerful medicine," purchased at an unnamed physician's suggestion, in Fritzie's suitcase when they seized it from Bernice's house. And with nothing else to report, another belated Fritzie-sighting materialized. Someone claimed to have seen Fritzie engaged in a violent confrontation with an unnamed girlfriend over a man's attention—FRITZIE IN HOT QUARREL WITH FRIEND, the *Sun* proclaimed—during the week before her death. Both leads fizzled.

By Thursday, January 25, ten days into the case, the Fritzie Mann story had lost its steam. The papers replaced it with a never-ending stream of mayhem and weirdness: *Drags Woman by Hair Through Street*; SHOOTS WIFE AND SELF IN ORGY OF JEALOUSY; MAN CONVICTED OF SLAYING AFFINITY, Bites Off Chunk of Wife's Nose to Keep Her Off Job. Plus, bizarre human-interest stories such as *Father, 86, Spanks Daughter, Aged 60, For "Flapperism."* "Pa is too old-fashioned," the woman said after charging her daddy with assault. "He doesn't take the modern view of things. He doesn't seem to realize that girls of my age must have some fun."

Behind the scenes, the investigation continued. DA Kempley returned from L.A. for the *habeas corpus* hearing, announced a "new angle" in the case, then rushed back north the same day. He returned two days later and immediately called a special session of the county grand jury.

***

Chapter Thirty-Two – We've Both Got 'Em Again

On Wednesday, January 17, the same day the Long Beach police had discovered the correspondence at Bernice Edwards' house, a man impersonating a cop had seized five pieces of the Fritzie-Jacobs correspondence and a letter Fritzie had sent to Bernice. The culprit turned out to be a reporter, or two reporters, from the *Los Angeles Examiner*. That a newspaper would be brazen enough to filch evidence under the color of the law strains credulity, but no worse than other capers Hearst's yellow paper had pulled off.

Less than a year before, *Examiner* reporters had used Chicago thugs to kidnap William Desmond Taylor's valet, Henry Peavey, and hold him all day. That night, in an effort to frighten him into confessing, they took him to Taylor's grave and forced him to confront his boss' "ghost." They apparently believed a stereotype that African Americans were deathly afraid of ghosts. It didn't work; Peavey laughed at the men, one of whom later died in the St. Valentine's Day massacre. The paper had gotten away with this outrage despite a formal NAACP complaint and DA Woolwine's threat to prosecute them. It got away with this latest outrage as well, even though the theft had a real, negative impact on a high-profile murder investigation.

Chief Patrick apparently didn't become aware of the letters until three days after the reporters stole them. He later sent a telegram to the *Examiner*'s editors demanding the immediate return of the evidence via registered mail. The editors took two more days to respond: *Letters given to U.S. [us] At Edwards. Have, are being taken to you today by Mr. Knickerbocker of the Examiner Staff. City Editor, Examiner.* But they never did deliver the letters. Chadwick and Sears would pick them up in L.A. the following week.

The identity of only one of the stolen letters is known, and it is known because the *Examiner* published it the same day their fake cop had confiscated it, before any other paper had reported the existence of the correspondence. The contents of the letter wouldn't be published in San Diego until the *Sun* finally published it on January 26. Incredibly, Chief Patrick didn't learn of its contents, among the most important evidence in the case, until the 25th—ten days into the investigation. Based on this letter, he modified his theory about Fritzie's death.

Almost certainly the last letter of her life, Fritzie wrote it on U.S. Grant Hotel stationary and mailed it to her chum Bernice on the afternoon of Friday, January 12, two days before her death. "Dear 'B -'," she began:

> *At last I have a chance to write you, after trying to get a minute to myself for the last year it seems.*

> *Now as to matter concerning myself we have decided that San Diego would be the best place, and all arrangements have been made accordingly. It will just take a few days and then I can come back and start right into every thing.*

> *I do not understand the whole thing about Minor, as she was there, and in fact was until yesterday. He made me call the Lankershim and they told me she has been there for the past two weeks. Something is Cockeyed some where and I'll be damned if I can figure it out.*

Any way, he has been wonderfully sweet to me, and does not seem to be able to do enough for me. He is trying so hard to make me see things the way he does. We have been together constantly and he's begging me not to go back to L.A. We both have gone through an awful strain and it has brought us together much more than we ever have been and I am somewhat afraid that we've both got 'em again – and a little bit too strong, but I guess it's all in a lifetime. We've had a marvelous understanding and things are going beautifully.

So, honey girl, I will let you know the outcome, and hope to be, in fact, I am sure, if all goes well, I'll be in Long Beach the first of next week.

As for the hat and dress, I am taking marvelous care of them, and am not wearing them as my darling mother has put them away and made me wear my own clothes, as she was very angry at me coming down in your things. In fact she still raves about it. So, old kid, your stuff am [sic] *more than safe in Ma's hands.*

So no more this time, sweetness, and I shall keep you posted on everything.

Give my best love to Carl and tell him I'm storing up a lot of good jokes for him. Ha! Ha!

My love to the folks, and worlds of it to you.

I am as ever your unforgetting Fritz.

Do not answer my letter as you know I won't be home

Fritzie is vague enough that without context an outsider couldn't be sure what she was planning or with whom. She notes the strain, but her tone doesn't sound suicidal two days before her death. The DA seized on this to reinforce his belief that Fritzie had been murdered. But the upbeat tone doesn't mean much in itself. It's not uncommon for a depressed person, after deciding to end her life and knowing her suffering will soon end, to behave this way before killing herself. But here Fritzie is making plans for the future. *I can come back and start right into every thing*, she wrote. This can only allude to her career. She may have planned to continue performing at the Palais Royal or to pursue other opportunities in L.A., Hollywood, or San Francisco.

For Chief Patrick, the letter answered some questions and raised new ones.

Clearly an abortion had been planned—or Fritzie believed an abortion was planned—for that Sunday night or the next day. This raised many questions.

After more than a month of stress-filled machinations in L.A., why had they decided on San Diego as the best place? And who was going to perform the operation, a local doctor or someone coming from L.A.? Perhaps the mysterious "man from Los Angeles" Fritzie had mentioned to her mother? Or someone pretending to be one of Jacobs' no-named friends from Kalamazoo? Or did they meet a doctor in La Jolla, perhaps after checking in at the Blue Sea Cottages? This might explain Mr. Johnston's remark to Albert Kern, that they were going out for half an hour. Or did Jacobs plan to perform the abortion himself? He specialized in the treatment of tuberculosis and other diseases of the lungs, but he also performed surgeries at the Camp Kearny hospital. And he had worked in the genito-urinary department of Hebrew Hospital in Baltimore after medical school, which may have given him the requisite knowledge of the procedure. Jacobs told Chief Patrick he'd refused Fritzie's request to perform an abortion, but maybe he'd changed his mind or decided he didn't have any other choice. Where was the procedure going to be done, at the cottage? In L.A., it would've happened in a doctor's office. Now it was going to be done at a La Jolla beach cottage? Mr. Johnston told Kern he needed a unit with running water. Or was the cottage a place for Fritzie to recover? Johnston had said he might need the cottage for two or three days.

Perhaps inconsequential to the investigation but curious was Fritzie's mention of the borrowed hat and dress, evidently a special garment to Bernice. Fritzie wore the dress to the "house party in Del Mar" two days after assuring her friend that her mother had put it away for safekeeping. Why? And why had she needed to borrow her friend's clothes, fancier than anything she owned, for the San Diego visit?

He is trying so hard to make me see things the way he does. Is she referring to her career plans and decision to stay in L.A., a point of recent conflict between the two according to Bernice? Or to the abortion, with Jacobs pressuring her to go through with the procedure despite her fears and her desire to get married instead? Or both?

I am somewhat afraid that we've both got 'em again. The meaning of this obscure phrase becomes clear once the Jazz Age slang is deciphered. The *Routledge Dictionary of Historical Slang* defines "Got 'em bad" as "To be in earnest; seriously affected (by illness, delirium tremens, love): low coll: from ca 1870. C.f. get them." Whatever Fritzie and Jacobs shared in earnest wasn't illness or delirium tremens. From Fritzie's perspective at least, they were in love. Or, rather, in love *again*.

Do not answer my letter as you know I won't be home. Before a letter from Bernice could arrive, Fritzie expected to be on her way back to Long Beach. *All arrangements have been made.*

***

Chapter Thirty-Three – Pretty Well Covered With Alibis

For three weeks the grand jury considered the case evidence in secret session. Reporters stalked the courthouse corridors and camped outside the grand jury room. Little of substance leaked out. The newspapers stayed quiet for the most part while they waited for something to happen. They occasionally commented on the comings and goings of witnesses, mostly familiar names.

A reporter described Amelia Mann, age fifty-three, as "slight, elderly," leaning heavily on her son's arm as she entered the grand jury room.

Reporters also noticed Wilma Minor. With her stylish attire, curvaceous figure, gray-green bedroom eyes and an actress' flair for the dramatic, Wilma commanded notice. After her testimony, she emerged from the grand jury room visibly distressed. She spotted Dr. Jacobs sitting in the corridor, dressed in his Public Health Service uniform, waiting to testify.

"Oh, it's too bad," Wilma said, extending her hand to him. "I'm so sorry!"

"Why?" the doctor asked, alarmed. "What do you mean?"

"Oh, you know—it's all so unpleasant—I'm so sorry!" She hurried away, down the stairs and out the front door to Broadway.

Reporters also noted Albert Kern. County Detective Wisler, the DA's investigator, had harassed him almost daily, Kern claimed. He said Wisler accused him of withholding information and tried to convince him to finger Dr. Jacobs as Mr. Johnston. Wisler even harassed him on the way to the courthouse for his grand jury testimony, Kern claimed.

"Now, you better come out with everything you know," Wisler said, according to Kern. "Somebody is going to the penitentiary for lying in this case."

"All this here is the straight truth," Kern replied, "what I've been telling you."

Kern wavered before the grand jury, especially concerning the identity of Mr. Johnston.

The grand jury didn't call any of the movie stars, directors, and producers the cops had questioned in L.A.— the cops had finally exhausted their Tinseltown leads. After all the rumor and hype, Chadwick and Sears had returned to San Diego with a long report but no new leads and no new suspects. The authorities never released the names of the Hollywood players they had interviewed.

After a week the press again lost interest. For the next two weeks, the papers uttered not one word on the Fritzie Mann case.

***

Camp Kearny had opened in May 1917, part of the war mobilization effort that also brought the Navy and one hundred destroyers to San Diego. The Army had built it on 8,000 acres of backcountry on the Linda Vista Mesa, a wide-open, relatively flat area twelve miles north of downtown. Six years later the neatly kept fifty-acre compound of U.S. Veteran's Hospital No. 64 was about all that remained of Camp Kearny. Sagebrush and chaparral had reclaimed the rest, leaving only the foundations of razed buildings laid out in neat geometric patterns.

On the morning of February 17, 1923, Dr. Louis Jacobs sat alone in the hospital cafeteria eating breakfast. He looked up to see two officers looming over him, one of whom waived a murder warrant. Jacobs recognized County Detective Wisler.

"I am not surprised," the doctor said.

They escorted Jacobs to his room at the officers' quarters. He swapped his uniform for a double-breasted suit and grabbed a pillow and a suitcase.

"If it wasn't for the inconvenience, this would be ridiculous," he muttered as he knotted his tie.

Jacobs retrieved his coat and hat at the hospital administration building. As the officers marched him out, a nurse told someone over the telephone, "The impossible has happened," expressing the astonishment of people who knew him that the doctor could've killed the dancer. Clearly, that haughty DA must be framing him.

Outside, a gaggle of reporters confronted Jacobs.

"I would not care to make a statement now. I am an old newspaper man myself," he said, apparently alluding to his time working on the Johns Hopkins newspaper. "... but I must see my attorney, Judge Wadham, before I have anything to say about this case. Later I may have a statement to make. The whole story will come out at the trial."

In response to a reporter's question, Jacobs said, "I am pretty well covered with alibis."

A reporter remarked that the grand jury must have received information that "changed things."

Jacobs looked perturbed. "I think they will change again."

Jacobs ran another gauntlet of reporters outside the county jail. As a cameraman snapped his picture, the doctor threw up his left arm, using his pillow to conceal his face. In the resulting photo, published on the front page of the *Sun*, all that can be seen of Jacobs' head is an anonymous silhouette of part of a hat, part of a face, and an ear. The police booked a visibly unnerved Jacobs into the county jail at 10:00 a.m.

***

JAIL DR. JACOBS ON MURDER CHARGE *CAMP KEARNY DOCTOR INDICTED BY JURY FOR FRITZI MANN SLAYING.* "Dr. Louis L. Jacobs, 30, dashing, debonair young captain in the United States public health service, was today arrested on a charge of murder of Fritzi Mann, petite San Diego dancer."

Again, articles under screaming headlines and pictures of Fritzie and Jacobs covered the front pages of all three San Diego dailies. Jacobs' arrest caught the public by surprise. Many people assumed the police had cleared the doctor after the *habeas corpus* hearing and since then the investigation had seemed to focus on Hollywood. The papers published the indictment—for first degree murder—and the list of twenty-five grand jury witnesses, but otherwise the DA stayed silent on his case.

***

"Dr. Jacobs would rather go before a jury and obtain complete vindication than to go through life with the least suspicion attached to him," Jimmy Wadham told reporters. "There is as much chance of convicting him as there would be of convicting me in this case. The arrest came as a great surprise to Dr. Jacobs."

His client, Wadham declared, had been forthright with the police since day one. Jacobs had approached them on his own initiative and tried to assist them in their investigation. He had told them everything he knew. Wadham stated that the case would probably go to trial within a month, but he'd be ready in a couple of days.

Dr. Louis Jacobs strode into Judge Spencer Marsh's courtroom on February 19, 1923, for his 10:00 a.m.

arraignment, confident and immaculate in a sharp business suit, his face closely shaved, his hair carefully combed. The only visible sign that he'd spent the past forty-eight hours in jail was a slight pallor to his face. He crossed the courtroom to where Jimmy Wadham sat, and the two men shook hands. Wadham whispered something to Jacobs and handed him two telegrams. They spoke in guarded tones.

"Louis L. Jacobs is accused by the grand jury of the county of San Diego," the DA said, "by this indictment of the crime of murder committed as follows: The said Louis L. Jacobs on the 14th day of January A.D., nineteen hundred and twenty-three, in the county of San Diego, state of California, and before the finding of this indictment, did then and there willfully, unlawfully, feloniously, and with malice aforethought, kill and murder one Frieda Mann, a human being: contrary to the form, force and effect of the statute in such case made and provided, and against the peace and dignity of the people of the state of California."

First degree murder.

How do you plead to the charge? Judge Marsh asked.

"Not guilty!" Jacobs said.

Heartened by telegrams from friends and relatives back east expressing sympathy and offering assistance, Jacobs appeared confident and cheerful. But he fretted at the thought of languishing in jail for an unknown period until the trial began.

Wadham made a motion for a speedy trial and announced his intention to fight for bail. Dr. Jacobs' tubercular patients desperately needed him at Camp Kearny, Wadham argued, stipulating that the doctor, if released, would be confined to the base.

DA Kempley, who planned to personally prosecute the case, vigorously opposed bail. Judge Marsh denied the bail request.

On February 24, the DA's office announced that the trial would begin between the 21st and the 26th of March.

According to rumor, a renowned L.A. criminal attorney would lead a high-priced defense team.

***

Chapter Thirty-Four – The Third Degree

A huge headline appeared in the March 10, 1923, *Union*: JACOBS' LAWYER ACCUSES S.D. OFFICERS OF 'THIRD DEGREE.' Jimmy Wadham had filed a formal request demanding the return of Dr. Jacobs' possessions, seized without warrant following his arrest when the DA's men had ransacked his Camp Kearny room. The items included a leather handbag containing two revolvers, a vest-pocket camera, and photographs of Jacobs' lady friends and a priest.

But that was nothing compared to what the cops did once they had the doctor in custody, Wadham told reporters. They subjected him to various acts of "frightfulness" designed to extract incriminating admissions. They had harassed the man without respite following his first arrest on January 18. On one occasion they marched him into a "star chamber" with chains and handcuffs displayed to intimidate him into confessing. Another time, County Detective Wisler, who Jacobs didn't know at the time, tried to trick the doctor into implicating himself by pretending to be a friend of Wadham's. On another occasion, just to annoy him, Wisler had rousted Jacobs in the middle of the night and threatened the doctor with a murder charge unless he came up with a better alibi.

The misconduct continued after Jacobs' release on the habeas corpus writ. The captain of the county traffic squad, Wadham claimed, had attempted to bribe a Camp Kearny telephone operator so police could eavesdrop on Jacobs' conversations. And officers trailed the doctor everywhere he went. The commanding officer eventually ordered them off the base.

The illegal treatment continued after Dr. Jacobs' arrest on February 17, Wadham complained. Just a few nights ago, Wisler and a deputy DA had rousted Jacobs from bed, ordered him to dress, and drove him to La Jolla in his own car. They forced him to drive his Hudson from the coast highway down Bonair Street to the Blue Sea Cottages, following Mr. Johnston's presumed path. Again, they forced him to reenact the police theory of Mr. Johnston's movements on the night of January 14 while depriving him of his rightful access to his attorney.

Wisler admitted to the nighttime crime reenactment but claimed he hadn't forced Jacobs to drive—the doctor had volunteered because he wanted the exercise.

While at the cottages, Wisler asked Jacobs to write "Alvin M. Johnston and wife" on a blue laundry receipt supplied by Albert Kern. The doctor consented. The detective stopped him and instructed him to write a printed capital "A," as it appeared in the register. As Jacobs had done previously with Chief Patrick, he had written the letter in cursive.

Spotting Jacobs' Hudson, Kern asked Wisler, "Is that supposed to be Dr. Jacobs' car …the car that he was out here in that night?"

"Yes."

"Well…it was never here."

Wadham concluded to reporters: "If my client survives the star-chamber methods of the police department and the district attorney's office, he will be ready for trial on the day set…but the treatment to which he has been subjected is a serious ordeal to a refined and educated man who is not physically robust."

Interestingly, an anonymous letter had arrived at police headquarters on January 20, when Jacobs and Clark were both in custody, stating that "one of the men under arrest will tell all if you apply the third degree."

The DA and Chief Patrick denied any mistreatment of the prisoner, but the allegations of skullduggery had just begun.

***

Part III – An American Tragedy

Chapter Thirty-Five – The Feast Of Pure Reason

The use of unsavory tactics in this case could've been predicted and probably was. Corruption and legal dirty tricks were so common that people assumed they were happening whether they were or not—a sign of the times but also of the city. As Chief Patrick once noted, as a border town, a Navy town, a tourist town, and a seaport, San Diego faced formidable law enforcement challenges that Prohibition had exacerbated. The bourgeoning population, augmented by a booming tourist trade and legions of sailors and marines, fueled an insatiable demand for vice. With easy access routes via the sea and the border, bootleggers and bookmakers rushed to fill the demand. So did bawdy house madams and opium traders. By the time of the Fritzie Mann case, vice had become commercialized, enabled by graft so prevalent and so open that it left sober citizens confounded. How could it happen? According to some, only one way: A cabal of power players lurked behind the scenes, manipulating events to facilitate illicit operations. Despite the protests of moral reformers and frequent pledges by city leaders to eradicate vice, the situation continued to deteriorate as the 1920s roared on. Chief Patrick tried but he was swimming upstream in filthy waters.

In early December 1922, six weeks before Fritzie's death, he'd delivered a letter to the grand jury requesting an investigation into "protected vice." The letter outlined a complaint from a "rooming house keeper," who claimed she'd been forced to pay a rival named Agnes Keller for police protection. Agnes ran the Dearborn Hotel, a notorious brothel across 3rd Street from the U.S. Grant. Included with the letter was an affidavit, sworn out by a representative of the San Diego Women's Civic Center, that documented immoral and illegal activities at the Dearborn. It would be four months before the grand jury issued its report. Along the way it would consider other matters, most notably the Fritzie Mann case. Sparked by the investigation, a heated mayoral campaign and the journalistic machinations of the city's chief muckraker, the situation finally erupted in an internecine civic battle during the two weeks before the Jacobs trial.

***

Abraham Sauer, editor of the *San Diego Herald,* had long mocked city leadership. To him, they made no effort to sanitize the vice trade or thwart the influential men he believed controlled it, men eager to maintain the status quo and re-elect the mayor. Sauer's diatribes tended to be blunt and hyperbolic, but in the March 15, 1923, edition he out-did himself: VICE IS RAMPANT IN SAN DIEGO, *Bootleggers' Paradise, Prostitutes' Oasis, Gambler's Monte Carlo.*

Sauer called San Diego the "most lawless and wide-open town north of the Mexican boundary." Mayor Bacon was either unaware of the situation, which made him clueless, or he knew about it and did nothing, which made him complicit. Clueless or complicit, he was unfit to be mayor. Moreover, though undoubtedly a KKK sympathizer, Bacon was also a hypocrite because he opposed a city council permit that authorized a Klan parade, just to curry favor with "Catholics, Jews and negroes" for the upcoming election. In a sardonic open letter, Sauer accused the mayor, the police, and the "higher ups" they answered to of corruption. And he chastised the *Sun* as the leader of the "Bacon for Mayor Club."

"There is less vice in San Diego today than there has been at any time in many years," an indignant Chief Patrick responded. DA Kempley agreed, calling San Diego "exceptionally free from vice of all kinds…strangely true in view of the proximity to Mexico, where there are no restrictions whatever on vice."

With suspicious timing, a group of citizens demonstrated how silly these statements sounded on the front-page of the *Union*, providing overwhelming evidence to support Sauer's rants in the *Herald*. They filed affidavits with the city clerk that documented examples, from just the past two days, of immoral conditions running "unmolested in the heart of the business district." The documents demonstrated in detail the ease with which anyone could purchase a drink, place a bet, or procure sex.

As the joke went, to find a drink just ask the nearest cop. According to Sauer, back-room gin joints carpeted downtown San Diego. The bell hops in almost every leading hotel doubled as bootleggers' agents. One affiant described how it took him only fifteen minutes to locate and buy two one-pint medicine bottles of whiskey from "Frenchie," a bellboy at the Panama Hotel. Another man paid the going rate of thirty-five cents for a glass of whiskey at the Italian Village. At the Belmont Hotel, a night clerk named "Frenchy"—apparently a popular nickname among those in the illegal liquor trade—served whiskey from bottles labeled "Old Monogram." No one mentioned it, but even the U.S. Grant Hotel, the most elegant and conspicuous establishment in the heart of downtown, resplendent with crystal chandeliers, hand-painted ceilings, and a white marble staircase with carved alabaster railings, ran a speakeasy in the basement. Bootleggers smuggled hooch into the hotel through tunnels beneath the streets that brought steam and salt water from the bay. The booze came into San Diego by sea and overland from Mexico and Canada. Rumrunners from mother ships off the coast landed launches on Silver Strand beach. Or they maneuvered boats into an ocean cave at Sunset Cliffs in Ocean Beach. From there men carried boxes of booze up concrete steps and through a tunnel to a bootlegger's house.

Prostitution also flourished. Bawdy houses, nearly ubiquitous downtown, employed enough "Sadies, Mabels, Mauds, etc, to make a dozen harems of the size which King Solomon boasted of," Sauer wrote. "There are 'ladies' boarding houses within three blocks of the police station... assignations houses in nearly every block down town." One affiant described how he had witnessed two painted ladies solicit customers on 3rd Street and escort them to the Belmont Hotel. Another man reported that he'd overheard a woman making arrangements for sex work with the landlady in the parlor of the Dearborn Hotel. During a twenty-four-hour period, only three people—all women—were registered at the Dearborn while at least forty men came and went without checking in. The Dearborn's colorful madam, Agnes Keller, openly boasted that she had the best-looking girls in town.

Gambling, too, was pervasive. Sauer wrote that bookmakers, slot machines, and poker games operated in almost all "cigar stores, many of the hotels and all of the bootleg joints." Affidavits described how citizens placed bets on Tijuana horse races at Allen's lunchroom, the Palm Candy Shop, the Turf Pool Hall, and the lobby of the Oxford Hotel. Of course, you didn't have to place illegal bets in San Diego. Instead, you could drive seventeen miles south on the "road to hell," as Dr. Jacobs often did, and bet legally at the Tijuana track. While there, you could enjoy top-grade liquor.

Spillover from TJ had long irritated San Diego reformers and law enforcement. Prohibition, though, had propelled the town into a golden age—the number of cantinas doubled between 1920 and 1924. The only way to discourage people from crossing the border to spend their money at the cantinas, racetracks, and brothels of TJ was to tacitly allow similar establishments to operate in San Diego. Moral issues aside, stopping the vice trade, even if it were possible, might've crippled the economy.

***

Warned of the incendiary contents in advance of the March 15 edition of the *Herald*, Chief Patrick tried to halt its publication. With Det. Sgts. Chadwick and Sears as back up, he stormed into the printing company office. An elderly night watchman, who described the chief's disposition as "loaded for bear," tried to stop them. The chief cursed at him, the watchman said, pushed him across the room, and put him in a headlock.

"After the chief had strong-armed me," the watchman said, "he gave me a shove and I went staggering out of the door into the street."

According to Chief Patrick, the watchman had "dared us to touch him" and moved for his gun, whereupon the chief pinned the man's arms while Chadwick disarmed him.

Threatening the print operators with criminal libel, Chief Patrick ordered them to halt the presses. More cops arrived and began loading stacks of newspapers into a patrol wagon, confiscating 8,000 completed copies, leaving thousands more incomplete copies. The chief warned the printers not to print more and posted officers outside to make sure they didn't.

The raid and the bruhaha that followed put the chief in one of the worst pickles of his long and otherwise distinguished tenure. News of the raid covered the front page of the *Union* the next morning under a huge banner headline. Chief Patrick had "pulled a boner," the *Union* said, and congratulated him for his "brilliant and eminently successful spilling of the political beans" with his unauthorized raid on the *Herald*. It gave "real news value to what otherwise would've been nothing more than the personal opinions of an editor of a comparatively obscure weekly." Two days later, bowing to the inevitable, the chief returned the confiscated newspapers to the printer and allowed Sauer to belatedly publish his March 15 edition. By then the *Union* and the *Evening Tribune* had published Sauer's polemic verbatim.

The chief stood by his actions. He'd had honorable motives—to stop Sauer from incurring another libel charge, since the journalist had been indicted only two days before for slandering a state senator. This was dirty politics, an eleventh-hour effort to defeat Mayor Bacon, the chief said, and he objected "to having the police department drawn into political fights." He threatened to reveal the identities of the "important men" who backed the *Herald*. He said the same about the Spreckels-owned *Union* and *Evening Tribune*, which were backing Bacon's main challenger and vilifying him. The DA and city attorney stayed mum, leaving the chief to twist in the wind. Only the Scripps-owned, pro-Bacon *Sun* defended him. The *Sun* accused the *Union* of hiring private eyes to dig up dirt for the grand jury investigation to make the administration look bad on the eve of the election.

The grand jury foreman denied any political influence on the vice investigation. But he said local officials had stonewalled the grand jury, so the full truth about vice and corruption might be beyond their reach. Frustrated, he asked the state attorney general to take over.

"Deceit and selfishness always conspire together to cover truth and I fear that the covers are thick in San Diego city and county," the foreman said.

Bacon won re-election in a landslide six days after the chief's raid on the *Herald*. Willis "Trusty" Shelton, owner of the Blue Sea Cottages, whose "shoe leather" campaign had involved visiting one hundred families per day and assisting them with chores, placed a distant third.

The mudslinging subsided as attention shifted to the Jacobs trial.

***

Chapter Thirty-Six – Corpus Delicti

Headlines on March 26, 1923, in San Diego and the rest of the world said *SARAH BERNHARDT DEAD*, but the only real news in San Diego was *The People of California versus Louis L. Jacobs*. Many expected it to be the most sensational trial in the city's history.

The trial began on a gorgeous day. Widely covered, it generated many sensations and controversies. DA Kempley battled a formidable defense team, led by high-profile L.A. attorney Paul Schenck, to a standstill. On a gloomy Monday morning, after twenty-three days of testimony, sixty-eight witnesses and passionate closing arguments on both sides, the case went to the jury. The jury deliberated for thirty-five hours. On April 17, they deadlocked, divided evenly between those for conviction and those for acquittal. The main contention: Whether the prosecution had proved *corpus delicti*, that is, proved that a crime had been committed. Some jurors believed that Fritzie had killed herself, so no crime had been committed. Others believed someone had murdered Fritzie, but Jacobs hadn't done it. Still others thought the DA had established the *corpus delicti* and connected it to Jacobs. When the jury foreman announced the hung jury, the defendant beamed, assuming he'd be set free. His smile vanished when the DA said he intended to re-try the case.

***

Both sides committed questionable acts before and during the first trial. The defense employed a squad of private detectives to do some of their dirty work. The detectives kept getting caught, with embarrassing and sometimes comic results.

ARREST IS MADE FOR THREATS TO WITNESSES IN MANN CASE read the headline of the Saturday, April 6, 1923, *Sun*. *A BOMBSHELL was exploded in the Fritzi Mann murder case to-day when Otis J. Smith, former newspaperman, was arrested on a charge of attempting to intimidate witnesses.*

Smith had knocked on Wilma Minor's door and identified himself as a feature writer doing a piece on the Fritzie Mann case. She could still be charged for conspiring to commit an illegal abortion, he warned her, even if Jacobs were acquitted. And if she left town, authorities would track her down. A man fitting Smith's description had also tried to intimidate Helen Whitney and Dorothy Armstrong. Later, a county detective spotted Smith loitering in the courthouse corridors and arrested him. A lawyer on Jacobs' defense team admitted hiring Smith, but only to interview key witnesses who had already testified, essential since the trial transcripts hadn't been made available to the defense. No one instructed Smith to do anything unethical. He posted Smith's bail pending an investigation.

The defense also had private eyes tailing the police chief, the DA, and other officials, apparently hoping to "get something on them." Instead, they exposed themselves.

An irreverent front-page story in the April 12 *Sun* made the private eyes out to be buffoons, hardly worth the ten dollars per day they were getting: COMIC OPERA ALL RAGE AS DICKS TRAIL, THEY'RE SO CLEVER, Hardly Anyone Knows What They Are Doing But the Public.

One private eye followed the DA down Broadway, but Kempley spotted him. The private eye ducked around a corner. The DA caught up to him, slapped him on the back, and shook his hand.

"Well, well," Kempley supposedly said, "we are getting better and better acquainted day by day. It's going to be pretty lonesome for me when you go off the job!"

One evening the DA and two associates met at the Golden Lion for dinner. The three men, each walking alone, arrived simultaneously by chance. Their separate tails almost collided on the sidewalk, "fairly trampling on each other's toes attempting to get out of sight."

None of the private eyes wanted to follow the police chief after Patrick pulled his pistol on one of them in a dark yard.

***

The grand jury had issued its report on protected vice midway through the trial. The next day a *Union* headline announced that someone had broken into the double-locked iron strongbox in the grand jury room and stole several documents, including the letter Chief Patrick had submitted the previous December, the Women's Civic Center representative's affidavit concerning the Dearborn Hotel, and probably other documents.

The Women's Civic Center rep had continued her investigation into the Dearborn since December. She had recently sworn out a new affidavit in which she described observing a continual passage of sailors coming and going from the hotel, obviously customers. The new affidavit, along with the theft of the first one, had triggered the latest raid on the hotel on April 14, this one led by the Gold Dust Twins, Chadwick and Sears. They arrested four women for prostitution but released the madame, Agnes Keller, due to insufficient evidence. The *Union* and the *Herald* cried foul.

Abraham Sauer accused the police of conducting a fake raid, implying that money had changed hands. True or not, few bought the official story from the police or the DA and no one believed Agnes Keller's denials. The Dearborn was the biggest open secret in a city full of those and Agnes never seemed to hide her profession unless threatened with a criminal charge. An infamous character of the San Diego and Tijuana underworlds with nine different aliases, she had a criminal record stretching back to her teens. She'd run so many brothels, she once said, that she couldn't remember them all. She'd been charged with every imaginable crime, from pick pocketing to murder, but almost always beat the rap or got off light. When things got too hot, she paid off corrupt officials, closed shop, and moved to a new place.

Agnes had got away with it again, or so the *Union* and the *Herald* insinuated. Things had been "settled nicely" in Kempley's office during a meeting with the Dearborn's owner, an elderly woman who claimed to know nothing about illegal activities in her hotel. The owner transferred the lease to another woman and the DA allowed Agnes to vacate the property with no charges. Six weeks later the cops busted her again at her new place, the Warren Hotel.

The *Union* stopped short of accusing Kempley of taking bribes but criticized his performance as DA. In three and a half months on the job, the paper said, he'd dismissed twenty-seven criminal charges, everything from grand larceny to lewd and lascivious acts to seduction under promise of marriage. Using the Dearborn Hotel incident as a prime example, the paper accused him and the police of lethargy for allowing commercialized vice to operate with impunity. Were "higher ups" getting paid to protect illicit operations? the *Union* asked. Why was the Dearborn raided on a Sunday night when everyone knew the place would be quiet? Why wasn't Agnes Keller, with her lengthy rap sheet and well-known to the police, arrested? Why did the DA allow her to depart in haste, without charge, the matter "nicely settled?"

The *Union*'s suspicions would seem prescient three years later when Agnes Keller would play a pivotal role in another high-profile murder case, a spectacular mob hit. She would claim that in 1923 she'd bribed the DA to escape the Dearborn charges. And that he'd tried to bribe her to give false testimony at the Jacobs trial.

***

After the first trial ended, the DA had turned his attention to gathering new evidence. Right away he got sidetracked by an unexpected development.

SAILOR HELD IN FRITZIE MANN MURDER CASE cried the headline of the April 20 *Union* over a headline about the Dearborn raid. The article, based on an Associated Press story, bore a Miami, Texas, dateline. The sheriff there had arrested a young man who gave his name as Lewis Franks after contacting the San Diego authorities. The man claimed to be Fritzie Mann's slayer.

Franks, a Norwegian merchant sailor, had been arrested in the Texas panhandle town for an alleged auto theft. When questioned, he startled the sheriff with information about the Fritzie Mann murder case, apparently due to a guilty conscience.

"I left her where I killed her," Franks was quoted as saying. "She keeps calling to me now and telling me not to kill her. I can't stand it any longer."

Franks claimed that a San Diego madame called Agnes Keller had ratted on him for the murder after "beating him out of $200." The Texas sheriff had contacted San Diego officials, who decided Franks' statements corresponded "fairly well with the known facts in the Mann case."

The DA took the report seriously enough to announce plans to travel to Texas, but soon dismissed Franks as a crank, obsessed with the case but with no real connection to it.

***

Chapter Thirty-Seven – The Dean Of American Medicine

On April 20, 1923, while waiting in jail, Jacobs wrote a letter to Dr. William H. Welch, director of the Johns Hopkins University School of Hygiene and Public Health. A distinguished physician and pathologist and founding professor at Johns Hopkins, he has been called the "Dean of American Medicine." Welch served as a professor of pathology at the university and pathologist-in-chief at the hospital when Jacobs was there. The letter is typed, with additions and the signature in Jacobs' hand. "Dear Dr. Welch," he began:

The writer of this letter, one of your former pupils, is being held at present facing a second trial for murder. The evidence against me is purely circumstantial, and the jury disagreed on the corpus delicti. They never balloted to determine my guilt or innocence. Needless to say, I have no doubt of the final verdict altho the case is enmeshed in a snare of local politics. The circumstances briefly, are as follows: -

Young woman, 20, found on the beach, body parallel to the water, hands folded (conflicting testimony as to exact position) legs close together. Pregnant – 4½ months. Color of body – PINKISH.

Slight, round, black-blue contusion outer end of rt. eyebrow. Dried, grayish-white matter on both lips (similar to appearance after taking cyanide.... (coroner)) Very small amount of water & <u>froth</u> in lungs, water in stomach. Probable time in water 12 hours.

Coroner's inquest "Death by drowning."

My queries are as follows: -

1) What effect would an anesthetic (ether, chloroform) have if taken shortly before being thrown in the water – on the above picture?

2) Can one drown in the surf without subsequently finding water or froth in the lungs?

3) Can one drown in the surf without sand being found in the lungs or stomach?

4) If sand is always present in the lungs of persons drowned in the surf – where would that sand be – in the alveoli – or bronchi?

5) If the sand be in the alveoli would a casual examination reveal it?

6) What effect would cyanide – taken just before drowning – have on (a) the general appearance of the body (b) the lungs, heart, stomach (c) rigor mortis?

7) Would it be <u>possible</u> for the waves to more or less fold the arms across the body? And rigor mortis <u>fix</u> them in a folded position?

8) In your experience – do physicians fold the arms of the dead – let us say – more as a matter of <u>habit</u> – than laymen – or any other class?

9) Can water enter the stomach of a person – unconscious or semi-conscious – when thrown into the ocean – within fifteen hours?

10) Is sand or sea-weed more apt to be found in the lungs or stomach of a person thrown into the ocean – if when thrown in she is (a) conscious (b) semi-conscious (c) unconscious?

These questions may sound trivial to you – and I know the answers to some, but I am very anxious to get your authoritative opinion – and that as soon as possible.

Needless to say appreciation precedes

Jacobs signed off "Respectfully, LOUIS L. JACOBS. '17. It's not clear if Dr. Welch responded, but Jacobs' questions show the criticality of the medical evidence. Each question reflects significant points argued at the first trial, either to support the defense theory of suicide by drowning in the ocean, or the prosecution theory of murder by drowning somewhere else.

The DA felt he had proved Jacobs' motive and opportunity to kill Fritzie at the first trial. Proving that the doctor had the means to commit the crime, was harder, as this depended upon the disputed manner of death. He had proved *corpus delicti* to the court's satisfaction at the first trial, but only just, and in the end the jury didn't buy it. This remained his biggest hurdle.

***

Chapter Thirty-Eight – A Disreputable Lot

In mid-May 1923, Dr. Louis Jacobs learned that he was no longer a commissioned officer in the U.S. Public Health Service. In February, embarrassed that a PHS officer had been indicted in a nationally publicized murder case, U.S. Surgeon General Hugh Cumming ordered Surgeon J.R. Hurley, the medical officer in charge of the San Diego Quarantine Station on Point Loma, to investigate. Hurley met with the DA, one of Jacobs' defense attorneys, and the Camp Kearny hospital commanding officer. He submitted a five-page report to Cumming that had undercurrents of anti-Semitism and misogyny.

Fritzie Mann was "a professional fancy dancer, of local fame," Hurley wrote, from "a Jewish family, but all are known as respectable people." The DA had "established that Miss Mann had not a loose moral reputation, or at least was not a common prostitute, which is partly substantiated by the fact that she had absolutely no money, and very few clothes—speaking from the feminine standpoint—and some of the clothes she had belonged to her friends." As for Jacobs, even if ultimately acquitted,

> *There is not a doubt in my mind that he has been guilty at least of conduct unbecoming an officer and a gentleman, and tending to bring scandal upon the Service. In fact he has already brought scandal upon the service, and it has been repeatedly published in the local press, and no doubt*

*disseminated broadcast by the Associated Press
and others, as well as being mentioned in common
gossip about town, that he is an officer of the U.S.
Public Health Service. His letters convict him of
attempting to procure an abortion for Miss Mann,
and in a newspaper interview...he admitted that
fact, and explained his reason for so attempting as
that he had been consulted professionally by Miss
Mann in the premises, and felt sorry for her in her
predicament, and in his action was actuated solely
by "damned altruism."*

During the early stages of the first trial, a colonel who'd
recently taken over as commanding officer of the Camp
Kearny hospital, had written to someone on the PHS staff. In
his opinion, whether or not Jacobs was convicted,

*I think he should be sent away from here just as
soon as possible. I think he should resign from the
service and save the embarrassment...Personally,
I think the fact that an officer should become
involved as he has with a disreputable crowd
should be sufficient to ask for his resignation.
The whole crowd to whom he has been giving his
money and writing letters and sending telegrams
in reference to illegal operation for the girl are a
disreputable lot. It was want of brains in the first
place that got him into the affair.*

The "disreputable lot" apparently included Wilma Minor,
Helen Whitney, Bernice Edwards, and Fritzie. Secretary of
the Treasury Andrew Mellon terminated Jacobs' commission
"for the good of the service."

***

Chapter Thirty-Nine – An Army Of Flappers

The county courthouse sat prominently on Broadway next to the hall of records and county jail and across the street from the Spreckels Theatre. Italianate in design, it featured tall arched windows and doorways and allegorical sculptures standing guard around the clock tower. On June 26, 1923, the courthouse again formed the center of gravity in San Diego.

Public enthusiasm and press coverage of the case had revived in recent days, and excited spectators began lining up at 7:00 a.m. for the 10:00 a.m. start time. When the doors opened, the unruly throng rushed inside and up the stairs to Department One of the San Diego Superior Court. Spectators instantly filled the seats reserved for the public. Others sat on the windowsills or stood on chairs around the periphery of the room. Bailiffs left the courtroom door open so the crowd in the corridor might be able to hear the proceedings, then struggled to keep a passage clear for witnesses as the crowd blocked the doorway.

The high frescoed ceiling, flanked on two sides by the big arched windows and small stained-glass windows high on the walls depicting the great seals of the states, lent the courtroom a stately air. The bailiffs left the windows open to compensate for the poor ventilation, but this also let in the streetcar noise from Broadway. The noise sometimes overwhelmed the echoing courtroom voices, requiring witnesses and lawyers to constantly repeat themselves.

Reporters remarked on the composition of the crowd. These weren't middle-aged "murder fans," as the *Sun*'s Magner White called typical court watchers, but a markedly younger and more female crowd. Surveying a sea of silken gowns and trimmed hats, a *Los Angeles Times* reporter called the crowd "an army of flappers."

Spectators craned their necks to see Fritzie's possessions, the ones they'd heard so much about, the ones she had died wearing. The DA had arranged her things on an ornate chair near the witness stand for maximum emotional impact. Her peacock blue nightgown was draped over one corner of the chair back, Bernice's brown silk crepe dress, now with a rent under one sleeve and broken rows of copper beads, over the other. On the seat lay her handbag, the open vanity case with its cracked mirror, her rumpled lacy brown stockings and garters, her brown French pumps and pink silk teddy.

The trial started with two and a half days of *voir dire*. Opposing council took their time selecting the jury, arguably the most important phase of a criminal trial. The defense team used its allotted peremptory challenges to dismiss women from the jury; they assumed women might be more sympathetic to the victim. They also dismissed persons already convinced that Fritzie Mann had been murdered. The DA tried to seat women and dismissed people who seemed skeptical of circumstantial evidence and expert testimony. He also dismissed a Jewish man named Samuel Schiller. Schiller served as secretary of the local branch of the Independent Order of B'nai B'rith. Although Jacobs wasn't a member, he had visited him in jail to ensure the doctor had adequate legal representation. At the end of *voir dire*, the DA had a more favorable jury than at the first trial. He managed to seat four women plus a woman alternate juror. Only one woman had made it into the jury box for the first trial.

***

The press rarely mentioned that both the victim and the accused were Jewish, preferring to highlight their more bankable aspects—she was a petite, beautiful dancer, he a debonair doctor. The press might have hyped the case even more if the victim had been a white protestant allegedly killed by a Jew. Schiller's concern about fairness was well-founded. Anti-Semitism existed in San Diego as it did everywhere, manifested in casual ways such as Surgeon Hurley's comment in his report to the surgeon general about the Mann family, and the more nefarious ways of the KKK. Though the DA's tactics made it unlikely that Jews would make it onto the jury, members of the Klan or those sympathetic to the group easily might have.

As it was across the nation, the San Diego area Klan was active and growing. By 1923 the local Klan was as mainstream as any fraternal organization—the San Diego Klan, No. 1 advertised in the newspapers alongside the Elks. The week of Fritzie's death, a Baptist minister gave a fiery lecture at the Klan hall at 13th and I Street. He said he wanted to present the "other side" of the organization even as he railed against Catholics, immigrants, and the "international Jews." The local Klan focused much of its effort on harassing immigrant Mexicans and trying to prevent them from obtaining political power. The bodies of murdered Mexican workers occasionally turned up, sometimes showing signs of torture, in the lemon groves east of the city. The killings instilled fear into the Mexican community but drew little press interest. The Klan intimidated their enemies in other ways. During the first Jacobs trial, three crosses made of heavy timbers covered in oil-soaked burlap had blazed in the night, one on Point Loma, one in Balboa Park, and one southeast of downtown on Grant Hill. And the Klan carried out sneakier activities such as trying to influence the district attorney and trying to seat members on grand juries.

The courtroom went silent as the DA, a tall, slender man of thirty-six with dark hair, a narrow face, and thickish lips, rose from the plaintiff's table. Another DA might've cursed his luck to draw one of the biggest criminal cases in the city's history one week after being sworn in. Not so Chester Kempley, an active player in local Republican politics with ambitions for higher office. Like most professional men of the day, he maintained memberships in numerous fraternal organizations. These included the familiar—the American Legion, the Elks, the Lion's Club—and the more esoteric— the Knights of Pythias and the Improved Order of Red Men. Unknown outside of San Diego until the Fritzie Mann case, Kempley would play a small but decisive role the following year in a more famous Hollywood death, that of producer-director Thomas Ince aboard William Randolph Hearst's yacht off the coast of San Diego.

The DA used a diagram of the Torrey Pines beach and the Soledad Lagoon to outline his case for the jury. He pointed out the locations of the coast highway, the slough bridge, the parking area south of the bridge, the items of evidence, and Fritzie's body. He then described the position and condition of the body and the autopsy results.

The prosecution would prove motive, he said, by describing the relationship between the defendant and the deceased, which resulted in her pregnancy.

"We will prove to you that he made repeated and almost frantic endeavors to have an abortion performed upon Frieda Mann," Kempley said.

He would discredit Jacobs' various alibis and demonstrate that shortly before her death, he and Fritzie Mann had stayed briefly at the Blue Sea Cottages. This would prove that Jacobs had the opportunity to commit the crime.

"Fritzie Mann was either unconscious or dead when the body was placed there on the beach," he said.

And he promised new evidence.

As Kempley spoke, Jacobs, as usual in a sharp suit with carefully coiffed hair and large tortoise shell glasses, shifted his eyes from the DA to the jury box and back, his expression unchanging. He occasionally shifted his position but always returned to a favored posture: He cupped his chin in his right hand and tilted his head slightly to one side, a pose Magner White likened to Rodin's "The Thinker."

The DA had not outlined his theory of how Fritzie Mann had died in his opening statement. This had been a key contention at the first trial and contributed to his failure to prove *corpus delicti* to the jury's satisfaction. At the end of the DA's statement, the defense asked the judge to direct him to state his theory. Kempley argued that he didn't have to; he need only state what he could prove and what the evidence showed. The judge agreed and the DA called his first witness.

In a replay of the first trial, the DA painted a picture of the beach crime scene through a series of witnesses, including San Fernando fruit packer John Chase, whose son found the body; motorcycle cops Clarence Matthews and Robert Bowman, the first policemen on the scene; garage man Harley Sachs; and Deputy Sheriff John Bludworth. On direct examination, Kempley focused on the bruise over Fritzie's eye, the location of her vanity case, overnight bag, and gold bar pin, and especially her folded arms, trying to coax tidbits from the witnesses to support a murder scenario.

***

Chapter Forty – Corpus Delicti Revisited

The opposing teams weren't evenly matched in numbers, experience, or panache. The DA shared the prosecution table with one man, a rather tall and stout assistant DA named Guy Selleck. But at any given time, up to six attorneys might be crowded around the defense table. Louis Shapiro, Jacobs' first cousin and a prominent Detroit attorney, was a constant presence. So were Jimmy Wadham, ex-San Diego mayor and Jacobs' first lawyer, and a junior partner of Wadham's firm, Clifford Fitzgerald. Another of Wadham's partners and an L.A.-based associate of the lead defense attorney, Paul Schenck, periodically joined the gang. Jacobs did not have a seat at his own defense table. He sat behind his lawyers, the defense team forming a symbolic gauntlet between him and the huge American flag that flanked the judge's bench.

Jimmy Wadham had recommended Paul Schenck, one of the top criminal defense attorneys in Southern California, to Jacobs. The pair had successfully defended two Chinese men accused of murder the year before. Schenck had earned a national reputation defending high profile L.A. and Hollywood clients and as a pioneer in the use of the insanity defense. He'd had heated exchanges in court with L.A. DA Thomas Woolwine, who had once punched Schenck in the face in the courtroom. Over his career he'd successfully defended scores of people facing a death sentence and never lost. Schenck, a largish man with a full thatch of white hair and wire-rimmed glasses, appeared older than his forty-eight years. His trademark light-colored suit, white shirt, black bow tie, and five-carat diamond ring made him stand out it in the group of conservatively-dressed lawyers in dark suits, as did his personality.

"Personality oozes from him like smoke from a fire," someone once said of Schenck.

Jacobs could not have afforded such high-priced legal talent plus a private eye squad on his PHS salary. The papers reported that wealthy relatives back east were financing his defense. But his immediate family wasn't wealthy, so members of his extended family may have pooled their resources to finance his defense, as they had done to help send him to Johns Hopkins. His affluent cousin, Louis Shapiro, may have helped finance the defense team and presumably worked pro bono.

Schenck forcefully cross-examined the beach witnesses the DA called, always trying to coax responses consistent with suicide and to create reasonable doubt. He highlighted uncertainty about the position of Fritzie's arms. Only two witnesses said her arms were crossed neatly over her breast. Others remembered her arms positioned over the body but not neatly. Others couldn't remember either way. This uncertainty helped to undermine one of the points that Kempley claimed proved murder.

Schenck also highlighted differing testimony on the state of rigor mortis, potential indicator of time of death than can be influenced by many variables, especially environmental conditions. Some witnesses, including the coroner, said the body was in full rigor. Others said it seemed relatively limp. The prosecution believed that Jacobs had murdered Fritzie or rendered her unconscious at the Blue Sea Cottages, then staged her corpse on the beach between 8:00 and 9:00 p.m. on Sunday night. If true, it meant that Fritzie had been dead for sixteen or seventeen hours when the Chases found her. The body should've been quite rigid, even on a chilly and wet beach. A relatively limp body might suggest a later time of death, tending to support the defense theory that Fritzie had committed suicide on Monday morning.

After the beach witnesses, the prosecution began to weave a chain of circumstantial evidence to prove *corpus delicti*. Through the testimony of patrol cop George Churchman, Albert and Mary Kern, cottage cleaner Mrs. Spencer and Amelia Mann, the DA tried to establish that Fritzie had spent a period of time between 6:30 and 8:00 p.m. at Blue Sea cottage number thirty-three accompanied by a man calling himself Mr. Alvin Johnston. He then called Det. Sgts. Chadwick and Sears to tie the two crime scenes together with the olive drab army blanket, missing from the cottage and later found on the beach embankment.

***

Spectators looked on with compassion as Amelia Mann, dressed in mourning black dress and hat, her face strained with grief, took the stand. Amelia spoke rapidly in her broken English, but so softly that even the court reporter sitting a few feet away had trouble hearing her. She described her interactions with Jacobs. When the police first arrested Jacobs, Amelia couldn't believe it—the respectable soft-spoken doctor couldn't have murdered her girl. She had since come to accept it.

Amelia described how Jacobs, beginning near the end of April 1922 when the family had lived in Golden Hill, often stopped by to pick up Fritzie. He would ring the doorbell, ask for Fritzie, and they'd drive off down 29th Street. He continued to call after the family moved a few blocks away to an A Street address in July, where they lived until moving to the Spruce Street house in November, around the time Fritzie left for L.A. He didn't visit after Fritzie returned to San Diego on January 8 but phoned almost every day.

The DA then had Amelia describe Fritzie's last day, her happy demeanor, of how she showed no signs of having "something in her heart" and might be contemplating suicide.

The worst part came when Kempley showed Amelia the brown party dress and asked her to identify it as the one her daughter left home wearing. He repeated the process with each of the personal items, devastating Amelia with each one. Her face blanched with suppressed emotion and her lips twisted as she tried to maintain her composure. It was hard for spectators to watch.

On cross, Schenck treated Amelia gently, keeping her on the stand only a few minutes. If he badgered the broken woman while trying to make her daughter look suicidal, he'd come off as a monster, especially after what the DA had just put her through. Instead, he used Amelia to drag Rogers Clark's name into the courtroom, asking about her habit of writing down the names of Fritzie's suitors. He would repeat this tactic time and again, part of his strategy to plant reasonable doubt. Was the wrong man on trial?

***

So far, the trial had been a virtual replay of the first. Covering familiar ground provoked fewer objections than before, so things moved swiftly. The information was so familiar that for the first time the crowd began to thin out. But then the testimony of two witnesses—autopsy surgeon Dr. John Shea and Blue Sea Cottages manager Albert Kern—caused a stir.

While cross-examining Shea, Paul Schenck gave his most impressive performance of either trial. In one fluid sequence covering seventy-two pages of trial transcript, he demonstrated that because of the non-specific findings of an inept autopsy, the cause and manner of Fritzie Mann's death could not be determined. Despite Schenck's badgering, Shea didn't change his opinion on cause of death—she had drowned, the doctor insisted. But he admitted that the condition of the body could reasonably indicate death by any of six other causes: acute pulmonary edema, or fluid in the lungs, a condition to which pregnant women are susceptible; eclampsia, or seizures causing unconsciousness, "strikingly peculiar to pregnant women;" spasm of the glottis, which closes off the passage of air, causing strangulation, perhaps due to the shock of her feet hitting the cold water; syncope, a sudden stoppage of the heart causing inhalation of water in a quick breath before death, possibly brought on by an underlying coronary condition; acute embolism of a coronary artery, blocking passage of blood to the heart; and poisoning by any of the cyanogen group of poisons, producing congestion of the lungs and death by asphyxia.

Death from any of those wouldn't be, strictly speaking, due to drowning, Shea said, even if water appeared in the lungs or stomach. The tell-tale sign of froth in the lungs indicated drowning. But it was often difficult—at times impossible—to distinguish at autopsy among these causes of death.

Especially, Schenck implied, *this* autopsy.

If the undertaker hadn't already drawn off the blood before the autopsy, Schenck said, "you would have been able to determine whether she died from syncope, or any one of the forms of asphyxiation due to poisoning or drowning or strangulation..." And also, whether she had drowned in salt water or fresh water?

"Yes, sir," Shea replied.

"The presence of clotted blood in the right heart, and the empty left heart, is not peculiar to drowning, is it?"

"Not by itself, no, sir."

Would it be present "in pulmonary edema, eclampsia, syncope and all the other causes mentioned, as well as 99% of all deaths from asphyxia?"

As a rule, I'd say yes.

Did you test for albumen in the urine, a mineral always present in deaths due to eclampsia?

No.

Any signs of convulsions before death?

No.

A person dying from any of the cyanogen group would likely die a placid death with no convulsions, right?

Right.

Have you heard of cases where an individual took cyanide, "folded their arms, and laid down and died, just as placid as though they are going to sleep?"

I've heard of a case where a girl took cyanide, laid down in her bed, and died.

"What was the color of her face when you saw it?"

"The face had a distinct reddening."

Was the bruise over the eyebrow post-mortem or ante-mortem?

"I would say it was ante-mortem." The bruise could have happened one minute before death and wasn't a contributing cause of death.

Was there blood in the corner of her eye?

Some blood may have oozed down from the superficial bruise.

Isn't uncoagulability of the blood also typical of the cyanogen group?

Yes, but other poisons as well, such as carbon monoxide.

Could cyanide have caused the pink color of her face or was that peculiar to drowning?

The pink color could've been caused by any number of things, not just cyanide or drowning. The sunshine may have caused it.

The inescapable takeaway from Schenck's masterful grilling of the doctor: The autopsy findings were inconclusive. Fritzie Mann might've died from any of seven causes. Because of this uncertainty and the botched autopsy, the cause of death was not only unknown but unknowable.

This put the DA's ability to prove *corpus delicti* in jeopardy. If you couldn't say for sure how Fritzie Mann had died, how could you say that someone murdered her?

But Shea saved the prosecution on direct examination. The issue was the condition of the lungs, specifically the amount of water in them and the presence or absence of sand or sea growth. Although not definitive, the small amount of water in her lungs suggested that she'd been unconscious when she drowned; a conscious person struggles against death and therefore tends to inhale more water. Also, if she had drowned in the surf, you'd expect to find sand and sea growth in the lungs. Shea didn't find either in Fritzie's lungs, so he thought it likely that she'd drowned elsewhere.

On balance, Shea's testimony favored the defense, but had the prosecution done enough to prove *corpus delicti* to the court's satisfaction?

The fate of the trial now rested with Judge Spencer Marsh. Sixty-eight, gray-haired and dignified, Marsh had served as the San Diego DA before his appointment to Superior Court Judge. Best known for his progressive ideals and interest in social problems, he wrote a notable legal opinion supporting women's right to serve on juries, a right finally won in 1917. His avuncular and unflappable personality hid a keen legal mind. A former grandmaster of a Masonic lodge, he was known to keep a tight rein on the outsized egos and bellicosity of opposing counsel typical in high-profile cases, a critical skill in the Jacobs trials.

Schenck and Kempley argued long and hard before the judge about whether the prosecution had met its burden on *corpus delicti*. To the DA's relief, Marsh ultimately agreed with California court precedence and applied a liberal rule requiring comparatively little proof of "criminal agency."

***

Chapter Forty-One – Star Witness

Albert Kern, ostensibly the DA's star witness, had been a headache for Kempley from the start of the case and turned into a migraine at the first trial. His nervous indecision on the witness stand had worsened as an aggressive prosecutor and meticulous defense counsel harassed him in a courtroom stacked to the rafters with flappers, reporters, and the dead woman's family and friends. Now, on the same day as Schenk's masterful cross-examination of Dr. Shea, Kern blew the DA's case out of the water.

"Now, would you say that the defendant, Louis Jacobs, was the man...out there that night with this young lady?" Kempley asked Albert Kern.

"No, sir," Kern said.

"That is...you are not certain whether he was the man or not?"

"I am sure he was not."

The DA had no choice but to use Kern as he was the only eyewitness at the cottages. At the first trial, Kern had testified that he couldn't be sure either way if Jacobs was the man. His testimony had been so weak that when Kern left the stand, Jacobs had settled back in his chair, a triumphant smile on his lips. This was the prosecution's star witness? Kern's testimony alone may have been enough to prompt the hung jury.

Now, dumbfounded and caught completely off guard by Kern's new-found certainty, Kempley asked, "You are prepared to say positively that he was not the man that was there?"

"Yes, sir," Kern said.

"Has anything occurred that refreshes your recollection as to who was there, since the last trial?"

"Well, I have always been positive that he was not the man."

He had stated on many occasions, he said—to Chief Patrick, to the grand jury, to various police officers and to the DA's representatives—that they had the wrong man. But for two or three weeks after his grand jury testimony, two of the DA's men, County Detective Wisler and another officer, had hounded him incessantly. They accused him of lying and tried to convince him that it couldn't have been anyone but the doctor. The harassment had confused him. Worse, the detectives had accused him of accepting an $800 bribe. Kern admitted that he didn't categorically eliminate Jacobs on several occasions, including at the grand jury and the first trial.

Furious and embarrassed, Kempley branded him a hostile witness. Then he cross-examined his own star witness, abusing the hapless Kern the rest of the day until court adjourned for the weekend. He resumed the assault on Monday morning, repeating many of the same questions he'd asked on Friday again and again, nitpicking Kern about anything he'd said to anyone at any time, intent on exposing the "motive" behind Kern's change of heart. Cowed, Kern answered slowly, almost inaudibly at times. He often answered with "I don't remember." He revised his story in real time and added new details, further angering the red-faced DA. For instance, he related a new detail about Mr. Johnston. Kern had noticed the man's hand when he signed the register. Johnston's hand appeared "rather heavy or large" and he held it in a "crooked position."

Schenck sat back and enjoyed the spectacle, happy to let Kempley's tirade run its course. Only after the DA had asked the same question with minor variations a couple of dozen times did Schenck finally start to object to questions as "already asked and answered."

Kempley got nowhere.

Schenck cross-examined Kern at length, mostly to counter the prosecution's inferences about defense improprieties.

Did the defense ever pressure you? Schenck asked.

No, Kern said. You asked me to come up to L.A. You met me at the train depot and drove me to a hotel. The next morning you took me to meet Rogers Clark, to see if he might be Mr. Johnston. You offered to pay my travel expenses, nothing more. I've had no other interaction with the defense since then.

Schenck also got Kern to say, "I would say that Clark resembled the man more than Dr. Jacobs did."

***

The next morning, Albert Kern stood outside of his office at the Blue Sea Cottages talking to County Detective Wisler and another officer, the same officials he'd accused of "confusing" him.

Kern looked across the open car at his smiling wife. "It's a warrant for my arrest!" he cried. "Perjury!"

Mary Kern's smile vanished. She glared at the detectives. "It's all right, honey," she said, her smile returning. "You are right, and when you are right, nothing can hurt you."

"Do you want to change your clothes?" Wisler asked Kern.

"Yes. Yes. I've got to leave the cottage, haven't I? I'll have to have a few minutes to put everything in shape."

Wisler and the other officer waited in the office for ten minutes while Kern changed clothes, and for he and Mary to prepare for his unexpected absence.

Mary climbed into the back seat of the car with her husband.

"What are those?" Kern asked, pointing at a rail on the back of the front seats.

"Handcuffs," Wisler said.

"Are you going to put them on me?"

"If you wish. Anything to please you."

"No, sir," Mary said. "You don't need them with Albert."

Kern declined to speak to Magner White, who had ridden along with the detectives. "I will have my say later... No more talking for me just now."

The officers marched Kern into the city jail.

"They've hounded him," Mary Kern told reporters.

She could not immediately raise the $5,000 bail. Albert spent four and a half days in jail until Mary managed to raise $3,000 to pay the reduced bail.

***

Chapter Forty-Two – Why, How Dare You Say That!

After the Kern debacle, the DA tried to resuscitate his case by concentrating on by far the strongest part of it, motive. He set the stage by using Chief Patrick to highlight Jacob's shifting alibi. More importantly, he used the chief's testimony to introduce the correspondence, reading each letter and telegram aloud in court.

On cross, Schenck pressed Patrick about his interviews with Jacobs until the normally staid chief lost his patience.

"Do you want me to go over the same story?" the chief said.

"No, I don't; but I want—" Schenck said.

"I don't know what you want me to answer."

"Why did you ask him where he was on Friday night, when Leo Greenbaum came down there and said, 'This is Jacobs'?"

"Well, why did he ask for an attorney?"

"I don't know."

"I don't know either."

"So…after you found out a man wanted to see an attorney—you thought he needed investigation right then and there, did you?"

"Wouldn't you have thought so?"

"No. All right, Chief, if that is the only reason you can give for it…"

***

The DA called Fritzie's chums Dorothy Armstrong, Bernice Edwards, and Helen Whitney. They provided essential if mostly uneventful testimony about Fritzie's last days and weeks and her relationship with the defendant. Reporters always commented on the appearance and comportment of young female witnesses as though narrating a fashion show instead of a murder trial, although not as much as they had at the first trial. Dorothy Armstrong wore a long dress with short sleeves, a fur tippet, and a flowered cloche hat that concealed most of her short black hair. Bernice Edwards, tall, slender, and pretty, took the stand wearing a full-length brown fur coat, a pearl-gray bonnet trimmed with flowers, and slippers with crossed straps. One reporter described her as "piquant." Helen Whitney wore "a stunning coat that dragged the floor, and a picture hat that made her face appear dainty and petite." She took the stand with "regal coolness, undraped her coat, leaned back in the chair and tilted her chin."

***

Wilma Minor, a "comely young woman dressed in black," testified to her L.A. trip at the defendant's behest, her five or six phone conversations with the doctor, and Fritzie's failure to meet her at the Lankershim Hotel.

"Did you have any conversation with Dr. Jacobs after your return from Los Angeles?" Kempley asked.

"Yes," Wilma said. "He telephoned me the day the body found on the beach was identified as that of Fritzie Mann… He asked me if I had heard the news, and when I said that everybody in town had heard it, he said: 'My God! What shall I do now?'" Wilma testified that she and Jacobs had never discussed the nature of Fritzie's condition or what assistance she might have rendered in L.A., implying she hadn't known anything about an abortion.

She'd been coy at the grand jury as well. She'd testified then that she hadn't been aware of Fritzie's pregnancy, nor had she "gone to Los Angeles to arrange with a doctor for an illegal operation upon the person of Fritzie Mann." Technically, she may not have been lying. She and Jacobs most likely spoke in euphemisms over the phone, never uttering the words "abortion" or "illegal operation," an ambiguity that allowed her to be disingenuous without perjuring herself. She never offered to help Dr. Jacobs to arrange an abortion, she insisted; she'd offered to help him find a doctor in L.A.—nobody said anything about an abortion. It hadn't fooled the grand jurors, who had seen the correspondence and Fritzie's last letter. And Jacobs testified at the grand jury immediately after Minor and admitted to "arrangements made through Miss Minor relative to a proposed abortion for Fritzie Mann which was to be arranged for by Miss Minor with a Los Angeles physician." Jacobs had denied making any abortion arrangements in San Diego. Rather, he claimed the plan was for Minor to take Fritzie back to L.A. personally. Wilma denied this.

***

The name of Rosie de Cacho, Fritzie's good chum, had never appeared in the papers related to the case until the first trial. Thirtyish, tall, with short frilly hair, her fur coat "could have been exchanged for the San Diego Courthouse and yet leave a generous profit in the County Treasury," according to one reporter. Rosie was the first witness to display open hostility toward the defense. She glared at the defense attorneys, she scowled at Jacobs. Observers likened her animated gestures and exaggerated facial expressions on the stand to those of a motion picture actress, a characteristic of actors during the silent era as they tried to portray a range of emotions without the benefit of words and sound.

The subject of her testimony concerned a conversation one evening between the 10th and 15th of October 1922, about the time Fritzie learned she was pregnant. Jacobs and Fritzie stopped by her house, Rosie said, the first and only time she had met the doctor.

According to Rosie on direct, she was upstairs hearing her small son's prayers when the doorbell rang.

"Go down and let Fritzie in," Rosa told her daughter, Alyce.

Alyce showed Fritzie and Jacobs into the living room, then Fritzie followed Alyce upstairs.

"Put some clothes on and come down," Fritzie told Rosie. "I want you to meet my doctor."

Rosie laughed when she saw Jacobs "standing in the library, looking in Miss Mann's vanity case, powdering his nose…"—the doctor seemed to be "dolling up." They sat down. Jacobs pulled a small bottle out of his pocket and offered to make punch if de Cacho would bring ice and fruit. She and Fritzie declined.

"Why, Rosie," Fritzie said, "what do you think of my doctor?"

Seeing Jacobs powder his nose had made an impression on Rosie. "It is hardly time to ask a question such as that. It might not be so very favorable to the doctor."

"I want you to like him very much," Fritzie replied, "because when we are married you are going to be the matron of honor."

"Oh, how nice," Rosie said.

Jacobs stood up and walked into the library. Fritzie followed. At first de Cacho couldn't make out what they were saying, but then she heard Jacobs shout, "I will marry no one!"

Taking him by the coat with both hands, Fritzie said, "You will marry me!"

"I will marry no one," Jacobs repeated. "I will assist you all I can, but I will not marry you."

Uncomfortable, Rosie motioned to Alice to go upstairs, then went to the living room and began playing the piano. The couple came into the living room and stayed for about twenty minutes until Jacobs announced that he needed to leave since he had to perform an operation the next morning.

Schenck's cross-examination of Rosie had caused the biggest sensation of the first trial when, out of the blue, he asked her if she'd been intoxicated to the point of "actually reeling" during that visit with Fritzie and Jacobs. She had squeezed the arms of the witness chair and shouted, "Why, how dare you!" The judge banged his gavel to quell the din and threatened to clear the room. De Cacho left the stand quaking with rage. She stopped by the defense table and stood glaring at Schenck for half a minute. He looked up and grinned. She rushed out of the courtroom in tears. Outside, Rosie sobbed to reporters, "Can you feature such a statement as that?"

Now the courtroom hummed in anticipation for another sensation. Schenck's staccato cross-examination did not disappoint at the end.

"Mrs. de Cacho, you were confined in Doctor Little's Sanitarium in July 1922," Schenck said, "and again in March 1923, on a charge of insanity, weren't you?"

"No."

"I will ask you if it is not a fact that at that time you were so overcome and affected by the use of alcohol that you did not even know what happened?"

"Why, how dare you say that!"

"Just answer the question 'yes' or 'no'," Judge Marsh instructed Rosie.

"Positively no."

***

Chapter Forty-Three – The Questioned Signature

The DA needed to prove that Jacobs had the opportunity to kill Fritzie. The only way he could put Jacobs at the Blue Sea Cottages with Fritzie was the register signature.

The press had dubbed I.N. Inskeep, a questioned documents examiner from L.A., "The Professor." A small man with gray hair and a grave disposition, he stood for much of his testimony, a pointer in one hand, a stick of chalk in the other, schooling the courtroom in the art and science of handwriting analysis. He demonstrated points he made by writing on a portable blackboard. Photographic blow ups of "Alvin Johnston and Wife, L.A." and samples of Jacobs' handwriting were pinned to a board behind the witness stand. The prosecution had magnified some of the signatures two hundred times—large enough to be readable from the back of the courtroom.

Inskeep identified more than forty characteristics—loops, angles, curves, slants, formations, lines, stroke emphasis, and other penmanship habits—to support his conclusion that Louis Jacobs had, beyond any doubt, signed the Blue Sea Cottages register. A dead giveaway was the peculiarity of the capital "J." Jacobs made the bottom loop first, a characteristic that occurred "once in thousands of individuals." Capital "Js" appeared forty-nine times in the checks, letters, and telegrams Inskeep examined, each formed in this peculiar way. The "J" in "Johnston" of the register signature had been made using the same rare technique. Moreover, Mr. Johnston's signature showed signs of deception. He had held his hand at an unnatural angle, writing "backhanded," in an attempt to disguise his natural handwriting. Also telling, in the exemplars he had provided to the police, Jacobs wrote the "Js in the proper manner, forming the upper loop first. Aware of his quirk, Jacobs had tried to conceal it.

As usual, Schenck had done his homework. As he did with the medical witnesses, he demonstrated an encyclopedic knowledge of the technical aspects of handwriting. But he could not sway The Professor.

Later, Milton Carlson, a "celebrated handwriting expert" from L.A. with a national reputation, concurred with The Professor—the J's and other quirks gave Jacobs' writing away, despite his attempts to disguise it.

***

At the first trial, Kempley had called a surprise witness between the two document examiners. The DA had been unable locate the witness for the second trial so the transcript from the first trial was read into the record:

"What is your name?" Kempley asked.

"Alvin M. Johnson," the witness answered.

"Where do you live, Mr. Johnson?"

"Quitman, Mississippi."

"Where are you at present stopping?"

"Camp Kearny."

"What portion of Camp Kearny—in the hospital?"

"Yes, sir."

"Are you acquainted with the defendant, Louis L. Jacobs, in this case?"

"I am, in regards to the hospital."

"State whether or not Dr. Louis Jacobs…was the physician in charge of the ward that you were in?"

"He was."

"I will show you People's Exhibit Number 12 and particularly the page headed January 1923—the name on there—'Alvin Johnston & wife, L.A.,' and ask you whether or not you wrote that?"

"No, sir."

On cross, Schenck asked, "That is not your name, either, is it?"

"No, sir."

"You don't live in Los Angeles, do you?"

"No, sir."

With Alvin Johnson sitting below the blown-up signature of "Alvin Johnston," the DA scored "a distinct psychological point for the prosecution," one reporter commented.

***

Chapter Forty-Four – The Goddess Of Blind Chance

A man named Bertie Thompson had reported a hot tip to police early in the case. He'd overheard two men in the restroom of the Elite Garage downtown, he said. Both men wore Army olive drab field coats and campaign hats. According to Thompson, one man said, "It is G---D D—M funny that the doctor should have burnt those papers and stuff Monday morning at 9 o'clock when no one ever seen him around there until noon any other time." One of the men mentioned "the Chef," apparently the source of this information. Unlike most of the tips from the public, the police had learned the identities of the men Bertie Thompson overheard, soldiers stationed at Camp Kearny, and judged the story credible.

Kempley called one of the men, William Miller, a boiler tender at the Camp Kearny hospital. He tended boilers in the kitchen, operating room, and laundry. Miller had testified at the grand jury, but for some reason the DA hadn't called him at the first trial.

Miller testified that he saw Dr. Jacobs in the hospital kitchen at 8:30 or 9:00 a.m. on the day Fritzie Mann's body was found.

"Doctor Jacobs come into the kitchen," Miller said, "walked up to the stove and put something into the stove."

Asked if anyone else was present, Miller said "I was speaking to the Chef while Doctor Jacobs come in—"

Objecting, Schenck tried but failed to keep the next exchange out.

"Just after that," Miller continued, "the Chef asked him a question." The Chef had asked Jacobs, in a joking manner, "'Well, that's the last of this affair, is it?'" Doctor Jacobs said, "yes," and walked out."

"Did you see what he put in the stove?"

"As close as I could make out, it was envelopes."

For unknown reasons, Kempley didn't call the Chef, a man named Meeker.

***

Toward the end of the People's case, the DA called another new witness, Mrs. Blanche Jones, a former nurse at Camp Kearny. The *Evening Tribune* described her as "an innocent human implement in the workings of the goddess of Blind Chance."

Kempley asked her whether she was outside the camp grounds on the night of the crime.

"Yes, sir," Jones said. "I had taken a ride that evening."

The DA indicated a map hanging on the wall behind the witness stand. He pointed out the road leading from La Jolla to Linda Vista. From there it branched off into two possible routes to the Camp Kearny Hospital. One, a rocky dirt road (labeled Route 2 on the map), branched off to the right and ran southeast 2.28 miles directly to the hospital compound. The other road (Route 1), also dirt, branched off to the left and ran east along the northern edge of the camp. Route 1 was almost three times as long at 6.33 miles but a much smoother ride. Kempley pointed to the spot on the map near the northeast corner of the base and the little settlement of Miramar, where Route 1 met the main inland north/south route. This road led north to a small city, Escondido, thirty miles north of San Diego, and from there to L.A.

"Now," the DA said, "with reference to where this Route 1 intersects the Escondido Highway, where were you about nine or nine thirty that evening?"

Sitting in her Chevrolet, she said, just south of the point where the road from La Jolla met the Escondido Highway. She'd been on the way back to the hospital from a drive toward Escondido and stopped for a time on the side of the road. Around 9:30 p.m. she heard a machine's noise and turned to see a car travelling very fast as it approached the intersection from the west. It slowed momentarily to make the turn to the south, then accelerated. It passed right by her car.

"Are you acquainted with the defendant, Louis Jacobs, in this case?" the DA asked.

"Yes, sir." She also knew his car, she said, a closed, shiny new Hudson coach. There was no other car on the base like it.

"Did you see the person that was in the machine?"

"I saw the outline of a man driving."

"What would you say as to whether or not the man driving was Dr. Jacobs?"

"I should say it was Dr. Jacobs."

"Where did the machine go after it passed you?"

"It went towards Camp Kearny," Jones said, travelling south for a short distance and then making a right turn into the camp.

"What did you do?"

"I followed it."

"Did you see the machine go clear into the hospital grounds?"

"Yes, sir."

During a withering cross examination, Schenck scrutinized every detail of Jones' story, attempting to rattle her. He tried to exploit her admitted inability to judge distances or recognize the sounds of a car's muffler. Jones' brow furrowed with the strain, but she remained outwardly calm.

"Was there any one with you on this occasion, Mrs. Jones?" Schenck asked.

"Yes, sir."

"Who was it?"

"A patient named McCauley."

Suspicious she'd waited until after the first trial to come forth, Schenck asked, "You and Mr. McCauley talked about it, didn't you?"

"Yes sir."

Didn't she write a letter telling McCauley that "you wanted his services in corroborating and substantiating you—asking and begging him to substantiate you in the testimony that you were going to give?"

"I wanted him to tell the truth."

The DA's objections prevented Schenck from questioning her further about the letter. Judge Marsh called the letter itself the best evidence.

"Were you in attendance upon the court the last time we tried this case?" Schenck asked, implying that Jones had a special interest in the outcome of the trial, and therefore inclined to lie.

"No sir...I was a spectator one day."

Responding to another question, Jones said she had let McCauley out of the car just outside of the gate.

"Well," Schenck said, "he got out so that he wouldn't get caught being out late, didn't he?"

Kempley objected—sustained.

"What did he get out for?" Schenck asked. "Why didn't he ride in with you?"

"He asked me to let him out."

On re-direct, Kempley reinforced the point about the car's high rate of speed as it approached the intersection. It had slowed to make the curve, then accelerated as it passed

Jones' car. Although she started up right after Jacobs passed, he beat her into the camp by at least five minutes.

The DA did some of his best work during his direct and re-direct examinations of Jones with succinct, focused questions. By contrast, Schenck's cross-examination rambled.

On re-cross, Schenck tried to trip up Jones by grilling her on her knowledge of the cars at the camp. This backfired, clearly taking Schenck aback. While often unsure of distances and other details, she knew by sight many of the cars on base. Responding to Schenck's questions, she described numerous vehicles in detail by make, model, size, and owner.

***

NURSE'S TESTIMONY IN JACOBS CASE MAY COST HER OWN HAPPINESS. The Magner White story appeared on the front page of the July 9, 1923, *Sun*. "Suppose you are a woman, happily married," the article began, "that you have a 21-months-old daughter, and that you know something valuable to the state in a murder trial." But if you revealed what you knew you'd "turn a shadow of rumor and suspicion upon yourself and possibly cost you your future happiness, your husband and your child. What would you do?" Keep silent and enjoy your happiness or testify and "bare yourself to the rudeness of the gossipers" and console yourself that you were doing your duty? "Mrs. Blanche Y. Jones, former Camp Kearny nurse, today decided this question. Jones' husband, a disabled man in a soldiers' hospital in Sawtelle, was said to be "brooding over the situation, heart sick."

"He was a friend," Jones told reporters. "I like to talk to him. He was a patient, and I took him for a ride in my car. I never took anybody else for a ride. We drove down the road, then stopped by the side of the road and talked. It was just a visit and that was all. I never dreamed it would turn out to be such a terrible thing as it has been made to appear. It would probably cost me my happiness. I have no interest in the Jacobs case. I wish I had never seen the man that went driving by in the car, for if I had not, I would not have been called in to testify in this case. I tried to keep out of it."

She hadn't wanted to testify, Blanche said, but the DA somehow found out about what she'd seen and compelled her to testify for the prosecution. She had determined to go through with it and tell the truth, which she did.

"I did write a letter to the man who was with me and ask him to testify in corroboration of my testimony," she said. "But I didn't ask him to do anything but tell the truth. I am sorry everything has turned out as it has. It is going to cost me much. I have done my duty, but it seems at a cost that is out of proportion to the results. I have done nothing to deserve the trouble that it has brought me."

***

The DA called Blanche Jones' passenger that night, Richard McCauley, a WWI veteran, and long-term patient at Camp Kearny.

She had picked him up outside the gate around 7:30 p.m. on January 14, he testified. The Escondido road north of the intersection with Route 1 was under construction. Someone had placed a board across the road that said, "Road closed—impassable." Jones drove around the sign. They drove north on the partially paved road for three to five miles, then turned around. Jones parked her open-bodied Chevrolet, with the top up, about 150 or 200 feet from the intersection. They had been there for about thirty minutes when they saw Jacobs' Hudson make the corner at a speed McCauley estimated at thirty-five or forty miles per hour—the engine noise of a car moving at high speed is what had attracted his attention. A few seconds after Jacobs passed, Jones started her car and they followed him back to the camp.

Schenck pointed out a discrepancy in the story. Driving up the unfinished highway for a few miles, turning around, and then parking for thirty minutes would not have filled up the two-hour period between 7:30 and 9:30 p.m. that McCauley and Jones said they were out. Schenck did not press McCauley but implied his point: McCauley and Jones must have stopped somewhere else on the highway toward Escondido for a period of time as well, which neither had mentioned. It was not material to the case, but a hint of scandal wouldn't help the witnesses' credibility with the jury. Although unspoken in the courtroom, this information provided grist for the "rudeness of gossipers" Jones had complained about and caused her husband to brood "over the situation, heart sick."

How could you be sure it was 9:30 when you got back? Schenck asked McCauley.

Because I had to be back at nine, McCauley replied. I had my watch in my hand and kept looking at it. My estimate is off by no more than five minutes.

Who did you first speak to about seeing this car?

Mrs. Jones and I discussed it.

"Have you a letter now, from her, in your possession, that refers to this case?"

McCauley didn't have the letter with him. The judge released him to retrieve it. When he returned, the letter, dated June 6, 1923, was read aloud in the courtroom:

Mac. No word from you, looked for a letter yesterday, wanted to see you, - I guess it is "and" talk over this affair we are perhaps unwillingly thrust into – you, at least, are. I do wish you could see it differently, and not with hold what evidence we have. Why feel that way? 'a life,' you said. Yes, I know, but think of the lives cut off over seas, for what? This man should not go free, if guilty, should he? Why should the woman always pay? Stand by, it's not so hard. It's principle, dear, that counts with God, not money. I beg of you to be and do what is right in the matter, and I know you will, at whatever cost, because I believe in you.

Of our own personal interests, whatever happens will have to be. I can only hope it may eventually mean happiness for us both together.

Yours always, Blanche

Jones had written something at the bottom "really of a personal nature," which both sides agreed to leave unread as not material to the case. Apparently, her husband had reason to brood.

The People rested.

***

Chapter Forty-Five – Field Trip

During the first trial, Schenck had proposed a field trip. The topography related to the case confused him, he told the judge. Calling it "the world's biggest court exhibit," he asked the judge to put the entire 9.29-mile area between the Blue Sea Cottages and the slough bridge into evidence. He wanted to demonstrate the reasonableness of the suicide theory, he said, and the unreasonableness of the prosecution's murder theory.

Kempley agreed, with one proviso. He wanted the jury to also see the shortcut road from the coast highway to Camp Kearny. Judge Spencer agreed.

They repeated the field trip for the second trial. A caravan of vehicles filled with jurors, the court stenographer and clerk, two deputy sheriffs, the defendant, opposing counsel, the judge, and newspaper reporters and photographers drove up the coast road to La Jolla. The jurors rode in an auto stage, an extended car with five rows of seats and large windows. The caravan turned onto Bonair Street and stopped near the Blue Sea Cottages office.

Judge Marsh narrated the visit. "This is the office that was referred to in the testimony of Mr. Kern, and perhaps others," Marsh said.

Someone pointed out the signature blue light outside of the office and the approximate spot Mr. Johnston had stopped his car on the night of January 14. They walked down the row of cottages to the end and stopped in front of cottage thirty-three. Albert Kern escorted them into the cottage. They went through the bathroom and out the adjoining cottage.

A Turkish cigarette clenched between his teeth, "Jacobs strode through the cottage unmoved in the slightest degree," according to a *Sun* reporter.

Kern pointed out the approximate spot Mr. Johnston had parked his machine.

After the brief visit, everyone piled back into the vehicles and the caravan headed north on the coast highway. It wound its way through La Jolla, past the Scripps Institute, and up the Biological Grade. The caravan continued north on the coast highway and twisted down the Torrey Pines Grade. At the bottom of the grade, they made a sharp right turn onto the straight section of highway along the beach. They parked at the southern end of the slough bridge.

The judge and counsel pointed out the relevant sites referred to in the testimony: the curving bridge spanning the slough, the big rock crusher, the approximate spots where Fritzie's articles and body were found. There was considerable dispute over the locations of some of them, particularly the body. The group walked down the rocky embankment to the beach. Schenck, the largest figure in a light-colored suit and plainsman's hat, stood out among the men, all dressed in dark three-piece suits and dark Homburgs or straw boaters.

Many of the first trial jurors had found the experience on the beach unnerving, their thoughts inescapably drifting to the young woman whose life had ended there. According to the *Sun*, the mood on the beach was different this time, as light-hearted now as it was somber during the first trial.

One juror held a piece of seaweed aloft and shouted, "Hey, I've found the *corpus delicti!*"

"We'll now proceed to get some sand in our shoes," someone said.

"We'll stipulate that," Schenck said.

Jacobs walked around in the bright sunshine, hat in his hand, the only hatless figure in a group of hatted men and women jurors, chain smoking and sniffing the salt air with relish. He did not join in the merriment but smiled often, happy to be anywhere other than his jail cell or the courtroom for the first time in three months. Later, some observers expressed surprise to see the defendant standing where his good chum's corpse had lain, exhibiting no hint of stress. They found his affable demeanor odd.

After a brief walk around the beach, the gaggle piled back into the vehicles and drove south on the coast road. They stopped at Rannells Oil Station. The station was located at a crossroads formed by the highway, the Biological Grade, and the unnamed east-bound dirt road some called the Linda Vista road—the short cut to Camp Kearny the DA believed Jacobs had used after dumping Fritzie's body on the beach.

**

Chapter Forty-Six – Alibis

Schenck called a series of witnesses to establish Jacobs' alibi. He first called Mrs. Ella Worthington, a "pretty young widow," as the papers described her. A wealthy Coronado socialite of forty-nine, she lived on Encino Row, a few blocks from John Spreckels' beach front mansion and his Hotel del Coronado. She lived there with her eighteen-year-old daughter, her sister and a female boarder. Jacobs had met her in April 1922, the month after he arrived in San Diego. As she explained it, since he was new to the area, "…we offered him the hospitality of our home…," as she had other servicemen with wartime service. How long he stayed at her house is not clear, but he remained close to the family until the present, often taking Mrs. Worthington for drives in the country, to clubs and the racetrack in Tijuana, and out to dinner. He also frequently visited their home after he moved out. He didn't meet Fritzie until May or June.

She and Jacobs had spent the afternoon of Saturday, January 13, at the racetracks in Tijuana, Worthington testified, returning late that night. Jacobs stayed over at her house that night. On Sunday, January 14, they went to Tijuana again, arriving back at her home ten or fifteen minutes before 6:00 p.m. Jacobs left at about 6:15, announcing his intention to catch the 6:20 ferry and meet friends at the train station at 6:30. This was corroborated by four others. Then Schenck called four Camp Kearny witnesses to testify that they'd seen the doctor at the hospital between 9:30 and 10:00

p.m. Schenck had to establish the beginning and end of the timeline, but Jacobs' whereabouts before 6:30 and after 9:30 were never in dispute. Only the gap mattered.

To fill the gap, Jacobs had stated and then abandoned three alibis. In his first interview with Chief Patrick, he said he went from the Santa Fe depot straight to Camp Kearny, but no one had seen him there before 9:00 or 9:30 p.m. Next, he said he visited a patient for two-and-a-half hours at the U.S. Grant Hotel before going to the hospital. That patient either didn't exist or didn't corroborate Jacobs' story. It never came out in public or at the trials, but he'd tried out a third alibi at the grand jury in February.

A waitress at Harvey's Lunch Counter in the Santa Fe Depot said Jacobs and an "elderly gentleman" (probably Jimmy Wadham) had visited her two or three times during the week before her grand jury testimony. They tried to convince her that she'd served him consommé and sandwiches at 6:30 p.m. on January 14, when Jacobs was supposedly there meeting friends from Kalamazoo. But she testified that she couldn't remember if she'd served him or not, intimating that the men had tried to plant a "memory" in her head. By the time Jacobs testified to the grand jury a few days later, he'd settled on his fourth and final alibi. His stop at the U.S. Grant, he claimed, had been two-and-one-half *minutes*, not *hours*. Then he went to Ye Golden Lion Tavern to cash a check and then stayed for a couple of hours before going to the hospital.

Schenck called several Golden Lion cashiers and waitresses, who placed Jacobs at the tavern between roughly 7:00 and 9:00 p.m. on the 14th, filling the gap nicely. If he was there, Rogers Clark might've seen him. As the police had confirmed, Clark and Gladys Taylor had dined at the Golden Lion between 8:00 and 10:30 p.m. that night. For both suspects to be there at the same time wasn't much of a coincidence. Located at the corner of 4th and F Street, two blocks from the Grant, the Golden Lion was one of the most popular restaurants in town, known for a stunning stained-glass dome over the bar. Jacobs, a Golden Lion regular, had been there on separate occasions with Fritzie and Ella Worthington. And Fritzie sometimes hung out there with friends. If Jacobs was telling the truth about visiting the Golden Lion, the probability that he and Clark would've spotted each other at the restaurant was high, as it wasn't a big place, and their visits would've overlapped by about an hour. This suggested the ironic possibility that Clark might've provided Jacobs with an alibi. Whether Clark and Jacobs knew each other by sight before their pictures started appearing in the papers isn't clear; they certainly knew *of* each other. The grand jury apparently didn't ask Clark if he saw the doctor at the Golden Lion, and neither side called him during the first trial. Kempley called him at the current trial to dispel any lingering doubts to the jury about the actor's possible guilt, which Schenck had worked throughout the trial to do. Surprisingly, Schenck's cross-examination of Clark was short.

The DA called rebuttal witnesses—other Golden Lion employees—to poke holes in Jacobs' new alibi. He also called County Detective Wisler to testify that one of the defense witnesses had changed her story since he spoke to her. Some of the witnesses thought Jacobs had been there on Saturday the 13th but not the 14th. One cashier said that Jacobs had cashed a check on Saturday or Sunday but couldn't say which. On cross-examination, this witness told Kempley that Wisler had shown him the cancelled check two weeks later. The date of January 14 had been written in pencil—by a different hand. He didn't recall if the date had been there when he cashed it for Jacobs, but everything else on the check was written in ink. That check had apparently been lost so Kempley couldn't introduce it into evidence.

The extensive Golden Lion testimony was confusing and unconvincing on both sides. Some of it, most notably the check backdated in pencil by an unknown hand, was suspicious. Given the tactics already used, chances are that one or both sides bribed or intimidated the Golden Lion witnesses or tried to. Just as likely, some of them were mistaken. Jacobs didn't even decide on this alibi gap filler until the grand jury, a few weeks or a month after the night in question. They were harassed repeatedly by attorneys, private eyes, and cops. In the end this conflicting mess probably favored the defense.

***

Chapter Forty-Seven – Neurotic Woman

Schenck called other witnesses, some of them new, to sow seeds of reasonable doubt, to reinforce his suicide theory or, as he had with the Golden Lion testimony, just to muck things up. One of the new muck witnesses was Ada Beach, a member of the grand jury that had indicted Jacobs.

Ada had contacted Schenck out of the blue earlier in the trial. Some of the prosecution witnesses had changed their stories from their grand jury testimony, Ada claimed, and she had her notes to prove it. "Preserve those notes with your life," Schenck had told her. "It may mean a man's life."

According to Ada, the coroner testified to the grand jury that when he first saw Fritzie Mann's body, rigor mortis hadn't yet set in, her arms weren't crossed, and both hands were clenched; William Mann that Rogers Clark, not Dr. Jacobs, had called Fritzie at home every day during her last week; and Amelia Mann that Rogers Clark had made Fritzie pregnant and gave her medicine to cause an abortion but instead had made her deathly ill. Kempley later called three of Ada's fellow grand jurors to contradict her testimony.

***

Schenck brought in David Rannells, owner of the oil station on the coast highway and one of the beachcombers who found the vanity case and handbag, to cast doubt on the beach crime scene. Rannells contradicted the other beach witness on almost every point. Fritzie's body was limp, not stiff. Her tongue had not protruded out of her mouth. The skin on her entire body was pink, not just her face. The brown party dress was crumpled or folded into a compact shape, not stretched out on a line toward the body. And he placed the body seventy-five feet seaward of the consensus location. These points favored the suicide theory.

Schenck also used Rannells to discredit the cops and infer corruption. He had been with Chadwick and Sears when they found the Army blanket on the embankment, three days after the body was discovered. In court, he inspected the blanket in evidence and decided that it wasn't the same the detectives had found. Moreover, Chadwick had also found an old, sun-bleached cap bearing the tag of a Tijuana dry good store within twenty feet of the brown dress but had deemed it unrelated to the case and discarded it. The prosecution tried to discredit Rannells, saying he held a grudge against the police. As he admitted on the stand, he'd been a "special officer" with the force for a brief period, but Chief Patrick had fired him.

Schenck also supported his suicide theory with medical evidence. As he had at the first trial, he called Dr. A. F. Wagner, the L.A. County autopsy surgeon. Wagner said he'd performed close to ten thousand autopsies—at least nine thousand more than Dr. Shea and Dr. Thompson, the prosecution's medical experts, combined. The frothy mucous Shea emphasized so much wasn't peculiar to drowning, he testified, nor was it the only important symptom in any cause of death. Cadavers often exhibited frothy exude from other causes. Just last week he'd seen froth bubble from the nose of a corpse as it lay on the autopsy table. The person had been run over by a truck. Wagner echoed Shea's testimony about edema of the lungs—any number of conditions other than drowning might cause it and pregnancy increased the risk. Based on the autopsy results and circumstances of Fritzie's death, drowning was not the definitive cause. But if she did drown, she might well have drowned in the surf. Among the numerous drowning cases he'd handled, only four or five contained sand or seaweed in the lungs. Moreover, sand in the lungs was hard to detect by sight alone. He'd recently confirmed this by drowning a large rabbit in the surf; he'd autopsied the rabbit and couldn't find any sand. Then he conducted a microscopal test and found sand. Sand might have been in Miss Mann's lungs, but no tests had been done. And she might have died of a drug or poison such as cyanide, but the autopsy was so inadequate there was no way to know.

Asked about the mental state of pregnant women, Dr. Wagner said they had a tendency toward "neurotic conditions."

"By 'neurotic,' what do you mean?" Schenck asked.

"That means their nervous system is not well balanced. Their tendency is toward insanity…to do things that they would not do in other conditions…to eat things and have appetites for unusual articles of foods. All these things are brought about by the condition of pregnancy."

"And what have you to say with reference to suicide?"

"Suicide is one of the neurosis, suicide and homicide, and anything that is…criminal or unnatural."

Schenck also used Wagner to counter the DA's contention about the position of Fritzie's arms and hands. The DA believed that when he put her body on the beach, Jacobs had folded her hands across her breast out of habit—it's what doctors did when someone dies in the hospital. Had Wagner heard of this?

"Never heard of such a thing," Wagner said. "That is the business of the undertaker."

Schenck brought in another new witness to support suicide. A young man named Ben Shelley said he'd known Fritzie briefly. They had met in June or July at the "Army department store" he ran and saw her several times until he left for Reno in November. He once took her to see her sister at the Paradise Valley Sanitarium. Another time he was at the Golden Lion with the "Schlossberg boys," Henry and George, when Fritzie and another girl came in. They all went to Rosie de Cacho's house.

They attended a party together on another occasion. Fritzie told him about her disappointment over her "secret marriage" in high school in Denver. She never told her family about it, and it was later annulled.

"Fritzie, why are you so blue?" he said he'd asked her. She had responded, "Oh...I am disgusted, disappointed...At times I feel like ending it all."

On cross, the DA asked Shelley if he'd told anyone about Fritzie's statement.

He'd told the Schlossberg boys when he returned to San Diego in March, he said. Since then, he'd mentioned it to Dr. Jacobs' friend, Leo Greenbaum, and recently to Jacobs' lawyer, Louis Shapiro. He said he didn't know about Fritzie's pregnancy. He never saw her again after their October conversation.

**

"Only the advice of my attorneys will keep me from going on the witness stand," Jacobs declared to a *Sun* reporter on Friday, July 13. "...if my chief counsel, Paul W. Schenck, will agree to it, I will take the stand. I have nothing to conceal."

Jacobs did not testify. His cousin Shapiro jumped in to explain. Schenck never allowed a client to testify since juries would tend to exaggerate the importance of "the slightest little slip in his testimony."

**

Chapter Forty-Eight – She Was Not A Gold Digger

Closing arguments began on the afternoon of July 16, 1923. The DA shared the prosecution's argument with his assistant, Guy Selleck, who went first. The prosecution didn't need to state a specific theory of Fritzie's cause of death, he said, responding to Schenck's earlier criticism; they need only to prove the death was criminal. He ticked off the six possible causes the defense had proposed and eliminated them each in turn. He ridiculed Jacobs' supposed altruistic motivation and changing alibis. The handwriting analysis proved the doctor had been at the cottages and his exemplars betrayed a guilty knowledge. He attacked the veracity of defense witnesses, calling David Rannells an habitual but poor liar. But the prosecution witnesses were credible, he said. Blanche Jones' reluctance to testify made her particularly credible.

"All I ask is that you should lay aside the idea that 'the man should not pay,'" Selleck said in closing, echoing Jones' letter to McCauley.

***

During an intermission, a *Union* reporter seated at the press table leaned over to Jacobs.

"Wouldn't it have been a good idea, doctor," the reporter asked, "to have provided a supply of scopolamine to give the witnesses before they took the stand?"

"It might have eliminated a lot of queer testimony," he said, laughing. "You know, some woman wrote to the district attorney and asked him why they didn't submit me to the 'truth serum' test. Kempley handed the letter over to me and asked me what I thought about it.

"I told him I was game. I said I would submit to the scopolamine test on one condition, that he would quash the indictment against me and drop the case if my testimony, while under the influence of the drug, showed that I am innocent. But Kempley wouldn't agree to that so I didn't take the test.

"As a matter of fact, the stuff is no good anyway. It is the same stuff that, mixed with morphine, is given to women as 'twilight sleep'…did you ever hear a woman in twilight sleep? I'll say she talks. Scopolamine produces all sorts of delusions, illusions and hallucinations, and it loosens the tongue…but there is nothing coherent in the conversation. It usually consists in all sorts of wild imaginary and impossible stories. It does not prevent inhibitions.

"Sure, I'd submit to the test any time. In fact I'll answer any questions anybody wants to ask me. But Kempley wasn't as game as I was."

Later, during an interview, the DA blasted Jacobs for refusing to take the stand in his own defense. "Jacobs has been quoted in the press as saying he offered to submit to scopolamine, the truth serum, under certain absurd conditions," he said. "He has only to take the stand and tell the truth. The use of opiates would be nonsensical where opportunity exists for truth telling with all faculties alert. Jacobs was present when Fritzie came to her death. He is the only eyewitness. Yet he refuses to take the stand and relate the facts."

***

The defense attorneys also took turns. Clifford Fitzgerald, a tall, twenty-six-year-old USC alumnus who had served as an officer during the war, and who had done a significant share of the defense work during the trial, led off. Referring to Fritzie's apparent change of plans when she called her mother from downtown, he asked, "How could it have been possible for Jacobs to have had anything to do with Fritzie Mann's change of plans?" He had proof that he was with friends until after 6:00 p.m. "There must have been some other man or person mixed up in the affair who saw Fritzie Mann and who caused her to change her plans."

Fitzgerald also accused the prosecution of dirty tricks. The defense had trouble getting witnesses to testify because they feared the DA's power of retribution. This was why they had no witnesses to rebut the testimony about Jacobs' alleged burning of letters in the kitchen stove—they were afraid.

The defendant was a man of standing, he said, with no reason to commit a heinous crime. And if he had, he was too smart to have done it in a way almost designed to draw suspicion on himself.

Louis Shapiro, a short, portly, man, spoke from a thick bundle of index cards. He made an emotional plea for his cousin's life. His attack dripped with sarcasm, and he often shouted at the jury and accused the prosecution of unsavory acts. He attacked the DA for unfairness, for presenting dishonest witnesses, for intimidating defense witnesses, and for withholding, misrepresenting, and manufacturing evidence. Fritzie Mann's condition, moreover, made her susceptible to a neurotic and unbalanced state of mind and therefore to suicide. Her note, "I am Fritzie Mann," indicated her intent to commit suicide and desire for her body to be identified.

Shapiro advanced two new theories. Fritzie had crossed her hands over her breast as she waded out into the waves, he said. The shock of the cold water caused her instant death due to syncope or heart failure, and rigor set in instantly. He made had an even stranger suggestion—nine-year-old Russell Chase had crossed her hands when he found her body.

***

Schenck, the defense closer, also adopted a sarcastic tone. He scorned the handwriting experts, savaged the coroner, and accused the prosecution of chicanery. The detectives found a blanket, allegedly from cottage thirty-three, three days later, after the beach had already been searched? How suspicious was that?

He said he couldn't answer the prosecution's theory of death since they never advanced one.

"If I hadn't stipulated it," he said, "they wouldn't even have proved that Fritzie Mann is dead."

He mocked Rose de Cacho and her "affected manner" on the stand.

"I never saw anything so pitiful on the stand in my life." He wheeled and shouted at the jury, "Would you hang a yellow dog on testimony like that? I wouldn't even spank a cur on that sort of evidence."

At the end he begged the jury to either hang Jacobs or set him free.

***

Kempley spoke all morning and into the afternoon, "With an eloquence that brought a hush over the courtroom and caused many women to brush tears from their eyes." He dismissed Jacobs' claim of altruism by reading from the correspondence where Jacobs had warned Fritzie not to tell anyone that he was a doctor. And the correspondence left no doubt—Jacobs knew he was the father of her unborn child and failed to do the right thing.

"Fritzie Mann knew who was the father of her unborn child and this man here (pointing) was not man enough to marry her. His social position: 'I will assist you but I will not marry you.'

"She was not a gold digger," he said, holding aloft the handbag found on the beach. "Do you think that the little girl who carried this tattered old handbag along with her on her trip from home was a gold digger? Did they find any rings on her fingers or anything else to indicate she was a gold digger, living off of the money from men? Was she a woman of the streets, and is there anything in the evidence to indicate she was that sort?"

The DA read Fritzie's last letter to the jury again to prove she had no plans to commit suicide but planned to return to L.A. soon.

The case went to the jury on Friday, July 20, 1923.

***

Chapter Forty-Nine – The Verdict

The attorneys anxiously wandered the halls as the jury deliberated. Many of the spectators hung around. Some wandered down to Judge Delong's court for Albert Kern's preliminary hearing on the perjury charge.

On Saturday, 21 July, after deliberating for twenty-two hours the jury filed back into the jury box.

Jury Foreman Rose C. Whalen said, "We, the Jury in the above entitled cause find the defendant, Louis L. Jacobs, Not Guilty." Rose. C. Whalen, Foreman.

Judge Marsh discharged the jury and ordered the defendant released.

"I knew it!" Jacobs said.

As the jurors filed passed him on the way out of the courtroom, Jacobs shook each of their hands and thanked them. Some of the jurors expressed belief in his "absolute innocence."

When asked about his plans, he said, "I don't know what I'll do now. I don't know whether I'll go back to Camp Kearny."

Once outside, Jacobs turned as if to head back to the jail behind the courthouse, as he had done nearly every day for five months. "I'll be darned if I'll go back to that place," he said to reporters.

"This vindication and acquittal has lifted a tremendous load from my heart," he said. "Truly, I would give anything in the world to know who was with my poor little friend that dark night back in January and what actually happened to Fritzie Mann. Perhaps that mystery will never be solved, but I hope the truth comes to light someday, and if she was murdered, the guilty person will be made to pay."

The trial players handled the recent strain in their own ways. Judge Marsh took a vacation. Kempley relaxed at Coronado Tent City. Schenck had a heart attack. Jacobs travelled to San Francisco and Honolulu with Shapiro and Shapiro's wife.

***

Chapter Fifty – An American Tragedy

If twenty-first century forensics and investigative techniques had been available and applied, the police would've quickly solved the Fritzie Mann case. They would've secured the crime scenes, systematically gathered and documented evidence, and prevented reporters and curiosity seekers from trampling on the evidence. Photographs of the body on the beach would've rendered the position of the arms moot. Analysis of the tire track impressions near the cottage might've established whether Jacobs' Hudson had made them. The lab may have obtained a DNA profile from the blood spot on the sheet or elsewhere in the cottage. Luminal might've indicated the presence of blood in the bathtub or elsewhere in the cottage. The autopsy would've been performed before the blood had been drained, which might've revealed the presence of toxic substances and a more definitive cause of death. Security camera footage, internet searches, cell phone records...and so on. As it happened, the DA didn't have enough evidence to convince the jury that Jacobs was with Fritzie when she died, much less that he killed her. The manner and cause of death remained debatable to the end.

Considering the evidence presented, the second jury reached the correct verdict. But it's one thing to find reasonable doubt on a charge of first-degree murder, another to believe in Jacobs' "absolute innocence," as some of the jurors expressed. Considering the moral code that compelled a man to marry a pregnant woman who had no legal or safe alternative, the apparent sympathy for Jacobs is mystifying. By getting Fritzie pregnant and refusing to marry her Jacobs left her with nothing but bad options. She could submit to an illegal and dangerous abortion, have the child and face life-ruining ostracism, and forfeit any chance of a career, or kill herself. Her only other option—pressuring Jacobs and threatening to ruin his life—carried its own risks.

Legal and moral questions aside, there is no doubt that Jacobs was directly involved in Fritzie's death.

But Kempley knew that his weak circumstantial case gave him a low probability of success, especially since he decided to pursue it as a capital crime. A lesser charge may have given him a better shot at a conviction. But first-degree murder sounded more dramatic, generated more publicity and produced a more sensational trial, which the politically ambitious Kempley desired. But the DA didn't have the option of going easy on Jacobs even if he had wanted to. The first trial coincided with a bitter mayoral election at a time public concern over crime and corruption had peaked. Except for the *Sun*, the papers were bashing the mayor, the chief, and the DA for failing to clean up the town and their apparently lackadaisical attitude toward crime. This is what Jacobs meant when he said his case was "enmeshed in a snare of local politics" in his letter to Dr. Welch. Although never revealed in public, anticipating the likelihood of an acquittal at the first trial, the DA had contemplated re-trying Jacobs on an accessory charge (accessory to what crime isn't clear). But after the jury deadlocked, he decided to pursue a first-degree charge for the second trial, for the same reasons as before.

Also unknown to the public and press, Jacobs had more at stake in Fritzie's pregnancy than his reputation and career. The "extra" incentive would've been easy for a jury to understand in 1923, a time before reliable and legal birth control, when Victorian morality and class consciousness lingered despite post-war sexual liberation and the advancement of women's rights. The motive formed the core theme of Theodore Dreiser's famous novel, *An American Tragedy*, published two years after the Jacobs trials.

Dreiser based his plot on a real case. In 1906, a man named Chester Gillette was convicted and executed for murdering a pregnant woman, Grace Brown, in upstate New York. The Gillette-Brown case, one of many similar crimes Dreiser had studied over a twenty-year period, represented an archetype of a peculiarly American crime that fascinated him. The root cause, he said, was young people's obsession with money and status, an obsession as much society's fault as the murderer's. According to Dreiser, one variation of the crime involved a…

> …young ambitious lover of some poorer girl, who in the earlier state of affairs had been attractive enough to satisfy him, both in the manner of love and her social station. But nearly always with the passing of time and the growth of experience on the part of the youth, a more attractive girl with money or position appeared and he quickly discovered that he could no longer care for his first love. What produced this particular type of crime about which I am talking was the fact that it was not always possible to drop the first girl. What usually stood in the way was pregnancy, plus the genuine affection of the girl herself for her lover, plus also her determination to hold him.

In *An American Tragedy*, Clyde Griffiths, a young man from a poor family, works at his uncle's factory in a fictional town in upstate New York. He starts dating Roberta, an innocent farm girl who falls in love with him. To keep from losing Clyde, she consents to have sex. When Roberta gets pregnant, she expects Clyde to honor his promise to marry her, but by now he has lost interest in her as he pursues a debutant named Sondra. Clyde tries but fails to arrange an abortion for Roberta, then procrastinates as his obsession with Sondra grows. Roberta finally threatens Clyde: Either he marries her or she reveals their relationship, creating a scandal, destroying his career, and ruining his chance to marry into wealth and status. Desperate, Clyde hatches a plan to murder Roberta by staging a boating accident to look like a suicide or an accidental drowning. He registers at an inn under an assumed name, listing Roberta as his wife. He takes her out onto a lake in a rowboat. He has second thoughts, but in the midst of an argument, he accidently strikes Roberta with his camera and capsizes the boat. Roberta, who can't swim, drowns as Clyde swims ashore. As it happened, knocking her into the water was an accident, but he had planned to kill her and didn't try to save her. Panicked, Clyde leaves a trail of incriminating evidence. He incriminates himself further by making confusing and contradictory statements to the police. The evidence includes Roberta's letters to Clyde, which are published in the papers and later read in court. To ensure a conviction, the authorities manufacture evidence against him. Clyde is found guilty and sent to the electric chair.

Dreiser may or may not have been aware of the Fritzie Mann case—it appeared in the national news while he was writing his book—but it fit his archetypal theme as well as the Gillette-Brown case. But he may not have recognized it as such because the portrayal of Fritzie's relationship with Jacobs in the press left out a key element: Jacobs had his eye on a bigger prize than a poor Oriental dancer and her pregnancy threatened to ruin his chances. The papers never mentioned this and likely never found out.

Fritzie got pregnant around the first of September 1922. Her relationship with Jacobs ended within a few weeks, probably before Fritzie knew she was pregnant and before she met Rogers Clark. Around this time, Jacobs became more interested in a woman he'd known before he'd met Fritzie. It was never made public, but Kempley expressed his belief that Jacobs was sweet on Miss Ella Worthington, an attractive eighteen-year-old debutante and daughter of the elder Worthington. Jacobs' close relationship with her mother—the dinner dates at the Golden Lion, the country drives, the days at the Tijuana tracks, his visits to her home— may have been part of an effort to win her daughter's hand. If Mrs. Worthington thought highly of him, Jacobs may have reasoned, she might encourage a relationship with her daughter, who at the time was dating a Navy Lieutenant. Kempley later concluded that Jacobs actually wanted to wed the widow, about eighteen years his senior. During the first trial, the DA had asked her several questions that reflected his suspicions of an intimate relationship between the two, although he never asked her outright.

As far as Jacobs' motive to kill Fritzie, it doesn't matter whether he wanted to wed the mother or the daughter. If the Worthington women discovered his relationship with Fritzie, a lower-class Oriental dancer pregnant with his child, it would've killed any chance to marry either. Or he feared, with good reason, that it would have. But Kempley had no hard evidence of a relationship, so he approached the wealthy widow with caution. The best he could do was to hint at his suspicions with a few oblique questions and suggest in his closing argument that Jacobs had refused to marry Fritzie because of her low station. Evidence of Jacobs' marriage plans would not have changed the outcome, only strengthened the DA's already strong proof of motive. But those plans are relevant to the mystery of what happened to Fritzie, as are other aspects of their relationship.

***

Fritzie threatened Jacobs twelve days before her death. She'd gone through enough, she said, "to embitter me more than ever." She was bitter that he refused to marry her, but it's possible to read more into her words. Had Jacobs pressured her to have sex or taken advantage of her after too many drinks? Or had he seduced her under a vague promise of marriage, a common enough scam? Or had he inferred a promise of marriage by declaring his love for her? To Fritzie, twenty years old and in love with a refined doctor eleven years her senior, it may have meant the same thing. Whatever the circumstances of their sexual relationship, Fritzie had assumed he'd marry her—it's what honorable men did. But when she informed him of her missed period, he balked. Their testy conversation at Rosie de Cacho's house took place between the 10th and 15th of October, soon after Fritzie had confronted Jacobs with the unwelcomed news. (Despite Schenck's efforts to make her out to be a drunk or a mental patient or a caricature of a silent screen star, Rosie appeared to be a credible witness, probably why he had treated her with more disrespect than other prosecution witnesses.) Jacobs said he'd never marry anyone. In truth he just didn't want to marry Fritzie—for the same reason Clyde didn't want to marry Roberta and Chester didn't want to marry Grace.

In her last letter, Fritzie said they had "both got'em again," but she was mistaken about his feelings. And Bernice Edwards was mistaken or being disingenuous when she told the police the "lovers' spat" between Fritzie and Jacobs was about her plans to return to L.A. It was over his betrayal. He wanted her out of his life, but once she threatened him, he had no choice but to treat her well, to spend time with her, to call her every day and to beg her not to return to L.A. until the threat passed. And perhaps he went so far as to pretend to be in love with her. Kempley implied this in his opening statement when he said Jacobs had had an *ostensible* affection for Fritzie. If he loved her, would he have left her on her own for so long in L.A., ill and facing a scary operation?

More than anything else, Jacobs' behavior during the final weekend of Fritzie's life and the days immediately after her death reveals his true feelings. He spent almost the entire weekend with Ella Worthington. On Friday evening, Jacobs met Fritzie at the Maryland hotel and went for a drive to La Mesa, no doubt to discuss the plan for Sunday evening. After dropping her off at home, he met Mrs. Worthington and another woman at the U.S. Grant, and they went to the Golden Lion for refreshments. On Saturday, he picked up Mrs. Worthington at her house at about 1:30 p.m. That afternoon, while Fritzie cried to Madame Hands about "a man keeping a promise," he was at the Tijuana tracks with his real love interest. They returned to Worthington's home late on Saturday night. He stayed overnight and spent all day Sunday with her in Tijuana, dropping her off at home just in time to catch the 6:20 p.m. ferry and meet Fritzie. This is not the behavior of a man who loves a woman, let alone a pregnant woman in a precarious state who was about to undergo a risky, illegal operation. And who had already endured months of hell.

Jacobs saw Mrs. Worthington at the Golden Lion on Tuesday, the day after Fritzie's body was found, apparently soon after his first interview with Chief Patrick. He visited her again the following day at her home. On neither occasion did he mention his involvement in the Fritzie Mann affair, the talk of the town. At the time he still hoped to avoid being implicated in the crime. Hoped they ruled it a suicide. Hoped Fritzie had destroyed his letters as he had destroyed hers. Hoped she hadn't told her friends or family the details about what was going on. Hoped the cops would go after Rogers Clark or another Hollywood player. If Fritzie hadn't kept Jacob's letters and telegrams, and if Bernice hadn't kept Fritzie's last letter, the police and DA may never have put a case together.

Until the end, Fritzie had hoped that Jacobs would change his mind and agree to marry her. In her last letter she wrote "he is trying to make me see things his way." That is, to get an abortion so he wouldn't have to marry her. Finally accepting the inevitable, Fritzie had decided to get the abortion, return to L.A., and resume her career.

"It will just take a few days and then I can come back and start into everything," she wrote to Bernice two days before her death.

**

Chapter Fifty-One – Why Should The Woman Always Pay?

Fritzie's last letter to Bernice left no doubt that an abortion was planned before she returned to L.A. Circumstances indicate that it was planned for Sunday night. Jacobs and Fritzie told others that they planned to meet someone at the train station at 6:30 p.m. and both were heading in that direction at the right time. They obviously met each other as planned, but did they meet a doctor coming in from L.A. or anyone else? Clearly, no. Among other reasons, had they met a doctor, Jacobs would've revealed the man's identity, if not at the beginning, then certainly by the time the grand jury indicted him for murder, and he faced a real possibility of being hanged. He would've told Chief Patrick, "We met Dr. So and So at the station, Fritzie left with him and I never saw her again." He had already admitted to trying to arrange an abortion and the damage to his reputation and career was done. Jacobs would've had every reason to name him and no reason not to.

Then why did Jacobs meet Fritzie at the train station? Because, by coincidence, it was the most convenient possible place for them to meet. Jacobs had already planned to spend the weekend with Ella Worthington and knew he would be coming from Coronado; he debarked the ferry and drove three blocks north to Broadway and Kettner. Fritzie took a streetcar to the end of the Broadway line and got off at the turnaround in front of the depot. He picked her up and drove north on India Street, the main route out of downtown to the coast highway. They didn't meet at one of their usual spots such as the U.S. Grant or The Golden Lion because they—especially Jacobs—didn't want anyone to see them. Did they meet a doctor somewhere else, say in La Jolla? No, because Dr. Jacobs was, with almost no doubt, the mysterious Mr. Johnston.

The handwriting analysis fell short of scientific proof and does to this day, but the testimony of the document examiners was among the most compelling evidence presented at the trials. Paul Schenck, who embarrassed other prosecution experts including Harvard Medical School graduates with ease, had no answer for the handwriting experts and didn't call an expert to counter them. In the first trial Schenck didn't even bother to cross examine Milton Carlson, an expert with a national reputation who he had faced some twenty-five times in L.A. trials on previous occasions. Schenck inadvertently admitted in court that Jacobs had signed the register when he said it *proved nothing but opportunity.*

But you don't have to be an expert to notice the striking similarity between the capital "J" in "Johnston" in the register signature and Jacobs' known signatures. Or that both were formed by the rare method of making the bottom loop first, a method contrary to what children learned in grade school copy books. The capital "L's" also look nearly identical. The only difference in either letter appears to be the angle. The experts said the register signature had been signed "backhanded" at an unnatural angle in an obvious attempt to disguise the writing, and Kern mentioned that Mr. Johnston had held his hand at an odd angle when he signed. Moreover, aware of his quirky "J's," Jacobs altered them in the exemplars he provided to the cops—it's obvious at a glance to an untrained eye. The exemplar "Js" look odd and nothing like those in his authentic signatures. He formed the characters in the exemplars the proper way, making the upper loop first, unlike in his authentic signatures going back to high school. He did the same in telegrams to acquaintances in Baltimore after his first arrest, blow ups of which were displayed at the trials along with the exemplars. Interestingly, he used his normal signature in his letter to Dr. Welch, presumably because he wasn't worried the DA might get ahold of it since one of his lawyers had mailed it from Jimmy Wadham's office. As the prosecution pointed out, his contrivances betray a guilty knowledge. This suggests guilt as much as his evolving alibi and lies to Chief Patrick. The pseudonym is also suspicious. He chose "Alvin M. Johnston," a name strikingly similar to a current patient of his. Needing an alias in the moment, the name of a patient came to mind.

Concerning the prosecution's "star" witness, it's hard to make sense out of Albert Kern's many and varied statements. But his initial description of Johnston, before he got "confused" by a marching band of detectives, lawyers and reporters, matched Jacobs in size, age, and appearance and nothing in it excluded him. A few details are telling. Kern described Johnston as dark complected with sunken cheeks, dark circles under his eyes, and a rather sharp nose. A PHS medical exam report listed Jacobs' complexion as "brunette" and the features described are consistent with a photograph of Jacobs taken at the time of the trials. Looking at this photograph it's easy to see how Kern might've described Mr. Johnson as dissipated and sallow like a consumptive or a dope fiend. Kern also mentioned a cold sore or dirt or something on his cheek. It never came out at the trials, but Jacobs had noticeable pockmarks on the left side of his face, several near the corner of his mouth, another at the level of his nostrils, visible in the same photograph. Another detail that didn't come out during the trials may be relevant: At the grand jury, Kern said Mr. Johnston wore an American Legion button. Jacobs was eligible for membership in the Legion and, like most professional men of his day, was almost certainly a member and may have worn his button. And Jacobs had the face of a changeling—his appearance varied markedly depending upon his demeanor and whether he wore a hat or glasses. He also appears to have gained weight between his first arrest and the second trial. Some of the photos taken in 1923 look like different men. Kern's failure to identify Jacobs is no surprise.

Kern's descriptions of the cars also closely matched. He described Johnston's machine as a closed, two-door coupe, either an Essex or a Velie, highly polished and apparently new, with a single seat in the front. Jacobs' Hudson coach was two months old. Neither Essex nor Velie coaches featured a single straight front seat then; the Hudson coach did. The Hudson company owned the Essex company and made closed coaches under both makes in 1922 that look nearly identical, with blocky, sharply squared off upper bodies, two same-sized rectangular side windows, and one rear window. It would've been easy to confuse these cars, especially at night under a harsh blue arc light. A Velie didn't look much like either of the other cars. And throughout the case, no one mentioned the color of the cars, which means the colors matched. Schenck would've pounced on so noticeable a discrepancy.

How did Kern recognize Fritzie's dead body but didn't recognize Jacobs alive and in person? Happenstance. Something about her happened to stick in his memory. Or because a middle-aged heterosexual man is more apt to pay attention to and remember a pretty, young woman than the man's she's with. Kern intimated to a reporter that he'd paid close attention to the woman but not the man.

***

Schenck didn't have to prove suicide because the prosecution couldn't prove a crime had been committed. Reasonable doubt was more than enough. But if Fritzie killed herself she didn't do it at the beach as the defense proposed—the posture and condition of her body argues against this scenario. If she'd waded into the ocean and drowned her body would've tumbled around in the shallows for hours before the ebb tide finally stranded it on the beach. Dr. Shea would've found more extensive cutaneous injuries and more damage to her clothes; her teddy, stockings, and shoes were on and intact. And he would've probably found sand or sea vegetation in her airways and stomach. The superficial abrasions on her elbows, forehead, and cheeks are more consistent with someone moving and positioning her body than from surf action. And the lack of corrugation ("washerwoman" wrinkling) to the palms and fingers indicates that the body hadn't been in the water for long. The arms folded across the body—neatly or not—is an unusual posture for a victim who drowned in the ocean and washed ashore; typically, the arms are away from the body. And as Chief Patrick pointed out, someone drove her to that beach.

Fritzie did not kill herself, but does this mean Jacobs killed her? As Dreiser pointed out, it wasn't uncommon for a man to murder his pregnant lover given the alternatives of an unwanted marriage or scandal. By mid-January 1923 Jacobs would've been desperate to solve his dilemma and worried that Fritzie might cause a scandal. But though he had motive, the evidence suggests that when they arrived at the Blue Sea Cottages around 7:00 that night, he wasn't planning to murder her, but to perform an abortion.

Jacobs told Kern that he wanted a cottage with running water and might need it for two or three days, which suggests plans for an operation and recovery. The cottage would've been a poor choice for a murder anyway—too many people could've seen him, even in January. Jacobs got lucky because Kern assigned him a cottage located on the alley, enabling him to park his car next to it, and didn't record his license plate number. Moreover, the cottage showed signs of panic. In his haste to flee, Jacobs left behind Fritzie's barrette and hairnet, failed to clean up the bathroom, and took a blanket that was later missed.

Jacobs may have acquired the requisite knowledge to perform abortions during his training. He may have witnessed abortions and childbirths during his "intensive" training at the genito-urinary department at Hebrew Hospital following medical school. In his interview with a reporter during the second trial he described the behavior of women in states of "twilight sleep" from an injection of morphine and scopolamine. Although controversial within the medical community at the time, this mix was often used to blunt the pain of childbirth while maintaining the consciousness of the patient. It could also be used for abortions. But even if Jacobs had the skill, he did not want to perform an abortion on Fritzie. He'd avoided it for months while investing considerable effort and money trying to find a specialist in L.A. Only out of desperation, after numerous attempts and Fritzie's threat to ruin him, did he decide to do it himself. He would've begun the operation by administering an anesthetic.

Before the case went to trial the DA had privately expressed a theory about what had happened at the cottage. Due to Fritzie's "importunities to perform an abortion on her he may have attempted it the night of January 14th at the Blue Sea cottage, and, after etherizing her, either got scared and lost his nerve, or believing he had killed her already with the anesthetic, hastily decided to dispose of her body, and so put an end to the annoyance."

Chief Patrick expressed a similar theory after he received Fritzie's last letter. He was "firmly of the opinion that an anesthetic was given in the La Jolla cottage in preparation for an operation, and that this either led to the girl's death or the belief of her frightened companion that she was dead."

Anesthetics in use at the time such as chloroform and ether are volatile substances with narrow margins for safety and a much higher death rate than current methods. Administering an anesthetic in a beach cottage without assistance would've increased the risk. Jacobs likely would've administered the drug by dripping the liquid from a dropper bottle onto a gauze mask placed over Fritzie's mouth and nose. It's possible that she died from cardiorespiratory failure from the anesthetic. Some of the autopsy findings typical of drownings, especially the presence of froth and the evidence of heart failure, are also common in anesthesia deaths.

But it's also possible that she drowned. Death by drowning is one of the most difficult diagnoses for pathologists to make to this day. As the medical experts pointed out at the trials, most of the postmortem findings indicative of drowning aren't specific to that cause of death. It's a diagnosis of exclusion with general and non-specific findings, some of which are present in Fritzie's death: the body found near or in water; the presence of froth, often blood-tinged, in the airways; congestion of the sclera and conjunctiva (reddening of the eyes and surrounding tissues); and water in the stomach. Shea didn't mention some of the other typical findings, which he presumably did not find: lungs heavy and hyper-inflated; pleural effusions (fluid in the space between the rib cage and lung); dilated "flabby heart;" middle ear hemorrhages; fluid in sphenoid sinuses (hollow spaces in the sphenoid bone behind the nose). The findings vary depending upon the circumstances such as whether the drowning occurred in fresh or salt water, how much the victim had struggled in the water, and the delay in discovery of the body. The most reliable sign of drowning is the presence of a fine white froth exuded from the nose and mouth and present in the lungs and airway. The froth and the location of the body are what convinced Dr. Shea that Fritzie had drowned. The beach witnesses described the froth oozing from her mouth and nostrils as resembling shaving lather or foam. Some of them mentioned bloody froth or a pinkish tinge, although Shea did not find this at autopsy, possibly because of the time lapse. All of this is consistent with drowning.

But if Fritzie did drown, she drowned in the cottage bathtub, not at the beach. There is circumstantial evidence to suggest this. The tub and towels had been used. Mrs. Spencer, who cleaned the cottage afterward, noted an iron rust discoloration of the water, which could've come from blood exuded with the froth at the time of the drowning. This evidence plus Dr. Shea's testimony that she drowned in fresh water, is what convinced the DA that Jacobs had murdered Fritzie. In this scenario, Jacobs would've incapacitated her with the anesthesia, then placed her in the tub in an unconscious or semi-conscious state.

Though Fritzie's friends said the doctor had treated her roughly at least once, apparently while intoxicated, he was a slight, "not physically robust" man who smoked cigarettes. Fritzie was a muscular, athletic woman. If he had attacked her and tried to hold her head under the water while she was conscious, he probably would've failed. If he had succeeded, her resistance would've produced obvious injuries such as bruises to the upper body, broken fingernails, and defensive injuries to the hands, arms, and feet. Her body showed no signs of a violent struggle. The single superficial bruise on the forehead suggests an impact incident to moving the body in or out of the tub or Jacob's car, not from an instrument or a fist. If he drowned her in the tub, he presumably would've put her head and upper body into the water, leaving her legs dangling over the side. Another possibility is that Fritzie was taking a bath and Jacobs suddenly yanked her by the ankles, rendering her instantly unconscious from a sudden rush of water into the mouth and nose, as in the infamous 1915 "Brides in the Bath" case in England. The marked congestion of her face is a possible indicator of drowning with her head lower than the rest of her body. Congestion of the face would usually suggest death by asphyxia from suffocation or smothering. But there were no indications of those methods such as petechial hemorrhages on the face and mucous membranes of the eyes and under the eye lids.

Whether Jacobs killed Fritzie accidentally with the anesthetic or murdered her in the tub, he decided to make it look like suicide by drowning—an obvious choice for a physician because he knew it would be difficult to distinguish at autopsy. A depressed pregnant woman found on a beach, apparently drowned, meant a high probability of a suicide ruling, and that almost happened. In his interviews with Chief Patrick, Jacobs emphasized Fritzie's despondency about her condition.

The DA didn't articulate it particularly well during the trials, but he probably had the beach scenario about right. Jacobs would've arrived there about 9:00 p.m. As he removed her body, wrapped in a cottage blanket, from the car, the bar pin fell out, where Bludworth found it two days later. He carried her down the embankment. He would not have carried her into the surf, as he wanted to minimize his time on the beach and avoid having to explain why his clothes were wet. And the slight Dr. Jacobs, panicked and exhausted, would've had trouble getting the dead weight of Fritzie's 130-pound body out of the car and down the rocky embankment much less out into the surf. He may have dragged her body down the well-worn path between the rocks and across the sand. The dress fell out of the blanket; it was found in dry sand near the bottom of the embankment and appeared to some witnesses to have been drug across the sand. He placed the body near the water's edge, enough for it to get wet. This was near high tide. Soon after he departed the tide began to ebb, leaving her body where he left it. The tide reached a low after 2:00 a.m. The next high tide, after 8:00 a.m. on Monday, was an unusually high one. The water would've reached the body sometime in the early morning hours. By that time the body had lain in the same position for perhaps eight or ten hours or more, enough time for rigor to set in, fixing her limbs much as Jacobs had left them. Her body would've floated and been moved around by the water some, but not tossed around in the surf. At mid-morning, the tide went out, leaving her body embedded in the sand about 150 or 200 feet to seaward, most likely in the same or nearly the same posture in which Jacobs left it.

On the drive back he tossed the blanket, handbag, and vanity case down the embankment and drove to Camp Kearny via the shortcut from the coast highway, taking the longer route to the eastern side of the base (Route 1 at the trial). He avoided the shorter route (Route 2 at the trial) because it was rugged and rocky and dangerous at night. The gate guard testified that he arrived at 9:30, with Jones and McCauley right behind him.

***

Jacobs may have killed Fritzie accidentally—it's impossible to know for sure. In the end, it doesn't matter. Either way it constituted a serious crime and made him directly responsible for her death. He slept with her, got her pregnant and refused to marry her, leaving her with no good options. In the end, only Fritzie paid the price.

***

Epilogue

In May 1926, the New York City *Daily News* published a two-page spread about the case with photos of Fritzie in a feathered headdress, the two suspects, and Dorothy Armstrong. The article gave a full re-cap of the case albeit one filled with errors and hyperbole. A month later the same article appeared in *The Atlanta Constitution* and perhaps other papers but not those in San Diego. With Jacobs' acquittal, new theories and rumors emerged around town, one of which had Fritzie murdered at the hands of a film colony drug syndicate, also responsible for William Desmond Taylor's death. But other than a passing reference or two in the local papers over the next few years, the Fritzie Mann mystery disappeared from the city's history until Richard Crawford unearthed it almost ninety years later. But some of the people involved in the case continued to make the news from time to time.

In late 1928, while working as a part-time *Union* columnist, Wilma Frances Minor submitted an article called "Lincoln the Lover" to *Atlantic Monthly* magazine. The submission included letters that Abraham Lincoln had reputedly exchanged with Ann Rutledge, who the future president had met in 1831. Some historians believed Ann was the love of his life. Minor also submitted a diary she claimed a friend of Rutledge's had kept, and a bible Rutledge had allegedly given to Lincoln. Some Lincoln scholars had theorized that Rutledge's death in 1835 accounted for the depression that plagued Lincoln from then on. Wilma's evidence seemed to confirm the theory. Lincoln biographers Ida Tarbell and Carl Sandburg quickly authenticated the letters, evidence enough for *Atlantic Monthly* editor and owner Ellery Sedgwick. Sedgwick edited out Wilma's purple prose and serialized her piece in three parts. The magazine paid her $1,500 for the articles and another $1,000 as an advance towards a book. Wilma became an instant literary celebrity. She gave talks and basked in the attention.

Other Lincoln scholars then came forward to call the letters crude forgeries. The handwriting in the letters, the experts noted, bore no resemblance to Lincoln's. Nor was the composer of the Gettysburg Address known to write sentences such as, "Night, like a black sinewy panther, crawled cautiously through the unbending straight directness of the saplings on the river bank." Embarrassed, Sandburg and Tarbell recanted their previous statements.

Wilma soon admitted that she had written the letters and the fake diary. But she had not committed fraud, she insisted, because she had help from the dead. A spirit guide in direct contact with Lincoln and Ann Rutledge, she said, had dictated the contents of the documents to her mother, Cora, a medium, making them as authentic as if the long-dead lovers had written them.

Cora, it turned out, was the mastermind behind the hoax. The editor of the Atlantic Monthly Press, Edward Weeks, described Cora as "...tall and beady-eyed, with hair suspiciously black for her age," who "reminded him somehow of a fortune-teller." The *Atlantic Monthly* hired an L.A. private eye to investigate the hoax. He described Cora as "...the hard nut of the two...a hard boiled old hen, who does not know what the word truth means." Wilma, on the other hand, "was very badly disrupted and plainly showed the ordeal she had been through. At one point Wilma seemed like she was ready to pass out."

The bizarre episode stamped a permanent black mark on Ellery Sedgwick's otherwise distinguished career. Apparently, he'd been duped in no small part by his electric attraction to the fetching Wilma and her gray-green bedroom eyes.

Wilma's celebrity-notoriety flamed out as quickly as it had ignited, and she drifted back into obscurity. She married three more times after divorcing Frank Minor, continued to write, became an artist and a scrap booker, and lived a quiet life in the San Diego area until her death in 1965. Her obituary, which doesn't mention the Lincoln letters, listed her age as sixty-seven. She was seventy-nine.

***

A few months after the second trial, Magner White wrote a fanciful account about a total solar eclipse. He researched the topic extensively ahead of time, enabling him to anticipate what could happen when the sun went dark, including that chickens might go to roost and the possible effects on a circus in town. He won the Pulitzer Prize for journalism the following year, a first for a San Diego journalist. He joked that he won the Pulitzer without having to leave the office. He later became editor of the *Sun*. After that paper died, he worked at the *Los Angeles Examiner* as a reporter and editor.

***

The remainder of Chester Kempley's tenure as DA proved to be as eventful as its start. The year after the Jacobs trials he played a small role in the fifth and final major Hollywood scandal of the early 1920s. On the evening of 16 November 1924, William Randolph Hearst's yacht, the *Oneida*, dropped anchor in San Diego Bay filled to the gunwales with Tinseltown luminaries. There is no reliable record of the passenger list, but it's thought to include

Hearst, Marion Davies (Hearst's mistress), Charlie Chaplin, writer Elinor Glyn, columnist Louella Parsons, actresses Aileen Pringle, Julanne Johnston, Jacqueline Logan and Seena Owen, actor-dancer Theodore Kosloff, and producer-director Thomas Ince.

The *Oneida* entered port after Ince became gravely ill. A water taxi delivered him and a doctor ashore. The pair boarded a train for L.A., but Ince's condition deteriorated to the point that they had to stop at the Hotel Del Mar. Ince died a few days later at home in L.A. Although the official cause of death was heart failure, the *Los Angeles Times*, the main rival of Hearst's *Los Angeles Examiner*, proposed a different theory: "Movie Producer Shot Aboard Hearst Yacht!" The story goes that Hearst had mistakenly shot Ince while aiming at Chaplin, who he suspected of having an affair with Davies. Hearst managed to squelch the initial reports, but rumors persist to this day.

Kempley conducted a cursory investigation of Ince's death. He spoke to a La Jolla doctor and a nurse who had attended to Ince during his stay at the Hotel Del Mar. Ince had blamed his condition on the copious amounts of bad alcohol he'd consumed aboard the yacht, not a gunshot wound to the head.

"I am satisfied that the death of Thomas H. Ince was caused by heart failure as the result of an attack of acute indigestion," Kempley announced, based on the doctor's opinion. "There will be no investigation into the death of Ince at least as far as San Diego County is concerned."

Whatever happened aboard the *Oneida*, the episode caused Hearst considerable angst, a small measure of poetic justice for the lives his papers had ruined.

In 1925, Kempley lost another high-profile murder case. A Chicago hood named McMahon had turned up dead near Old Town, shot and beaten and with a knife protruding from his chest. He'd apparently died shortly after he and an accomplice robbed two women of thousands of dollars' worth of jewelry in their room at the U.S. Grant Hotel. The DA charged two Chicago mob hit men named Johnson and McGovern with the murder. It looked like a slam dunk case. But then the knife disappeared, and the accused's blood-stained suits mysteriously shrank to the point they no longer fit. The thugs were acquitted, instantly prompting grand jury scrutiny of Kempley's conduct of the case. He was indicted and along with his deputy, Guy Selleck, stood trial, charged with accepting a $40,000 bribe to tamper with the evidence in the Johnson-McGovern trial. Star witness for the prosecution: former San Diego madame Agnes Keller, an inmate at San Quentin.

In the few years since the 1923 Dearborn incident, the cops had busted Agnes so often for such a wide range of crimes that it almost became comical. Possession of liquor at the Sunset Supper Club in Ocean Beach. Social vagrancy. Reckless driving. Running a disorderly house at the Warren Hotel. Running a disorderly house at the corner of 5th and A. As usual, Agnes beat most of the charges and got off light on the others. Her luck finally ran out after the cops busted her for robbing $560 from a customer at yet another brothel, this one located at 818 8th street. Kempley and Selleck convicted her of grand larceny and the judge sentenced her to ten years in prison.

Kempley's successor as DA brought Agnes in from San Francisco for the trial of the *People of California vs. Chester C. Kempley et al.* Agnes testified that in 1923 she had bribed Kempley to drop the charges against her from the Dearborn raid. She further claimed that he'd tried to bribe her to testify at the Jacobs trials, that she'd supposedly seen Dr. Jacobs at The Barn on a certain date. She had also "employed" Selleck to intercede in her son's legal troubles. Furthermore, she claimed that the DA and his assistant had paid her to perform several illegal tasks during the McMahon murder case. These tasks included shrinking the accused hit men's bloody suits, acting as liaison to the Chicago mob, and obtaining a diamond stud, a ring, and $3,000 being held by Coroner Schuyler Kelly. She advised the mobsters that to save Johnson and McGovern from the gallows would cost them $20,000 apiece.

The jury found a stunned Kempley and Selleck guilty. How could the jury convict them, they asked, on the testimony of such a celebrated scoundrel as Agnes Keller, now serving ten years at San Quentin? The California Supreme Court agreed. In overturning the verdict two years later, the court noted Keller's motive for revenge against the defendants and her unsavory character. "Numerous witnesses testified that her reputation in San Diego for truth, veracity, and integrity was extremely bad."

Chief James Patrick considered that an understatement. Once, on his way home from a national police chief's convention in Indianapolis, the chief stopped by Kansas City, Agnes' hometown.

"Do you know a woman named Agnes Keller?" Chief Patrick asked the Kansas City Chief of Police.

"Hell yes!" the Kansas City chief said. "She just turned things inside out here. I hear she's in California."

"Yes, she's in my town."

"You have my sympathy."

Paroled in 1930, Agnes became a fortune teller in San Francisco under a new alias. She was later convicted for swindling and posing as a spiritualist. The judge sentenced her to another ten years in San Quentin.

Chester Kempley moved with his family to L.A. a few years later and established a private practice. He died in 1960 at the age of seventy-three.

***

Schuyler Kelly also got caught up in the machinations surrounding the Johnson-McGovern and Kempley-Selleck trials. At the latter trial, Kelly testified that Agnes Keller and a Chicago mobster named Johnson, brother of one of the co-defendants, had repeatedly tried to get him to turn over the thirty-five pieces of evidence he was holding for the McMahon trial. This seemed to corroborate some of Agnes' testimony.

"Johnson met me one day and told me it would be well worth my while to turn over the exhibits," Kelly testified, "but I told him chances were mighty slim. Later, if my memory serves me correctly, it was Agnes Keller who offered me $10,000 for the evidence, particularly the knife found in McMahon's breast."

"Why did you not tell the authorities of this offer instead of keeping it quiet?" the prosecutor asked. "Did you not know you were committing a criminal act in not making this known to the officials?"

"I knew it was not exactly right, but I didn't think much of it."

"Well, what about the People of California?"

Kelly said he hadn't paid much attention to the bribe because that sort of thing happened all the time.

Earlier that year, Kelly had played a chief role in sparking an international brouhaha. It involved a bizarre and tragic episode known as the "Shame Suicides." To neighbors and acquaintances, the Peteet family—Thomas, his wife Carrie, and their grown daughters Clyde and Audrey—appeared to be pious and respectable. But on 30 January 1926, they rode the Highway to Hell south to Tijuana and checked into the San Diego Hotel. According to witnesses, they spent the next four evenings "eating, drinking, gambling, and carrying on in a manner unfit for polite society." On the fifth night, while drinking and dancing at the Oakland Bar, Peteet and his daughters lost consciousness. Thomas awoke in his hotel bed. Audrey and Clyde claimed they'd been taken to separate locations and raped—one by the Tijuana chief of police, the other by the Oakland Bar bartender. Two days after the Peteets returned home, police found the four of them lined up neatly on the kitchen floor on pillows and blankets, dead or dying from gas asphyxiation. At the autopsies, Dr. John Shea found evidence confirming the rape allegations. Thomas Peteet's suicide letter stated that "Death was always preferred to dishonor to our women."

Schuyler Kelly stated in public that "the suicides justified murder charges." He urged the U.S. Secretary of State to pressure the Mexican government. Seven men were eventually charged with rape, kidnapping, and other crimes. A Mexican judge ultimately dropped the charges against three of the men. The other four were acquitted during a trial in which the defense blamed the tragedy on Thomas Peteet and trashed the "loose" characters of his daughters.

***

A year after the Jacobs trials, Paul Schenck defended millionaire mining magnate Jack White against motion picture actress Ann Luther, who was suing White for $100,000 for breach of contract. Schenck conjured up William Desmond Taylor's ghost in the courtroom. Luther, he claimed, had threatened White by telling him to pay up or *watch out for what happened to Taylor.* The judge dismissed Luther's lawsuit.

In 1932, Schenck defended the infamous "Trunk Murderess," Winnie Ruth Judd, in Phoenix. Judd had shot two friends to death, dismembered their corpses, stuffed the body parts into trunks, and boarded a train for LA—with the trunks. William Randolph Hearst, it is said, convinced Schenck, who had been planning to retire, to join Judd's defense team. Over the objections of the other two defense lawyers, Schenck insisted on using the insanity defense—a novel defense in Arizona at the time. The jury found Judd guilty, the first and only murder trial Schenck ever lost. Although Winnie Ruth was initially sentenced to death, she ended up serving her sentence at the Arizona State Asylum. After the trial, the other lawyers kicked Schenck off the case.

A few months later, Schenck represented movie actress Helene Costello in her divorce from actor and director Lowell Sherman. Costello accused Sherman of constant nagging and, worse, of being a "ham actor." Sherman accused Costello of being a violent drunk who collected dirty books. He brought a dozen books to the courtroom as evidence. During the trial, someone stole two of the books, including *Memoirs of Fanny Hill*. The judge demanded to know who had filched the books.

"I'm too old to be interested in such reading," Schenck said.

Seven months later, Paul Schenck died of a heart attack at the age of fifty-nine.

***

James Patrick served as police chief until the end of Mayor Bacon's term in 1927, giving him a tenure of over eight years, the longest in the city's history. The record would stand for almost thirty years, an impressive achievement considering the incessant cutthroat politics and corruption he endured during his tenure. Underscoring this achievement, in the seven years after Patrick left the job, a new police chief would be installed on average once every eleven months. After his term, Patrick reverted to the rank of lieutenant and served under the title of assistant chief until he retired in 1932. He died in 1960 at the age of seventy-nine. He is considered among the best police chiefs in the city's history.

***

Det. Sgt. Richard Chadwick's daughter, Florence, became world famous for her long-distance swimming feats, most notably as the first woman to swim the English

Channel in both directions. A one-time swimming coach, Chadwick accompanied Florence to France and England in 1950 and 1951 to help her train. He died of a heart attack in 1951 at age sixty-nine.

His partner, Det. Sgt. George Sears, was appointed to police chief in 1934. Pliny Castanien, a former police officer and long-time police reporter for the *Union*, described Sears as "something of an enigma—to his friends a shrewd and seasoned political tactician, to his critics a corrupt cop on whom they could never get the goods." Was Sears—or any of the cops or lawyers in 1920s San Diego—as corrupt as they were often portrayed or simply pragmatic? It's hard to say; corruption and violence so permeated Prohibition America that even the most honest cop could scarcely escape it. Sears was not alone in his belief that it was in the city's best interest to keep San Diego an "open town" to support the tourist trade and population of sailors upon which the city depended. He also knew that if the city shut down the gambling joints and bawdy houses the vice would spread all over town, as had happened in 1912 when the city tried to clean up downtown in preparation for the 1915 Panama-California Exposition. Keeping the vice corralled to downtown at least made the situation somewhat manageable. At any rate, Sears' tenure as police chief was marked by controversy. He resigned in 1939 before the mayor, an old political enemy, could fire him.

***

Abraham Sauer continued his muckraking ways, routinely pissing people off with provocative headlines such as "Stupid Mayor and Incompetent Police Chief Responsible for Failure to Suppress Crime," until his death in 1933 at the age of eighty-two. Many people had tried to exact revenge on Sauer over the years for hurling journalistic bombs their way. During his career he appeared in court as a defendant nineteen times for various civil suits or criminal libel charges. In 1927 he swore out a charge of battery against Det. Sgt. George Sears. Miffed at something the editor had written about him, Sears allegedly punched Sauer. Sears was tried and acquitted. Numerous witnesses, mostly police officers, swore on the stand that Sears had been out of town at the time of the alleged crime. The judge at Sears' trial, however, claimed to have overheard the detective remark, "Next time the old man prints a piece like that he won't even be able to be his own witness in court." In 1920s San Diego, who knows what actually happened.

***

Al Flowers' efforts to keep Rogers Clark away from his stepdaughter ultimately failed. Clark married Gladys Taylor while the second Jacobs trial was in session. They moved to Altadena, California and later divorced. Clark married twice more. He returned to the paper business and retired as an executive for Crown Zellerbach. He died in Santa Barbara in 1953 at the age of sixty-eight.

***

In November 1923, Dr. Louis Jacobs wrote to Surgeon General Cumming. He asked Cumming to restore him to duty in the Public Health Service to enable him to resign honorably. Cumming denied the request. Jacobs then appealed to Eliot Wadsworth, Assistant Secretary of the Treasury, who also denied the request. Jacobs moved back home to Baltimore and appealed in person to U.S. Senator O.E. Weller of Maryland. He followed up with a letter. "Entangled in the local political situation the first trial resulted in a hung jury," Jacobs wrote. "This jury never voted on my guilt or innocence but disagreed – 9 to 3 – that no crime had ever been committed! The second jury acquitted and also voted NO CRIME." Jacobs describes himself as an "innocent victim of a political intrigue," wrongly held in jail for five months. He asked Weller "to remove this odious and unmerited handicap of dismissal so as to allow me to pursue my profession untroubled by the constant malevolent influence and damning insinuation that such an injustice invariably breeds!" Weller attempted to intercede with Cumming on Jacobs' behalf. Cumming responded that the Public Health Service's treatment of Jacobs had been justified.

Despite the blight on his record, Jacobs managed to build a private practice in Baltimore. He worked out of a house on Eutaw Place. He used the front rooms for his examining and waiting rooms and lived in the back with his sister and mother. Around 1936 he married a wealthy widow said to be twenty years his senior.

Jacobs wrote to the Surgeon General again in 1942. Inexplicably, he asked for a copy of the resignation letter he claimed to have submitted to the Public Health Service in 1923. Such a letter didn't exist, and he knew it so the purpose of this request is unclear. The Surgeon General's office replied that there was no resignation on file and sent him instead a copy of the letter from the Secretary of Treasury that had placed him on inactive status.

The last mention of Jacobs before his death came in January 1959, in a letter San Diego Police Chief A.E. Jansen wrote to Irwin I. Greenfield, the District Supervisor of the Treasury Department, Bureau of Narcotics, in Baltimore. Jansen's letter responded to one from Greenfield. The letter referred to Dr. Louis Llewellyn Jacobs of Baltimore, MD, and a case number. The letter briefly summarized the Fritzie Mann case and its outcome thirty-six years before. Jacobs was apparently involved in a Bureau of Narcotics investigation in some unknown way. He died the following year at age sixty-nine.

***

Fritzie's big sister Helen Mann died two months after the end of the second Jacobs trial, aged twenty-four, of consumption and a broken heart. Amelia buried her beside her sister at the Home of Peace Cemetery. Shortly after Helen's death, Amelia and William moved back to Denver. In 1930, Amelia relocated the remains of her two girls to the Denver Congregation Emmanuel Cemetery and reburied them beside their father. Amelia died in 1955. William died in 1981, apparently having never married.

***

San Diego is now the eighth largest city in the country and carries the boasty slogan "America's Finest City." Many of the places associated with the Fritzie Mann case are gone, others have changed little.

In 2015 and 2016 the city celebrated the centennial of the Panama-California Exposition at Balboa Park, which remains the pride of the city.

The U.S. Grant Hotel is still in business on Broadway. The basement room once occupied by the Plata Real Nightclub, a speakeasy, is now called the Celestial Ballroom.

The building that housed the Golden Lion Tavern 1923 is now home to the Hard Rock Café. The stained-glass dome still graces the ceiling over the bar.

No trace of the Blue Sea Cottages remains. Unlike some other well-known La Jolla cottages, the former site, now occupied by apartment buildings, isn't designated as a historical landmark.

Mrs. Worthington's house still stands on Encino Row in Coronado, as does the tiny house on Spruce Street where the Mann family lived when Fritzie left home for the last time.

The county courthouse was razed in 1959 to make way for a new one at the same location.

The Horton Plaza shopping mall now covers the site of the old 2nd Street police station.

The coroner finally got his own facilities. The county switched to the medical examiner system in 1990.

The Camp Kearny hospital closed sometime before 1930. The government used the old parade grounds on the base as an airfield. Charles Lindberg's plane, *Spirit of St. Louis*, conducted test flights there in 1927. In the early 1930s, the Navy installed an airship mast to moor dirigibles. This project came to a quick and tragic end when four line tenders were pulled into the air, killing two of them, during the airship *USS Macon*'s first mooring attempt. The site has been the home of military air stations since World War II. It was the Naval Air Station Miramar, home of the Navy's "Top Gun" school, for many years before becoming the present-day Marine Corps Air Station Miramar.

All of Fritzie's known dance venues are gone. The Point Loma Golf Club was demolished soon after Fritzie's 1922 performances to make way for construction of the Naval Training Center, which opened the following year. The Barn burned down in 1924 of suspected defective wiring. The city kept the Civic Auditorium in Balboa Park open despite warnings that it was a fire hazard; the beautiful building burned to the ground on Thanksgiving eve, 1925. The San Diego Natural History Museum now occupies the site. The Colonial was demolished in 1928.

The beach where Jacobs staged Fritzie's body remains much as it was, although the area is now heavily travelled. The beach is packed with people on nice days, which is most days. The estuary, now called the Los Peñasquitos Lagoon, has been preserved although it has lost more than half of its original habitats due to human activity and land use changes and continues to deteriorate. The wooden slough bridge was torn down long ago. The bridge over the slough now goes straight across to Del Mar instead of curving off toward the railroad viaduct as the wooden bridge had. The viaduct still stands; it marks the entrance to the beach parking lot. From there, a short stretch of road called McGonigle Road meets Carmel Valley Road, which winds up the hill to Del Mar along the original route. "Garage men" still fix cars in Harley Sachs' original building, now called the Del Mar Car Service.

The little parking area at the south end of the slough bridge is still recognizable, although cars now park all along the side of the road from there south to the Torrey Pines Grade. The rocky embankment is basically the same. Smooth gray rocks averaging the size of a fist are scattered around the embankment and on the beach. In places the rocks are concentrated, the surf backwash rattles them, making a pleasant sound, like a thousand billiard balls clattering together, until the tide goes out and leaves them embedded in the wet sand.

THE END

Sources

The most important primary sources are trial transcripts and contemporary newspaper articles.

The transcripts for *The People of the State of California, Plaintiff, vs. Louis L. Jacobs, Defendant* (March-April and June-July 1923) are located at the San Diego State University Library, Special Collections & University Archives.

Scores of newspapers across the country covered the Fritzie Mann case. I relied heavily on the major San Diego and Los Angeles papers that existed in 1923. I found these in various online archives or on microfiche at the San Diego Public Library (Marilyn & Gene Marx Special Collections Center), the Los Angeles Public Library (Central), the UCLA Charles E. Young Research Library, and the San Diego History Center. Newspapers:

San Diego Sun

San Diego Union

San Diego Tribune

San Diego Herald

Los Angeles Times

Los Angeles Evening Express

Los Angeles Evening Herald

Los Angeles Examiner

Los Angeles Record

Other papers in southern California provided important information, most notably the *Long Beach Press*, *Long Beach Daily Telegram*, *San Pedro Daily Pilot*, and *Riverside Daily Press*. I found these at historical societies and libraries or in online archives. Of papers outside of southern California, among the most useful were the *Denver Post*, *Baltimore Sun*, *San Francisco Chronicle*, and *Chicago Tribune*, all found in online archives.

Documents from the archives of government agencies, universities, historical societies, and other organizations provided essential information. These include court records, vital records, immigration records, military records, employment records, student records, and coroner's records. Some of these documents contain information unknown to the jury and public in 1923 that sheds new light on the mystery.

The most important of these documents are from U.S. Public Health Service files obtained from the Department of Health & Human Services, Division of FOIA Services, and the Department of the Treasury. Among the files are personnel and administrative records related to the USPHS service of Louis L. Jacobs, plus reports and correspondence between senior USPHS officers and other high government officials.

Likewise, files obtained from The Johns Hopkins Medical Institutions, The Alan Mason Chesney Medical Archives, contain critical new information. These include student records, a biographical file, and a letter from the William H. Welch Collection concerning medical aspects of the case. Also, a student file from Johns Hopkins University, Sheridan Libraries Special Collections.

The handwritten San Diego County Grand Jury minutes between December 1922 and March 1923, which can be found at the San Diego History Center, contain key facts that did not come out at trial or in the press.

Additional primary and secondary sources include books, pamphlets, journals, magazines, photographs, maps, city directories, oral histories, yearbooks, websites, and personal observations at actual sites.

One challenge to writing about a century old case is finding people who knew the characters, particularly true in this case because many of the principal characters have no surviving descendants. I managed to speak to or correspond with several friends and relatives of some of the characters. I'm grateful to Miriam Zarefsky, Beth Young, Lila Mae Edwards, Penny LaDue, and John Diebel for their reminiscences.

I also consulted several experts, most notably a former San Diego County Medical Examiner and a certified forensic document examiner and handwriting expert.

I received assistance from dozens of organizations. Among the most helpful:

San Diego History Center (Special thanks to Lauren Rasmussen and Chris Travers)

San Diego State University Library, Special Collections & University Archives (Special thanks to Jesica Brubaker and Robert Ray)

San Diego Public Library, Central Branch, Marilyn & Gene Marx Special Collections Center

Los Angeles Public Library, Central Branch

University of California at Los Angeles, Charles E. Young Research Library

The Johns Hopkins Medical Institutions, The Alan Mason Chesney Medical Archives

Johns Hopkins University, Sheridan Libraries Special Collections

Department of Health & Human Services, Division of FOIA Services

Department of the Treasury

San Diego Superior Court Central Records

San Diego County Medical Examiner's Office

San Diego Law Library

San Diego Police Department

University of Denver Library, Special Collections and Archives

Denver Public Library

La Jolla Historical Society

La Mesa Historical Society

Coronado Historical Society

Many more libraries, historical societies, and other organizations.

See JamesStewartAuthor.com for a bibliography and a full list of sources and organizations.

Acknowledgements

I owe a huge debt to everyone at the UCR Palm Desert Low-Residency MFA program, especially program director Tod Goldberg, associate director Agam Patel, my professors, and my fellow nonfiction students who provided invaluable feedback in the early stages of the book. Special thanks to Jill Alexander Essbaum, who taught me that prose writers absolutely must study poetry. Most of all, I'm grateful to my mentor, Deanne Stillman, for helping me navigate the maelstrom of narrative nonfiction.

I'm also indebted to my English and literature professors at National University, especially Dr. Wanda Addison, Reneé Weissenberger, and Scott Nesbitt.

Also, big thanks to my editor, Rowe Carenen, and to Steve Jackson, Michael Cordova, Ashley Kaesemeyer, and Natalie DeYoung at Wild Blue Press.

Thank you to Dr. Glenn Wagner, former Chief Medical Examiner of San Diego County, for his expertise and insights.

Thanks to San Diego historian and author Richard Crawford for publishing the article "1923 Death of Butterfly Dancer Becomes Shocking Mystery" in the *San Diego Union-Tribune* on June 23, 2011, which first piqued my interest in this case. Also, thanks to Karen O'Connor for being the first to suggest Fritzie's story.

I'm indebted to countless librarians, research specialists, archivists, and other people at libraries, historical societies, universities, and other organizations. Please see the Sources section.

Finally, to my wife Maryann, who in so many ways made this book possible, and my son Ashton, two of the best and bravest people I know.

For More News About James Stewart,
Signup For Our Newsletter:

http://wbp.bz/newsletter

Word-of-mouth is critical to an author's long-term success. If you appreciated this book please leave a review on the Amazon sales page:

http://wbp.bz/blueseacottagea

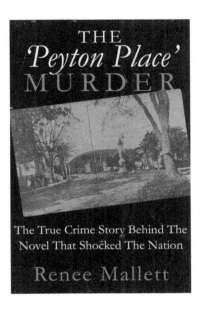

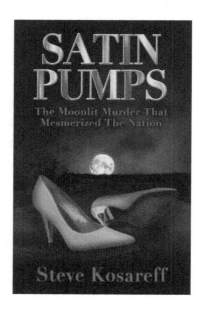